BOB FLOWERDEW'S
ORGANIC
GARDENING BIBLE

BOB FLOWERDEW'S
ORGANIC
GARDENING BIBLE

Successful growing the natural way

KYLE BOOKS

To my twins Malachi and Italia; may they inherit a greener fairer world than it seems today

Published in Great Britain in 2012 by
Kyle Books
23 Howland Street
London W1T 4AY
www.kylebooks.com

ISBN: 978 0 85783 035 7

10 9 8 7 6 5 4 3 2 1

This is a revised edition of *Bob Flowerdew's Organic Bible*, first published in 1998.

Design: ketchup
Photography: Pete Cassidy
Project editor: Sophie Allen
Editorial Assistant: Laura Foster
Production: Lisa Pinnell

A CIP record for this title is available from the British Library.

Colour reproduction by ALTA London.
Printed and bound in Singapore by Craft Print International Ltd.

contents

introduction

ABOVE LEFT *Apples – is there any crop which requires as little effort to produce?*
ABOVE MIDDLE *Damsons crop well almost anywhere with no attention at all.*
ABOVE RIGHT *Akebia quinata, a scented climber and a future crop.*

Since I wrote the first edition the whole world has faltered, and people's consciousness altered with it. The effects of climate change are becoming obvious to almost everyone, with weather-related disasters striking people in countries across the globe. Food prices are escalating, pushing yet more of the developing world into hunger and threatening even the more affluent with prospective shortages. Water resources are running out in places used to growing products to send to us, while their own people descend yet further towards starvation. We watch aghast as our young become swollen couch potatoes, their obvious discomfort caused not by disease but by self-inflicted excessive consumption, leading to malnutrition. The looming threat of GM foods multiplies previous concerns about toxic residues, micro-biological contamination and animal welfare. Consumers are rightly suspicious of deceit, malpractice and even criminal behaviour by some in the food chain. We stand by helpless as family concerns are swallowed up by multinational agri-chemi-medi-corporations possessing no ethics or morality other than the bottom line.

All this is but a foretaste of more impending disasters yet our leaders do little. It is no wonder the affluent have abandoned the cities for homesteads in the country. Those who cannot flee have sensibly retaken the allotments whilst gardening guerrillas tend vacant and unused patches of land wherever they can be found. We are obliged to think and act greener if we wish to leave a world worth living in for our grandchildren. For, despite all the negativity, hope persists. We are becoming greener, albeit too slowly, but nonetheless we are moving in a more positive direction. The fact that you are right now reading this gives us hope. We can save the world, but it will take just as long as it has taken to make this mess in the first place. And it is for each of

us to do our part. To reduce our excessive consumption to more modest levels. To tend and nurture our resources and steward the beautiful creation this planet still is. And most of all to take control and grow our own food and flowers in natural, organic and sustainable ways.

Fortunately, provided you can find a bit of ground, it is actually very easy. Growing your own is simple, straightforward and rather enjoyable. The healthy fresh air and exercise is far superior for your body and soul than the sterile gym or supermarket aisle. With birdsong and butterflies and nature all around you it is amazing how good you soon start to feel. And growing your own has become even easier. In place of poisons we have methods of wit and cunning to outmanoeuvre pests and diseases, we can encourage or purchase natural predators to assist us, while improved resistant varieties and innovations such as horticultural fleeces keep other pests at bay. Indeed it has never been easier to feed yourself with tasty, home-grown nutritious food.

In this revised edition I have made a myriad of small changes reflecting these newer varieties and improved methods uncovered over the last decade. I have also included many more tips on encouraging wildlife in our gardens. In particular, I have noted which plants you can choose for encouraging more birds and beneficial (and beautiful) insects, especially butterflies and moths. Many books note which flowers these frequent but few have indicated which plants their caterpillars require. I consider seeing more butterflies about again is almost as worthwhile a result as more food, and I willingly exchange the small damage caused for their glorious presence. My heartfelt best wishes to you all.

Bob Flowerdew   Dickleburgh, Norfolk, England

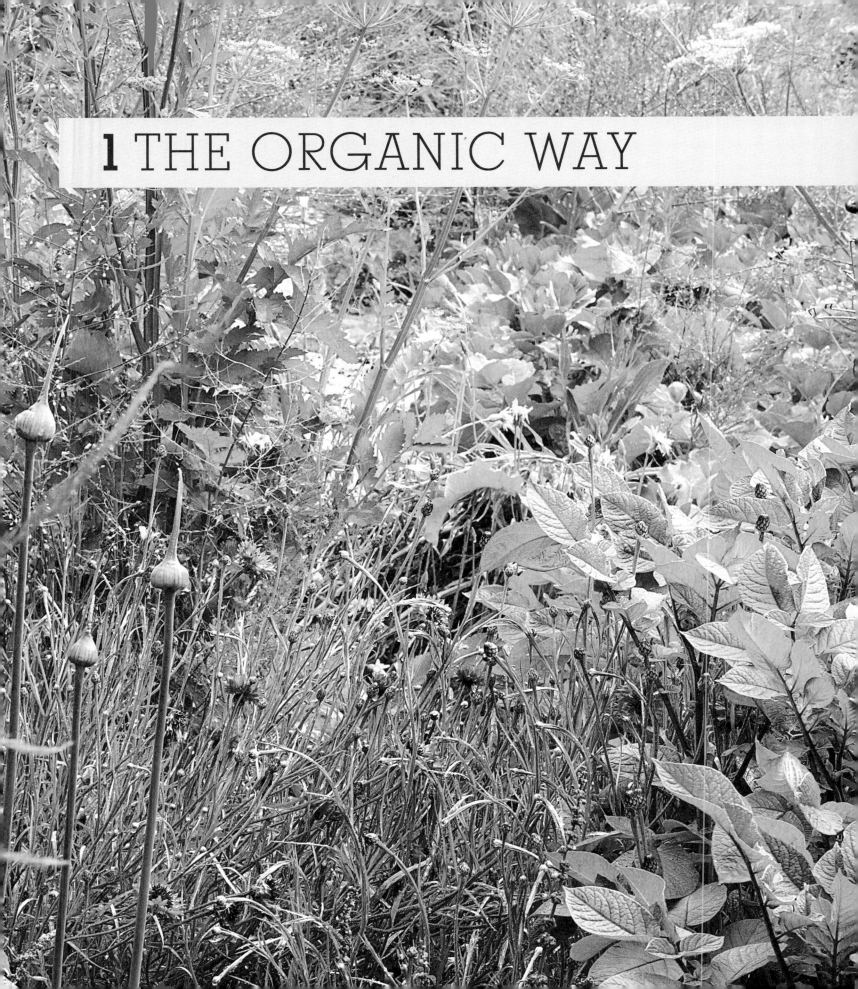

1 THE ORGANIC WAY

How we can all become successful organic gardeners, benefiting both us and our environment

Whereas a few decades ago organic, biodynamic and natural gardening was ignored entirely or regarded almost as an aberration, it has now become mainstream. Indeed, although not all gardeners wish to be hard-line organic growers, most now try to be greener and more ecological. Questions on BBC Radio Four's *Gardeners' Question Time* were once dominated by such questions as 'What should I spray for this problem?''Now, few pose questions in this way and many specify they are looking for a greener answer.

Having an organic garden is an enjoyable and practical way of caring for the environment and, in many ways, it is one of the most satisfying and worthwhile occupations we can find. However, over the last half-century much of the gardener's and farmer's harmony with nature has been displaced by a chemical approach to both gardening and farming. We were misled into believing that pesticides and weed-killers were essential to farm and garden practice. This resulted in a vast industry, with an unsustainable reliance on petrochemicals, that polluted

ABOVE LEFT *Borage is good for bees, and makes a grand liquid feed.*
ABOVE RIGHT *Peento (flattened) peaches are productive and easy to produce.*

our water, destroyed wildlife and wildflowers, and produced food and soil short of essential ingredients and contaminated with residues.

But, with an increasing awareness of green issues, ecological and environmental concerns and the search for a healthier way of life, many people are deciding to guard and nurture their own small plot of earth. Although each garden may seem insignificant, it is not. If every single gardener in the UK stopped using chemicals (it is estimated we spend tens of millions of pounds a year on them), then all the gardens put together would produce a conservation area the size of a large English county.

Cultivating our gardens organically has many benefits, including the production of fresh, tasty produce and beautiful flowers free from contamination and residues, as well as a healthier lifestyle that makes ecological use of our time. Organic gardeners gain satisfaction from saving on work and money by using their wit and cunning, rather than chemical treatments. Simply by recycling household wastes for composting, for example, we can significantly reduce the amounts of pesticides and fertilisers polluting our water, rivers and ponds.

LEFT *Grapes crop heavily and deliciously, these ones ('Muscat Hamburg') are best undercover.*

Creating an organic garden also enables each of us to encourage wildflowers and wildlife at a local level. We can save old varieties of fruit, flower and vegetable from extinction, especially as these are no longer grown commercially. Most of all, each of us can make our own small part of the earth richer with plants and more teeming with life than it was when we found it.

RIGHT *Onions from seed (left) and sets (right) spreads the risk and cropping.*
BELOW *Flowers bring in beneficial insects to patrol the sweet corn, and add beauty.*

What organic is all about, and what it is not

There is no single Organic Design or Organic Method that you can copy by rote. Organic gardening is a different approach, a choice of methods within a set of guidelines. This approach has been scientifically developed over many decades in response to the damage wrought by 'conventional' methods. Bad soil management, a profligate use of chemicals, and overcropping have resulted in the desertification and loss of productive land the world over. For instance, the American dust bowl, the silting up of the Mississippi, and a widespread loss of wildlife have all been caused by inappropriate and short-sighted methods of agriculture.

Once the farming system had been coerced into such foolishness, gardeners were gulled into copying the same methods to wreak havoc upon the ecosystems in their own gardens. Yet, the result was an increased dependence on artificial methods to obtain the same yield as before. Gardeners who annually applied vast amounts of soluble fertiliser and mixes of chemical poisons to their land rarely did much better than their forefathers. Increases in yields have usually always come from better varieties of plants rather than the methods used to cultivate them. Those same gardeners may also have wondered why there were fewer songbirds, butterflies and other wildlife to beautify the world, even while they were simultaneously poisoning both them and their own children and grandchildren. The steadily increasing lists of once approved and supposedly 'safe' pesticides now withdrawn make salutary reading, as do the lists of disclaimers on the packets!

Organic gardening is a sustainable, ecologically sound and environmentally friendly approach that has been carefully and scientifically evolved by the Soil Association in the UK. Other similar bodies operate abroad, and EU and international standards for organic products are in force. In practice, the approach in some countries, though called by another name, is still much the same. In Europe, their system is often called, or based on, Biodynamics and this started with the work of Rudolf Steiner. Otherwise, much like most organic farmers and gardeners, they pay close attention to companion planting, astrological timing and the more spiritual interactions between man, plants and the universe.

Permaculture is another approach that originated in sunnier lands and aims to use many layers of plant life to create a permanent but flexible ecology that is productive and low-maintenance. On the gardening side, permaculture was modelled on the tropical jungle and works in areas with high rainfall and powerful sunlight. Unfortunately, the light and rainfall levels in the UK are much lower, and attempts to create enduring, productive, layered gardens have resulted in poor yields, as most of our preferred food crops require open, sunny conditions. Where serious cropping ability is desirable, then a fruit cage, a herb bed, and an open and dedicated vegetable growing area make more sense, as is explained in Chapter 3.

LEFT *Simply growing strawberries in pots on stands eliminates the slug problem.*
ABOVE TOP *Fine netting gives crops 100% protection from pests.*
ABOVE BOTTOM *Beds with fixed paths eliminates the need for regular autumn digs.*

The principles of organic gardening

Guarding and increasing the life in the soil is the first and most important organic principle on which the others depend. Without healthy soil teeming with life, civilisation as we know it would disappear. We are dependent on our topsoil to feed us; if it becomes overworked and abused, it will blow, wash and erode away. The only way to maintain and increase topsoil is by actively encouraging the multitudes of life in the soil which convert inactive minerals and water into their own forms. It is their dead bodies and by-products which build up the humus-rich, water-holding, loamy soils that produce healthy plants. Chemical fertilisers and overcropping burn off this store and destroy the very organisms that could create more.

Thus, organic gardening follows the policy of feeding the soil with organic material. The burgeoning life in the soil utilises this organic material, mineral matter and the greater amounts of retained water to produce more life. Our plants then feed on the by-products and breakdown materials to make their own growth and, as a result, are more healthy and resistant to pests and diseases than those growing in denatured soil pumped full of chemical fertilisers. The effect of adding organic material is also accumulative: as more is introduced, it further encourages increased populations of soil flora and fauna. These larger populations then support yet more tiers and chains of life.

To protect this soil life, organic gardeners use no poisonous substances that can harm them, except certain, mostly 'natural', ones as a last resort. These are regarded as safer because they are less wide-ranging in their toxicity and break down rapidly and naturally after use. However, it is not their 'naturalness' but their effect on soil life that is important. Thus, nicotine, a plant product, is not allowed because it is too harmful to many forms of life, while Bordeaux mixture of copper sulphate and lime is allowed. This 'chemical' is relatively safe for soil life and is an effective fungicide. However, it should only be used if needed and ALL other measures have failed.

The increasing life in an organic soil then goes on to support more and larger forms of life in the garden and surrounding environment. After all, if you want blackbirds, then you need to have worms. The effects on this bigger scale are also accumulative. As more larger forms of life come to the table of your soil, they concentrate and bring in minerals and nutrients, further enhancing your soil's fertility. For example, birds shed feathers, leave eggshells, nesting material, copious droppings and, eventually, their bodies, all of which contribute to the soil's fertility. At first glance, this may not seem like much but, if you add up the daily amounts, then the annual production of just one extra bird family in your garden is a bucketful of very rich fertiliser.

Other creatures, such as frogs, toads and hedgehogs, all take part in the same processes and add to the overall fertility, and all give off precious carbon dioxide. This is a problem if pumped into the upper atmosphere but, released slowly in little breaths by all these creatures, it is rapidly reabsorbed by garden plants. Animal life of any size in or on the soil gives off carbon dioxide continually and, thus maintains plant growth.

LEFT *An inverted funnel made from a large plastic bottle helps feed this courgette the water it craves.* **RIGHT** *Extra early new potatoes in a bag of compost. An undercover crop before Easter when everyone else is starting theirs.*

Natural methods of pest and disease control The third principle is derivative, to an extent, of the first two; we wish to foster life in the soil and give our plants the best conditions we can. We, therefore, need to control pests and diseases but spurn the use of pesticides which may harm the life in the soil or even the plants themselves. Organic gardeners aim to prevent pests and diseases ever reaching the point where they need to use even an organically approved pesticide. They do this by building up a wide variety of plants to create ecosystems that are more stable, encouraging predators and parasites which then automatically control the pests. By growing more varied plants and mixing them we also prevent diseases and their spread.

Our most important skill in this area is using our wit and cunning to outmanoeuvre pests and diseases. Simple traps, sticky bands, careful timing and mechanical barriers can defeat many pests, while good methods, such as hygiene and crop rotation, prevent pests and diseases building up.

Minimising ecological damage and making best use of resources, time and money The fourth principle is to minimise our bad effects on the environment. Even gardening is not exempt as, left to itself, the soil would produce much more plant growth. Given a season or two of neglect, bare soil disappears under a tangle of weeds and brambles, and tree and shrub seedlings soon turn it into dense woodland. All of this growth increases the soil underneath, while it fixes sunlight and extracts more carbon dioxide from the air. A healthy natural soil can be destroyed by bad practice in a few decades.

Organic methods aim to increase plant cover as much as practicable by interplanting between crops and green manuring before and after. This natural soil cover ensures soil stability, preventing wind and water erosion, while building up the soil annually. The increased mixture and variety of plants not only aids pest and disease control, but also provides a conservation area from which beneficial wildlife can move out to recolonise the surrounding environment. Home-grown fertility from green manures and compost easily replaces bought-in chemical fertilisers and, with subtler pest and disease control, there becomes no need for direct intervention with ecologically expensive agrochemical pesticides.

Good husbandry – growing plants well Good methods and conditions get plants off to a flying start and keep them growing without check or hindrance. Plants that are slowed down in their growth never do as well as those growing consistently; their tissues harden and further growth is restrained. The aim of an organic gardener is to give the plants the best conditions and to prevent plants coming under stress from, for example, extremes of heat and cold and, most importantly, a lack of water. You can avoid water stress by increasing the organic matter in the soil, which then acts like a sponge and holds on to rain from times of plenty. Avoiding early stress and keeping down competition from weeds will produce healthy plants that grow well in spite of any pest and disease attacks.

ABOVE *Healthy well grown plants shrug off pest and disease attacks.*

Becoming an organic household

So, to convert your home and garden to an organic one may be easier than you thought. Can you do these four things?

1 Most important of all: recycle all garden and household wastes for compost and reuse. A household and garden that puts valuable material in the dustbin is throwing away its fertility. Anything that has ever lived can be converted back into fertility with a compost heap. Composting is the accelerated rotting down of once-living things and converts wastes into a brown, soil-like mass that is pleasant to smell and use. This mass is a perfect plant food and in a form readily available to their roots with no risk of overfeeding or imbalance as can be caused by chemical fertilisers. Moreover, the vast number of different microlife forms that have broken down the compost go on to inoculate and colonise the soil once the compost is added, thus further aiding soil fertility.

2 Stop using all soluble fertilisers, all herbicides, most fungicides and most insecticides. Although not necessary anyway, a few are permitted as a last resort, as is explained on page 232. Although not allowed under most organic standards per se, existing stocks of chemical fertilisers are best disposed of by being used. Once diluted down to a very weak solution, they can be watered onto grass sward during spring when the nutrients can be rapidly taken up with little danger of run-off. To dispose of unwanted chemical pesticides, fungicides and insecticides, contact your local authority for advice; please do not pour them down the drain.

ABOVE RIGHT *This was secondhand and has since outlasted four plastic rivals.* LEFT *A compost bin is full of fresh fertility, and all for free.*

3 Consume wisely and save nature. Stop, or at least reduce, your use of peat, especially from important wildlife sites. Don't buy ecologically unacceptable plants, such as imported wild bulbs and mass bedding plants; choose materials from renewable sources; and avoid plastic products wherever natural or longer-lasting alternatives are available. (My second-hand galvanised watering can has outlasted four plastic companions so far.)

4 Use wit, cunning and companion planting to grow healthy plants and outmanoeuvre pests and disease problems. Use the methods recommended on page 17 and maximise your natural ecosystem checks and balances by growing a wider variety of plants, especially more trees and shrubs. This helps create more habitats, especially if water is supplied with ponds and pools. Make nest boxes and nest sites; simple piles of rubble or rotting logs hidden under evergreen shrubs or in hedge bases will soon be colonised by many forms of wildlife.

All the benefits wildlife brings us

The greater part of good gardening method is encouraging all the forms of life in the soil and surrounding environment. The more wildlife in the garden, the more plant life it can support and this, in turn, supports more life and more plants. Our soil life may be nurtured with watering, mulches, compost, planting the best companions, and avoiding soluble fertilisers and pesticides. The multitude of insect and scurrying life forms is increased by growing many diverse plants that provide food, water, shelter, nesting and wintering sites. Larger forms of life are thus enticed to these and can be encouraged with yet more plants. However, a well-planned garden is not just filled with all the plants that benefit wildlife, but every nook and cranny is packed with nest boxes for birds, bat roosts, hedgehog dens, frog and toad pits, piles of rotten logs in shady corners and ladybird nests. More pests are supported in the average garden than would be in the wild because of

the diversity of food sources. These, in turn, support larger populations of predators and parasites which keep them in check. The balance point reached is not necessarily one that suits us, so we endeavour to move it in our favour by deliberately aiding the beneficial insects.

Although we cannot control which forms of wildlife we have, we can encourage them, and the more we can gather into our garden, the more it will throb with life and the more it will produce as the plants feast on their wastes, by-products and, eventually, their bodies. This is contrary to the conventional view where almost every creature is regarded as a threat and needs instant annihilation. The mixture of inhabitants in a healthy garden is amazingly varied, from the larger creatures down to countless varieties of bacteria, fungi and other forms of microlife. All of these prey on each other, the plants and all the breakdown products in between, yet all are solar powered, in the end, by photosynthesis capturing sunlight.

We can categorise these creatures as pests, predators, pollinators and recyclers but, in reality, they are all part of nature's interactive chain of life. For example, butterflies, who pollinate, were once caterpillars eating leaves, and a blackbird may be a pest when it is eating fruit, but is a predator when it eats wireworms or leatherjackets. Such creatures are continually recycling living and dead materials and excreting wastes. The value of all that fertility is easily equivalent to many handfuls of an organic fertiliser, but is distributed unnoticed in a healthy garden where material is quickly incorporated by the soil life. Our aim, as organic gardeners, is to get as many chains of life going as possible, attracting wildlife of all forms to our garden for the hidden fertility they bring with them and the checks and balances that come from building up the natural populations.

ABOVE *One of nature's jewels, the Azure Damselfly.* **LEFT** *Butterflies sip nectar so they can flutter for longer. That's their real name you know, flutterbys.*

Wildlife control and encouragement: aiding nature's ecosystems

To maximise the number and variety of life forms in the garden we have to provide for their needs by replicating their natural habitats. You can do this in a number of ways, as follows:

- Provide as varied and dense a planting as we can without choking the plants.
- Under and within this planting, provide shelter for the creatures to escape from our tidying and to overwinter.
- Create damp corners, warm dry spots and shady overgrown areas and avoid over-cleanliness and uniform tidiness – even a strip of long grass beside a hedge or along a fence provides a surprisingly good habitat for beetles, spiders and other predators. Add bulbs for spring interest and you provide pollen and nectar into the bargain.
- Make nest boxes for birds and hedgehogs.
- Hide nests of dry twiggy material for small creatures in every evergreen, as well as bundles of hollow stems.
- Provide extra food for the recycling system by adding organic material and natural fertilisers to the soil.
- Plant a wide variety of flowers to provide pollen and nectar over a long period for pollinators.
- Grow berrying plants and provide food scraps in winter to sustain birds who are useful allies.
- Provide water which will lure and retain more different forms of life than any other attraction. Especially useful are plants such as teasel, lupins and *Alchemilla mollis*, all of which capture rain and dew in their leaves and leaf joints. Birdbaths, water features, fountains, a deep pond, a shallow pool, a muddy stagnant ditch or a sunk-in sink will all appeal to different creatures. An old bath, once dug in and camouflaged, makes an excellent small pool. Do remember to make an easy way out for small creatures with a sloping bit of rough wood. Garden pools probably now account for the majority of breeding sites for frogs, toads and newts countrywide.

Pest subsystems Pests are an essential part of the ecology. Pests are only pests when they eat our crops or ornamentals, otherwise we would see them as wildlife, recyclers and pollinators. Often, they are part of several systems but at different stages of their lives. Woodworm in a dead log is a recycler, in a tree or table it becomes a pest. Some pests are also friends; thrips and capsid bugs damage some plants but eat tremendous numbers of red spider mites.

Plants in nature come to a balance with their pests; it is when we grow monocultures or eliminate the natural controls that they run rampant. However, pests seldom do much harm to healthy plants that are growing well; most things we grow are remarkably trouble-free after all. The pests we find most troublesome mainly concern a few vegetables and fruits, and these can be readily controlled by the methods described in Chapter 10. We need a background level of pests or there is nothing to keep the predators alive and, without them, any new pest would soon escalate into a problem. After all, if there were no snails there would probably be no songbirds, and even snails are useful, converting diseased and wilted material to manure.

Predator subsystems The predators and parasites in a stable system need pests to live. They control pest numbers effectively left to themselves in a complicated web where they prey not only on the pests but also on each other. This is particularly true of larger predators, such as hedgehogs and toads, which will eat almost anything. Ladybirds are well-known predators, but almost all beetles are predatory and deal with slugs and other small pests and their eggs. Spiders are all predatory, and number many million in a large healthy garden. Hoverflies, lacewings, anthocorid bugs and predatory wasps all help control red spider mites, aphids, caterpillars and other pests. Similarly, there are numerous parasites, wasps and other creatures that live on even in living pests. But, as all of these breed more slowly than the pests, if a pesticide is ever used and they are killed along with the pests, then the pests resurge out of control. It can take many years to

LEFT *A pile of sticks is home to a multitude of small creatures, each adding it's own value.* RIGHT *Even a water butt can be 'dead' or 'alive and throbbing'.*

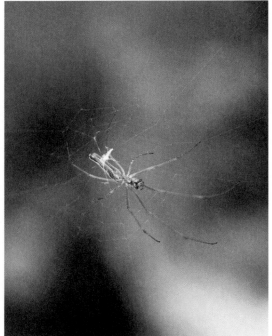

LEFT *Ladybird pupa and newly emerged adult.* MIDDLE *ALL spiders are friends, they do not eat any part of any plant, only insects.* RIGHT *And what will you become?*

rebuild a complex, self-regulating system if it is badly disrupted; thus, all pesticides are preferably avoided, even the less toxic, organically approved ones. By growing a wide variety of plants – especially sacrificial plants such as honeysuckles, sweet cherries, nettles and native hedges to which pests do little damage – you can maintain a background level of predators that control the pests on other plants in the garden. Ground-cover plants are particularly important for walking predators, such as beetles, and even simple strips of rough, long grass will increase their numbers. We can provide flying insect predators with nectar and pollen to attract and keep them working in our garden by planting wisely (see page 19).

Pollinator subsystems Bees are the most well-known of the pollinators but of course hoverflies, flies, butterflies, beetles and wasps all visit and pollinate flowers, as well as being predators. Bumble bees are more important to early flowerers than honey bees, which only fly in warmer weather, and so bumble bees can be bought commercially in cardboard 'huts' to hang in greenhouses. Obviously, the main requirement for encouraging more pollinators is more flowers, not just in mass but also throughout the longest season possible.

Recycler subsystems This is the largest system; the vast majority of small creatures are recycling material discarded by larger forms, although the larger creatures are often recyclers as well. Pollinators are not only pollinating the flowers, but recycling pollen and nectar as more

pollinators. These, too, then live and die, adding their droppings and bodies to increase soil fertility. This is not insignificant; a colony of honey bees contains from thirty to a hundred thousand bees at any one time and most of these live for only six to eight weeks in summer. Thus, a colony loses about ten thousand bees a week to natural death and predators. Insect bodies are rich in chitin (which makes up much of their tough skin) and is thought to be beneficial to soil and plant health.

In a sense we are all recyclers; everything living depends on absorbing bits from other, now dead, things. Plants build up their materials from air, light, water and the nutrients released from organic matter as it decomposes. All other life breaks down plants, other creatures and their by-products. The faster the turnover and the more forms of life we encourage, the more our garden will support. Most of nature's recyclers live on or in the soil surface where most things fall at the end of their life. Without them the world would long ago have filled up with smelly little corpses. Recyclers spend their lives converting dead and diseased material into plant food. These processes go on most rapidly in aerated, warm, moist conditions as found under ground-cover plants, a layer of leaves or a mulch. By duplicating these conditions we aid recyclers and if we supply them with organic material they will convert it into fertility.

However, remember that the predators are just as keen to eat the recyclers as the pests, so provide some refuges as well. Small piles of rotting logs, rocks, bricks or even bottles can be hidden under hedges and evergreens, providing shelters in which creatures can build up their numbers. Recyclers such as snails, often regarded far more as pests, can be found and dispatched of more easily if you create these convenient collection points.

Encouraging our best friends

Butterflies are often pests in disguise. However, they are usually pollinators and their beauty alone is reason enough to encourage them. Many flowers can feed them as they have long tongues and, of course, some rely on specific plants for their caterpillar stage. Buddleias, *Sedum spectabile*, golden rod, valerian and lavender are amongst the best floral attractants. Others include *Dianthus*, *Hesperis*, hyssop, lilacs, *Lonicera*, *Lychnis*, *Lythrum*, *Myosotis*, *Origanum* and violas. Many other flowers are visited, especially those in shades of yellow, orange or red. Night-scented flowers are appealing to moths who can smell them from further afield in the still moist air of evening.

Bees are under threat because the widespread loss of native wildflowers deprives them of their foodstuffs. Each of us can include a few bee plants and it is really in our interests to do so. In the short run, we benefit from the pollination of our fruits and more honey but, in the long run, we may save ourselves. If bees die out, whole families of plants may disappear and the chain of ecological damage may take us with it. Bumble bees are even more valuable but, of course, provide no honey. They fly in colder conditions and pollinate earlier in the year than honey bees. A third group, the leaf cutter bees, pollinate early fruit. They benefit from the same plants as the bumble bees and honey bees.

All bees need continuous supplies of pollen and nectar, so many different flowers should be grown to spread the season. See Chapter 9 for plants for honey bees. Bumble bees like much the same flowers but also go for all dead nettles, comfrey, flowering currants, fuchsias, globe artichokes, jasmine, knapweeds, mallows, thistles and wallflowers. Bumble bees need flowers most in early spring, such as *Aubrieta*, *Berberis*, bluebells, dandelions, flowering currants, wallflowers and white dead nettle. From early summer, they go for brambles and their hybrids, buddleias, clover, comfrey, *Cotoneaster*, fuchsias, globe artichokes and cardoons, golden rod, jasmines, knapweed, lavenders, mallows, Michaelmas daisies, raspberry, rhododendrons, thistles and vetches.

Hoverflies are the best aphid eaters; the larvae eat many more in a day than ladybird larvae. The best plant to bring them in is the low-growing, self-sowing annual *Limnanthes douglasii*. This should be grown as much as possible, filling the garden with hoverflies and feeding bees. Buckwheat and *Convolvulus tricolor* are excellent at supplying nectar

ABOVE *Lilacs provide masses of blooms, choose single not double flowered forms.*
BELOW *Borage is most useful, self-seeding and long-flowering.*

Beetles are a very large group; they are mostly friends, such as ladybirds, but there are exceptions which are pests, or recyclers, at certain stages of their lives, such as the wood-boring varieties. Beetles are good pollinators in cold, wet conditions when other creatures can't fly, though some, such as pollen beetles, can rob too much. Ground cover helps stop many useful ground-dwelling beetles from being spotted by bigger predators. Dense-foliaged plants that collect dew are, thus doubly good. Plants with hiding places between their leaves, under rough bark, in congested twiggy areas and even in deadwood will hide or hibernate beetles and other creatures.

Frogs, toads and newts eat many pests; they need water and wet places. They will be keener to patrol the garden if there is good ground cover, preferably moist underneath. Have a lush, overgrown corner in the greenhouse and you can have them living and dining there. Newts are useful and interesting to watch, especially at mating time. I made the end of my polytunnel abut the pond and a low log wall provides access, so all these friends can come into the warm and eat pests while visiting. In general, newts and frogs will not breed in the same small pond so, if you have the option, consider having two small ponds.

later in the season. Most flowers benefit hoverflies: *Alyssum*, *Arabis*, *Aubrieta*, cornflowers, *Cosmos*, *Eschscholzia*, *Geranium* (but not *Pelargonium*), golden rod, grape hyacinths, *Heliotrope*, honesty, *Iberis*, all marigolds, Michaelmas daisies, *Nemophila*, *Nicotiana*, *Petunia*, *Phlox*, all poppies, *Rudbeckia*, *Sedum spectabile*, Shasta daisy, stocks, sunflower, sweet rocket, sweet William and sweet Wivelsfield, tansy, all the mints and wallflowers. Letting celery and carrots go to seed will also encourage hoverflies and many other beneficial insects.

Ladybird and lacewing adults eat aphids (as do their larvae). They take nectar or pollen from the same plants as hoverflies, but also like *Allium*, *Anthemis*, fennel and yarrow. Lacewing adults fed only on aphids do not lay eggs. The best encouragement is plenty of tempting food. Grow plants that are regularly laden with aphids and soon there's plenty of predators. Aphids can be encouraged on patches of nettles, honeysuckles, sweet cherries, vetches and lupins which then maintain a healthy level of predators and parasites. The overwintering adults hibernate in conifers, evergreen hedges and dense culinary herbs. Nest boxes of hollow stems are useful and should be secreted in dry places.

Wasps are very good friends, eating pests in the spring and summer but, when autumn comes, they also rob our fruit! Dead rotting wood will provide wasps with raw material for their paper nests. All the nectar-producers for hoverflies will benefit their relatives: the predatory wasps which parasitise caterpillars, beetles, aphids and spiders.

Spiders are friends and are very sensitive to pesticides. The best way to encourage them is to provide the right type of habitat. Under cover, I supply strings to start their webs in convenient places, water in old bottle caps and hollow stems for nests.

ABOVE *Nasturtiums are easy space fillers, loved by insects and their flowers, seeds and leaves are all edible and tasty too.* **BELOW** *Sunflowers are fun, good for bees and butterflies and later for birds, or snacks for us.*

LEFT *Dense hedges and fences clad with ivy are full of tiny critters.*
RIGHT *A pool provides a garden with many different pest controllers.*

Birds Gardeners often wish to get rid of birds but, on the whole, they are beneficial (apart from the wood pigeon). Most other birds are hungry friends, always looking for snacks, most of which are pests, and they control more pests than they spoil crops. Individual crops may need protecting but, in the end, we all benefit from more birds. We can attract birds by providing the right habitat and a reliable food supply, but water is essential.

If you want to attract birds, grow fruit of any sort. As is all too soon apparent, birds prefer cultivated fruit to the wild fare nature provides. Redcurrants and cherries disappear fastest, but hardly any fruit makes it through winter. Berries of any sort are equally appreciated, though yellow ones apparently confuse the birds for a while before disappearing rapidly. Often they are just after the succulence, so you can reduce potential damage by providing water. The more fruit you grow, the less damage your resident population can do, so plant sacrificial crops of berrying trees and shrubs and enjoy all the wildlife that this brings. Seeding plants, especially sunflowers and wheat, will also feed them, and some heads can be saved for the winter.

Birds favour all dense-growing hedges, evergreens, and climbers because they provide useful nooks and crannies for nest building and shelter. Suitable nesting sites in the wild are increasingly rare, so provide nest boxes in your garden. Encourage the most useful birds, such as blue tits, great tits, tree sparrows, and other small insectivorous birds. The ideal nest site for most small insectivorous birds is an old woodpecker's hole, but few are available. The inside shape is most important; opt for a rounded, bowl-shaped bottom, which is easily made with papier-mâché or plaster. Robins, flycatchers and wagtails

prefer their box to have a bigger, wider, more open front. Boxes ought to resemble natural holes and be fixed to trees, safe from cats and other predators. Many of the other birds, such as blackbirds and thrushes, find ample nest sites amid dense evergreens or thick hedges. Bend suitable branches down out of sight and tie them together to form a nesting platform or prune them back hard to form clusters of splayed shoots suitable for lodging a nest.

Swallows and house martins bind their nests together with mud, of which there is now a shortage as garden ponds rarely have muddy edges. There are also fewer piles of strawy dung or livestock leaving their hair on hedges, which deprives house martins of the other material they need. If they make them out of mud alone, the nests have nothing to strengthen them, so they fall off when the mud bakes and shrinks. So, hang hair trimmings and put out bowls of mud by the pool edge for these useful insect eaters. Grow thistles, cardoons and artichokes, old man's beard and other downy, seeded plants for 'fluff'.

Worms Remember, if you want to hear songbirds, you need worms! Worms are probably the most important creatures in our gardens. Their casts provide ten tons per acre per year and more of the very best soil texturisers and fertilisers. Worm casts are water stable and have a granular texture that promotes root growth. Their burrows act as aeration and drainage channels and, when abandoned, are followed down by plant roots for their rich lining. Their digestive process reduces mineral particles in size, which makes these more accessible to micro-organisms. Encourage worms by keeping the soil moist and covered with a mulch. I feed all bare soil and most mulched areas with a handful of grass clippings every month or so as they need 'greens', as well as organic material such as compost or well-rotted manure. Ground seaweed, blood, fish and bone meal, and hoof and horn meal will also feed them. It is better not to rotavate and to practise minimal digging as these processes kill worms. In acid soils, add lime every four years or so unless you grow lime-hating plants. Adding lime for the worms is most important for the vegetable bed and for the most hard-wearing grass swards.

Hedgehogs and bats Hedgehogs do not thrive on the traditional milk and bread; dog or cat food is a better treat! Plant dense-growing shrubs with dry centres (such as brambles and conifers) for them to hibernate in. Hedgehog boxes can be put underneath these shrubs or hedges. Make them waterproof from above, at least a foot cubed, and full of dry leaves with a fist-sized entrance hole. Overall, I suspect hedgehogs are not very helpful. They eat many earthworms, as well as the occasional slug and snail. An examination of their droppings indicates that they do eat many beetles. Larger beetles are, on the whole, beneficial because many eat crop pest eggs and young, so losing them is not helpful.

Bats eat tremendous numbers of flying pests and are best encouraged by providing both roosting and hibernating sites. The former are flat wooden boxes that open underneath and are attached high up on warm walls, while the latter are harder to create. Trees, like limes, with large crops of aphids, will shower them off into the breeze and these attract bats.

RIGHT *Redcurrants are useful fruits for us and also grateful snacks for birds.*
OPPOSITE *Grapevine ('Boskoop Glory') trained over an old apple tree keeps the birds off another vine on a wall nearby.*

CHOICE PLANTS TO ATTRACT BIRDS

TREES AND SHRUBS

Amelanchier Edible berries in autumn

Beech, *Fagus* Hedges; good cover for nests and perches, even during winter

Berberis Nest sites and berries

Conifers Nest sites, roosts and weather protection

Crataegus Nest sites and berries

Elaeagnus pungens Nesting places and hard weather protection

Elderberry Perches, nests and berries

Firethorn, *Pyracantha* Loads of berries

Holly, *Ilex* Evergreen growth and winter berries if you plant both sexes

Laurel Hard-weather shelter, but not for nesting as it is so easily climbed by predators

Mahonia Grape-like fruit

Shrub roses Nest sites and rose hips

Sorbus (which includes the rowan and whitebeam) Plentiful berries

Yew, *Taxus* Nesting trees and berries loved by birds, although toxic to us

CLIMBERS AND WALL SHRUBS

Ceanothus Nest sites

Clematis Nest sites/nests; the seeds and many have fine floss that can be used for nesting material; for varieties see page 51.

Cotoneasters Nesting and a wealth of berries

Garrya elliptica Dense cover for nests

Honeysuckle, *Lonicera* Dense growth which is good for nests and they berry freely

Hydrangea petiolaris Good nest sites

Ivies, *Hedera* Shelter and berries late in the year, see page 51

Roses Good shelter from predatory cats, good nesting sites and hips

Virginia creepers, *Parthenocissus* Nest sites and berries after hot summers

Wisteria Good nest provider, with the old twisting stems producing many nooks and ledges. Although slow to flower, these are worthwhile

SACRIFICIAL FRUIT AND VEGETABLE COMPANIONS

These are much loved by birds and so are well-suited to the wild garden:

Top Fruit	Soft Fruit
Apples	Blackberries and
Cherries	tayberries
Mulberries	Grapes
Peaches	Loganberries
Pears	Raspberries
Plums	Strawberries
	Worcesterberries

When fruit fails to satisfy the birds' appetites, you can sow some of the following vegetables for tasty little seedling snacks:

Beet, Brassicas, Lettuce, Peas, Spinach

A time for everything – working with the yearly cycle

There's an old saying in gardening that there's a right time for everything and it was usually last week. It certainly can feel like that, as most jobs come in rushes and everything needs to be done at once. Less panic comes with practice and the familiarity of the yearly cycle. Certain tasks are not only best done at the right time of year, but can also be much easier or more effective when done at the precisely optimum time. We mostly do heavy pruning in the dormant period of winter when the plant is least shocked but, then again, we prune in summer to control growth or promote flowers or fruit. The timing of sowings is, of course, often critical. Cauliflowers need to be sown a year before they are wanted almost to the week and biennial flowers, such as foxgloves, two years before. Japanese onions must be sown as soon as the days shorten to less than fourteen hours. In my garden in Norfolk, that's the third week in August. It should be then, and only then, if they are to make good crops.

I was surprised when investigating sowing according to astrological timing at how strong the results were. Although there was much contradictory evidence as to the actual best date to sow any given thing, it soon became evident what a difference sowing a few days apart made to the final result. I now conclude that we ought to sow in at least three batches, each a few days apart. The best are then selected, usually with never a doubt.

Other tasks have their own schedule; for example, cutting a grass lawn for neatness becomes progressively more difficult the later in spring we start. Clearing an overgrown area is much easier in late winter when all the growth is dormant. And, of course, we can only collect leaves when they fall in autumn.

Working with seasonal changes in activity soon enables all gardeners to pace their workload so that it never overwhelms them. Indeed, one of the joys of gardening is that it can be done at so many levels depending on the amount of time and effort you are able or willing to put in. Growing vegetables is a make-work scheme compared to a design based entirely on evergreens. But, even so, the same result can be had by a lot of hard work ill-planned and too late or by a little in good time. And, it takes but a moment's thought to remember not to plant fruit trees that crop right in the middle of your summer holiday.

ABOVE LEFT *Pick tomatoes as soon as they ripen then more will set.* **ABOVE RIGHT** *Starting off in pots, trays or cells then planting out later can be much more efficient than sowing in situ.* **LEFT** *Pick early apples asap, and late varieties as late as possible.* **RIGHT** *Asparagus in bloom with leek heads about to flower.*

2 THE FLOWERING OF THE GARDEN

The pleasure garden of flowers; aesthetics, colour and design, and combining these in the productive garden

Perhaps the biggest change in recent years has been a burgeoning interest in native plants and wildflowers, as well as a desire to encourage wildlife into our gardens. Almost every gardening book now devotes some space to these themes, especially to attracting more birds and butterflies (though few seem as keen on caterpillars). Sterile, double-flowered varieties are being replaced by their more useful nectar- and pollen-bearing originals, while fewer gardens are being designed around plants such as conifers and evergreens which were once vaunted as 'low-maintenance'.

Gardens can be works of art. Everyone's taste is different and, in the end, it doesn't really matter as long as you like what you have to live with. Some prefer order, symmetry and regimentation, others like subtle shading and soft lines, or blazes of bright colour. All are equally valid, but what sits uneasily on the eye are mixtures of great diversity, unless these are skilfully blended with smooth transitions. What makes for a pleasing garden is a feeling of naturalness or oneness with the surroundings – as if the garden has always been as it is and could hardly be otherwise. If we create a harmony of shapes, colours, scents and sounds, then it helps us to relax and become more at ease, as well as giving us great satisfaction. The gardener's art lies in combining what few resources there are to hand to create this beauty, not only in the front garden or one particular bed but in each and every part. Although some areas may be given over to pure ornamentality, a garden is only complete when every bed, view and vista is a pleasure to the eye.

Furthermore, as we become more ecologically aware, then even purely ornamental areas are seen to benefit the rest of the garden. Indeed, they can be a source of fertility with grass clippings, leaves and

BELOW *The old greenhouse became a hen house and the rose garden the chicks' playground – I still get roses for the table, and chicken too!*

prunings being composted for use elsewhere and by encouraging and sustaining many more forms of life that then go on to contribute their own by-products to the garden's ecosystem.

When showing visitors around my garden, I am pleased and bemused by a frequent remark, 'I never expected to see so many flowers'. As I am perhaps best known for my organic fruits and vegetables, they never expect anything other than stark utilitarianism, but, of course, I do grow flowers, but mostly edible or scented ones – I just don't have space for the rest. Those flowers and non-crop plants that are a pleasure to see are also the dining tables to keep my tiny garden friends at home. Ornamental plants can provide for the wide variety of species that create balanced ecosystems, which control pests and diseases in the other parts of the garden and neighbourhood. The sheer diversity of plants and their many interactions means that purely ornamental areas are also easy to manage organically, with few pests or diseases ever causing problems. However, it becomes a little more complicated when you also want to grow crops in that same garden.

COTTAGE GARDENS IN MYTH AND REALITY

Often offered as the epitome of garden design is the 'cottage-garden style', frequently simplified to masses of mixed planting with flowers predominating and allegedly also producing useful crops. Perhaps this vision offers some escape to a supposedly simpler time and indeed the concept has some intrinsic merit, which we can learn from. Charming as these mythical cottage gardens are, however, they have done much to mislead gardeners. Wonderful masses of flowers combined with fruits and vegetables look terrific when staged at flower shows such as Chelsea, but are incredibly time-consuming to maintain.

Over centuries, the genuine cottage garden evolved from a primitive kitchen or herb garden outside a rustic hut. As we now understand and utilise more of the ecology involved, then utilitarian gardens such as this are enlightening. They were purely functional and probably developed with very little influence from the gardens of the rich and powerful, which relied on scale, order and geometry and on man imposing his designs on nature. With the Victorian period there came a desire to recreate a Rustic or Gardenesque style, but these were contrived from and not wrought with nature. Similarly, at the start of the twentieth century, Wild Gardening, as promoted by William Robinson (1838–1935), was concerned not with cultivating our native ecology but almost solely with growing exotics in a native setting.

Of much greater interest to us now is the pragmatic and mixed

ABOVE *It's a lot easier to grow flowers in the vegetable plot than to grow vegetables in the flowerbeds.*

planting used by 'ignorant' peasants. Early cottage gardeners did not grow plants to provide their staple food, but lived on beer, bread and roots grown elsewhere. Instead, their gardens largely provided herbs for flavouring and medicine, with few of our modern vegetables and fruits being grown. Now we may be searching for a similar harmony with plants that superficially resembles this humble cottage garden, but the compositions are necessarily changed. Some of the old herbs could be retained but not the many medicinal plants, and our modern choice of vegetables, fruits and flowers is likely to differ greatly from their traditional few. Thus, the modern cottage garden may be completely different from the original in content if not in its idyllic appearance. The only drawback is that serious quantities of food are not easy to produce when combined with a cottage-garden appearance, particularly because of the intense plant competition. Nonetheless, there can still be valuable contributions to the household of herbs, flowers and tree fruits. And, as long as the plants are well chosen, having such a wide variety of plants provides the diversity that makes for a stable ecology, so that pests and diseases become much less of a nuisance.

ORNAMENTAL VEGETABLE GARDENS AND POTAGERS

For serious crop production, it's important to give more emphasis to the needs of the productive plants. A great mixing of different plant types is suitable for non-productive areas, but vegetables require the very best of conditions in order to grow well. Although they benefit in pest and disease control from mixing and mingling with flowers and other plants, food crops must never be crowded or they fail catastrophically. Saladings can make quite attractive bedding in open spots but, unless you choose a cut-and-come-again variety, eating any inevitably leaves a gap. Many forms of fruit may be grown with flowers, but they will be unlikely to do as well as in a specially prepared and protected area. Also, ripe crops can be hard to find among other plants, unsightly to protect from the birds, and difficult to harvest.

If you decide to mix food crops and flowers, then the food crops must be the priority in terms of planning and position, with flowering plants included in spare niches you may have available amongst them. Basically, this means giving the vegetable patch an appealing design, adding companion plants and flowers, and surrounding it with trained fruit. If you attempt to grow common food crops amongst existing ornamental plants, then this nearly always gives poor results due to fatal competition from the established plants. There are alternatives; delightful gardens can be made almost entirely of ornamental edible plants, though I find few of them very palatable. You can, of course, forego the productive side entirely and go for a naturalistic garden that runs itself ecologically and take what you can glean.

FOREST GLADES

These offer the nearest we can get to a totally naturalistic garden given the parameters of a modern plot. We can easily recreate the effect of a sunny open space caused by the fall of a major tree within shady woodland. We can replicate such a glade with high fences and borders around a lawn and make it attractive to wild creatures by planting predominantly native trees and shrubs and then filling the border with woodland companions like foxgloves. The main drawback is that a small-scale forest glade soon becomes too shady for herb or vegetable production. However, as long as the sides don't get too high, then the central sunny glade area is suitable for most vegetables, while soft fruits (which usually grow on the woodland's edge) will thrive in a fruit cage.

WILD GARDENS

Leaving a plot to go 'back to nature' does have some merit: it is remarkable how rapidly a niche is colonised and, although a junk-strewn vista of weeds and brambles is not what most of us aspire to, it offers a vast number of interesting habitats – but only if left completely undisturbed. The art lies in concealing all the junk where it can be of service to the various forms of wildlife, while also offering them nest sites and water, as well as plants that will provide food and cover. A well-planned wild garden that looks appealing while also attracting wildlife is a great achievement rarely wrought by neglect!

LEFT Onions need hot, bare soil underneath to ripen but companions can occupy the edges of the beds. **CENTRE** *A wild garden may still need careful weeding occasionally.* **RIGHT** *A vegetable bed used for flower crops for a year or two, then returned to vegetables, benefits from the break in rotation.*

The golden compromise – selective companion planting for the health of the garden

Although plants compete with each other, they are not all after exactly the same niches. This, theoretically, allows us to squeeze more plants into a given area without them choking each other. Low-growing, shallow-rooting, ground-covering plants can exist in the light shade of deeper rooting trees, while climbers can grow up the latter, thus creating three planting tiers. Shrubs can be added, but will do poorly unless the trees are well spaced or open between, in which case four tiers of plants can be built up. This gives a rich habitat for wildlife and uses soil and light so efficiently that few weeds then get a chance to appear. It also provides the stable habitat that resists pest and disease problems.

Unfortunately, such a garden produces very little that is tasty and can even be unsuitable for many ornamentals. Some groups of plants just need to be isolated from the more vigorous woody and shade-forming ones – for example, most of our favourite herbaceous plants are best grown in their own border; silvery and culinary herbs thrive in their own dry sunny bed; and vegetables grow most successfully in their own open, sunny, airy plot. Vegetables, in particular, benefit from having the right permanent companions around the edges of their

ABOVE LEFT *Pot and French marigolds jostle with a self-sown asparagus plant on the end of this bed.* **ABOVE RIGHT** *Tobacco, Litchi tomato, borage and cabbages contend for space in this sunny corner.* **BELOW** *Strips of carpet make neat paths between beds, conserving valuable moisture and saving weeding all summer.*

growing areas and their own preferred companions inside (see page 161 for the best vegetable companionships).

Even building up good teams of perennial plants can only be successful if the order of planting is controlled to allow each form of plant time and room to establish. This applies to purely ornamental mixed beds and borders and to perennial productive combinations, but is definitely not recommended for most vegetables. First, prepare the area well, removing all weeds and rubbish and improving the soil, as outlined in Chapter 4. Once the site is marked out and ready, plant trees (preferably fruiting as well as purely ornamental ones), and ensure that each has ample room to develop. After these have established for a year, plant shrubs and fruit bushes between, again leaving each plenty of room. After another year, plant herbaceous plants, ground cover and bulbs in the available spaces. Several years later, when the trees and shrubs have reached sufficient size, climbers can be grown over them. Careful weeding is then needed until the plants cover the soil, although thick mulches will minimise this and aid growth.

You will be tempted to plant up the apparently enormous gaps while the main plants become established, so add more colour and interest in the first year or two by growing annual flowers in the gaps. These must not be vigorous and encroach on the main plantings. Alternatively, sow batches of green manures in the gaps instead, allowing a few fine specimens to flower and composting the rest.

Choosing useful as well as beautiful flowering and scented plants

You can *only* have so many plants, so make them all multi-purpose and only choose the best. For instance, don't choose a plant for its flowers if you can have one with equally good flowers *and* scent and, better still, with some part you can eat or which benefits wildlife. When choosing plants, remember that organic gardeners try to go with nature rather than force her. For this reason, plants are divided into several groups so that we can best understand their needs and help them to flourish.

Family ties We name and know plants from their genus and species; there is also often a cultivar name that gives further information. Most species in a genus are similar with minor differences and so, once we

know one, we can often guess at the needs and attributes of the others. For example, clematis and jasmine are thought of as climbers and the needs for most varieties and species are similar. However, there are herbaceous and shrubby clematis and even an evergreen shrubby jasmine, *J. humile* 'Revolutum'.

The important thing to remember is that closely related plants (those with the same first name) usually suffer from the same pests and diseases. Furthermore, the more widely any of them and their relations are grown, the more pests and diseases there are to plague them. For example, members of the Brassica family – such as cabbages, cauliflowers and broccoli – are all common and closely related, so are attacked by the same large number of pests and diseases. Any plants related to common native plants will similarly be subject to their pests and diseases, but these will usually be controlled by natural systems that have evolved with them, provided we have not inadvertently destroyed those.

Annuals and perennials Annuals live, flower and die in a short period, usually from spring to autumn. They provide some of the prettiest flowers and also make up many of our vegetables where we eat the fruits or seeds, such as sweet corn, peas and broad beans. (To complicate matters, many perennials are grown as annuals, discarded or killed by frosts, and then replaced the following year.) Annuals generally prefer direct sowing and resent root disturbance; most are normally only propagated from seed. The frost-resistant hardy annuals can usually be sown the autumn before to flower and crop sooner than spring sowings.

Biennials live longer than annuals, growing one year to flower the next. Many vegetables, such as the roots and onions, are biennials but are eaten before they complete their cycle. Some of our most attractive flowers are biennials – foxgloves, Canterbury bells, hollyhocks and sweet rocket are all examples. Some effectively biennial plants, such as wallflowers, Brompton and East Lothian stocks, and Sweet Williams, might live for another year or two before dying away, but are usually replaced with fresh plants. Moving biennials while they are dormant seldom harms them.

True perennials should survive for at least a year or two; most are much longer lasting. However, some are fairly short-lived, such as gooseberries, thymes and many daphnes, while other apparently perennial plants are monocarpic (and die once they have set seed). Those plants that spread with creeping roots (such as bamboos) are continually forming new plants at their margins and are effectively immortal. Some trees live for more than a thousand years and many for a century or more; however, few garden trees are very old at all. Perennials tend to make up the bulk of the ornamental and fruiting plants in most gardens, as they are semi-permanent, do not usually need annual replacement, and their established root systems help them endure poor conditions. Most can be moved when young, but grow increasingly resentful of this when older and larger. It is often easier to propagate and plant a new perennial than move an old one.

OPPOSITE *This jungle of tobacco and sunflowers leaves no room for weeds.*
ABOVE RIGHT *Gooseberries fully ripened are a succulent treat unknown to those who've never grown them.* BOTTOM RIGHT *This Romanesco broccoli has now sadly gone over – but note how clean it is, the Borage has kept the caterpillars away if not the wood pigeons.*

YOU CAN TELL A LOT ABOUT THE REQUIREMENTS OF A PLANT FROM ITS APPEARANCE

Soft or shrubby? Perennials can be divided into those with soft growth that dies back in winter and those with shrubby or woody growth that re-grows each year. The former, bulbs and herbaceous plants spring again from the roots and are mostly propagated by division or root cuttings, as they then come true. Some also come true from seed and in a fairly short time. Bulbs and herbaceous plants form larger clumps, but do not grow taller each year and thus need no pruning, only a tidy up in autumn. Woody and shrubby plants grow larger each year and may need pruning. They are mostly propagated from cuttings or layering, though some need grafting or budding onto suitable rootstocks. Shrubby perennials grown from seed may be variable and slow to flower or fruit.

Deciduous or evergreen? While overwintering herbaceous plants are protected by the soil, most woody plants drop their leaves in autumn and go partially dormant. This is usually a good time to prune or move them, as they recover much better than when moved in leaf. Although they appear totally dormant, they will start to root immediately unless the soil is frozen. Evergreens drop their leaves a few at a time and suffer in hard weather from drying winds and frozen soil. The moisture is sucked out of their leaves and cannot be replaced, causing scorched foliage or even death. So, evergreens have evolved waxy coatings on their leaves to prevent water loss, which makes them slow to break down and hard to compost. Their dense cover provides excellent winter shelter for ladybirds and other predators, big and small, so include some evergreens in the garden. Most evergreens are only pruned or moved in early spring once the soil is warm enough for them to recover quickly, as they are never dormant.

Tender or hardy? Plants that can survive in the open garden with some degree of frost are considered hardy. Hardy annuals are a large group of flowers grown from seed each year that do not need protection and can be sown direct once the soil warms up in spring. Many can also be sown in the autumn to overwinter for an earlier display. Most garden perennials are effectively very hardy and survive many years in favourable positions, only being killed by extreme winters. Given a very good position against a wall, some surprising plants, such as *Opuntia*, the prickly pear cacti, pelargoniums and palms, can be grown, especially if they are protected during the worst frosts. Similarly, other less hardy plants such as fuchsias can survive bad weather if you mulch the roots thickly with straw or loose airy material.

Plants that have been grown hard (outdoors), with strong but not too vigorous growth, tend to withstand frost and temperature change better than plants grown soft (indoors or on a warm patio) or lushly (overfed and watered). Never feed plants heavily in late summer or autumn, as this promotes soft growth that does not ripen well and is prone to disease as well as frost damage. Most plants are more frost-resistant if they are not wet at the roots; well-draining soil and a warmth-retaining mulch will protect roots against many degrees of frost. Often, it is not the frost that causes the most damage, but the warm damp period that follows, which encourages rotting. For silver and hairy-leaved plants, rotting from damp is the problem and they will survive almost any weather if the rain is kept off with a cloche or just a sheet of glass on two bricks.

Plants are shocked by changes of temperature, so keep these as gradual as possible. When moving plants from a warmer place, harden them off by putting them outside in the day and bringing them in at night for a few days. Similarly, do not move plants from outside to a hot room in one go but adjust them more gradually.

Half-hardy is used to describe those bedding plants that need sowing in warmth and hardening off before planting out after the last frosts in spring. Tender plants die with the least touch of frost and do badly if at all cold, while stove- or hot-house plants require real heat (see Chapter 8 for advice on growing under cover).

OPPOSITE *Sweet peas are one of the easiest and most prolific flowers for cutting.*

PLANT POLLINATION

One rarely needs to consider pollination, except when saving seed or in the fruit garden (see Chapter 6). A few plants, such as holly and *Skimmia*, are dioecious and need both male and female plants to berry. Otherwise, encourage as many pollinators as possible into the garden to take care of the mechanics. Pollinators can also be enticed under cover if companion flowers, such as marigolds and sweet alyssum, are grown to attract them. However, to be sure, hand-pollination with a cotton-wool ball is a good idea for plants growing under cover or early in the year when pollinators are few. Most flowers last longer if they are not pollinated though, so cut-flower growers may be better off without pollinators.

My favourite annuals, biennials, bulbs, herbaceous trees and shrubs, climbers, marginals and pond plants

Butterflies and moths are such delightful garden visitors. So, I've noted where specific varieties of larvae feed on the foliage (and other parts) and are also likely to be seen on the blooms of my favourite plants. I consider the small amount of damage they do fair exchange for their later beauty, as few of them become serious pests anyway.

ANNUALS

These are invariably better sown in situ, but it is often more convenient to sow them in small pots and plant them out early or use them to fill gaps. Most will self-seed, and autumn-sown seedlings overwinter and flower earlier than spring-sown plants, so extending their season.

Alyssum maritimum Sweet, honey-scented plant that is loved by insects. The rose, purple and dwarf forms are more attractive and compact, but less well scented. Foliage sustains larvae of Bath White butterflies and Gem moths.

Centaurea cyanus Cornflowers are a most wonderful blue colour and good for cutting. Foliage sustains larvae of the Black-veined moth.

Convolvulus tricolor Like a petunia, but hardy, so does not require greenhouse space. White, blue and yellow trumpets attract bees, hoverflies and other beneficial insects. Foliage sustains larvae of Garden Carpet moths.

Lathyrus odoratus What is summer without sweet peas? Grow the old-fashioned ones with a strong scent. Sow in situ and in pots in autumn and spring for a succession of flowers.

Limonium Statice or sea lavender is excellent for cutting and drying. Foliage sustains larvae of Ground Lackey, Rosy Rustic and Rosy Wave moths.

Matthiola Ten-week stocks are highly scented, but for colour, ease and the most divine evening scent, sow mixed Virginian and Night-scented stocks.

Nicotiana Poisonous but beautiful, evening-scented sweet tobacco *N. alata*, *N. affinis* and *N. sylvestris* have sticky stems and leaves that trap small pests. Foliage

ABOVE TOP *Cornflowers are vibrant, good for insects and an excellent cut flower.* **RIGHT** *Shirley poppies are selections from the wild with improved colour.* **LEFT** *Matucana is an original sweet pea variety, has few blooms per stem and only in this colour combination but has a powerful sweet perfume.*

sustains larvae of Pearly Underwing, Scarce Bordered Straw and, sadly, the troublesome Cabbage Moth.

Phacelia tanacetifolia is a wonderful bee plant and good space filler with masses of bluey-purple flowers.

Tagetes patula French marigolds provide good colour, are long flowering and attract beneficial insects. The other *Tagetes* marigolds are also useful plants. Foliage sustains larvae of Death's-head Hawkmoth and, irritatingly, the Small (Garden) Swift moth.

Tropaeolum Sow nasturtiums direct in late spring and do not overfeed or they will be all leaves. Dwarf forms are often well scented, trailers can cover large areas with flowers, and all parts are edible, including the seeds.

Zaluzianskya capensis Cape phlox is little known, but has the most heavenly evening scent of sweet rich vanilla.

BIENNIALS

Start these off in a seed bed in early summer and plant out in their final position in autumn. Start them off two years running and most can be left to self-seed.

Cheiranthus Wallflowers are really perennial but better discarded once straggly. They have more scent value than most, especially as they flower so early. Foliage sustains larvae of Garden Carpet moths.

Dianthus Classic cottage-garden plants, I equally like Sweet Wivelsfield and Sweet William. Foliage of most species sustains larvae of Tawny Shears; Deptford Pink foliage supports the Mullein Wave moth.

Digitalis Foxgloves that self-seed are always best; they feed bees, thrive in woodland settings, but will fit into most odd corners. Foliage sustains larvae of Heath Fritillary, Lesser Yellow Underwing and the Small Angle, while the flowers are the only known

sustenance for the Foxglove Pug moth larvae.

Hesperis matronalis Sweet rocket is an undemanding, old-fashioned plant with tall, stock-like flowers. It dies out, but will self-seed everywhere.

Matthiola Brompton and East Lothian stocks sown in July and August give gorgeous heads of scented flowers the following spring. However, many are lost over winter, even if cloched; *M. incana* is the original and best (and semi-perennial).

Oenothera Evening primrose produces evening-scented, pollen-laden flowers. Foliage sustains larvae of Silver-washed Fritillary, Orange-Tip and, sadly, Green-veined Whites.

TOP LEFT *Foxgloves could not be easier but take two years, and are thought to be beneficial to other plants nearby.* TOP RIGHT *Evening primrose, easy self-seeding, long-flowering biennial with copious scented yellow flowers full of pollen.* BOTTOM RIGHT *Sweet William is good for cutting, so grow some in the vegetable bed.*

BULBS AND CORMS

Grow these like herbaceous plants in a border and naturalised in grass or under deciduous shrubs. Wherever they grow, do not remove the leaves before they have started to wither, as this reduces vigour and flowering. When planting, err too deep and also bed them on sharp sand in heavy or wet soils.

Allium The onion family produces reliable flowerers with ball-shaped flowers loved by beneficial insects. Many are edible, such as garlic and chives, which are also believed to benefit other plants, especially roses. There are many more ornamental alliums, such as *A. moly*, with lovely yellow flowers.

Crocus These are often grown through grass, but quickly die out if the leaves are removed too soon. The common Dutch crocus are best planted in groups and are useful to beneficial insects in early spring. Other varieties flower in the autumn and through winter.

Cyclamen These have beautiful, sometimes scented, flowers and usually attractive foliage, especially *C. europaeum*.

Galanthus Snowdrops are best divided and moved or bought while 'in the green', as dried bulbs die away. Divide them annually and they will increase rapidly; especially nice is the double *G. nivalis* 'Flore Pleno'.

Hyacinthus These are noted for their powerful scents and bright colours, but they are expensive. Hyacinths forced for indoor use can be hardened off and planted out, but after a few years degenerate to resemble bluebells, though they are a different species. Grape hyacinths, *Muscari*, are smaller, earlier and seed freely.

Lilium Lilies need well-drained, rich soils. Some need acid conditions and most prefer full sun or partial shade. The easiest are the Turkscap, *L. martagon*, and the Regal lily which is outstanding; it can even be grown from seed to flower in two years. Lilies are much troubled presently by larvae of the bright, orangey-red lily beetle. Hand-picking these off or growing the plants under fleece or cover are the best solutions.

Narcissus Daffodils come in many forms, from the early dwarf *N. bulbocodium* with rush-like foliage, through the sheets of 'King Alfred' at Easter to the late-flowering, gloriously scented Jonquils and *N. poeticus* or Pheasant's eye, *N. poeticus* var. *recurvus*.

Ranunculus ficaria Celandines can be more of a weed than most, spreading by tiny tubers carried from place to place on shoes and tools. They bring early cheer with sheets of gold for beneficial insects and look stunning with blue grape hyacinths. Foliage

sustains larvae of the Flame Brocade and Twin-spot Carpet moths.

Scilla non-scripta Bluebells are useful woodland self-seeders. Foliage sustains larvae of Autumnal Rustic and Six-striped Rustic.

Tulipa Their strong colours can be overpowering in some settings, but give tremendous impact on drab spring days. Cottage tulips can be naturalised in rough grass.

OPPOSITE CLOCKWISE FROM TOP LEFT *Leeks left to flower are attractive, and appealing to wildlife. Ornamental alliums are good companions to fruit trees. Snowflakes,* Leucojums, *are good for cutting and grow well in moist shade.* Cyclamen *are one of the most attractive ground covering plants and are good for shade.* LEFT *Lilies can be grown in pots undercover where they are safer from the dreaded lily beetle.* RIGHT *Nothing does or looks better in dappled shade than bluebells.* BELOW *Celandines are often regarded as a weed – but they are early-flowering, good for beneficial insects, and pretty in leaf.*

HERBACEOUS PERENNIALS

Herbaceous plants suffer from the competition if grown with other plants, so are usually best grown in their own bed or border. Of course, some bulbs and smaller shrubs can be used and are regarded as herbaceous to all intents. Tidy the plants in late autumn and divide or move them in the spring. When cutting back in autumn, wait until the stems have withered so that all the nutrients have been reabsorbed, then cut them off about a hand-span high. This leaves the old stem bases to support and protect the young shoots as they emerge, and marks their position. Clean mulches, good spacing in between, and planting in groups of three, five or seven produces the best effects.

VERY LOW-GROWING HERBACEOUS PERENNIALS

Ajuga reptans Carpet-rooting mats of blue bugle make excellent ground cover and attract bees, but are very invasive.

Alchemilla mollis Lady's mantle provides good ground cover with mounds of soft yellow-green and traps water droplets in its foliage. Foliage of wild species sustains larvae of Red Carpet and Knot Grass moths. Flowers are eaten by the larvae of Dark Marbled Carpet moths.

Alyssum saxatile Trailing clumps of grey leaves and masses of golden flowers are good for rockery ground cover but rather vigorous and invasive; cut back immediately after flowering. Foliage sustains larvae of Bath White butterflies and Gem moths.

Armeria maritima Thrift resembles evergreen cushions of grass until it flowers with pink balls on stems; it makes a good edging. Foliage sustains larvae of Ground Lackey, Feathered Ranunculus, Sweet-Gale and Black-Banded, and it is the sole known sustenance for Crescent Dart larvae.

Aubrieta Similar to *Alyssum*, this has thick mats of evergreen leaves and masses of flower in red to blue.

Bergenia cordifolia A tough, evergreen ground cover with large leaves; survives almost anywhere. Pink flowers in very early spring.

Gypsophila paniculata forms hummocks of tiny flowers loved by insects and flower arrangers alike.

Helianthemum nummularium Sun roses are very similar to *Cistus*, the rock rose, and are really shrubs. Ideal for dry walls or banks, they are evergreen but short-lived; prune them hard after the reddish flowers fade. Foliage of wild species sustains Brown Argus, Wood Tiger, Square-spot Dart, Ashworth's Rustic and Annulet. Both foliage and flowers sustain larvae of Green Hairstreak, and the withered leaves are the sole sustenance for Silky Wave larvae.

Iberis sempervirens Evergreen candytufts are really dwarf shrubs with lax evergreen foliage and masses of white flowers. The foliage sustains larvae of Garden Carpet moths.

LOW- TO MEDIUM-GROWING HERBACEOUS PERENNIALS

These mostly stand up on their own or look best left to form their own shape. In windy areas, on strong soil support may be necessary, in which case tie them up early.

Aquilegia hybrids Columbines are cottage-garden plants with beautiful, low, fern-like foliage and tall, graceful, spurred flowers in many colours and combinations. Foliage sustains attacks from larvae of Grey Chi moths.

Aster novi-belgii Michaelmas daisies provide late flowers for insects in reds and blues. Foliage of wild species sustains larvae of the Wormwood Pug, and the flowers the larvae of the Starwort.

Brunnera macrophylla Perennial forget-me-nots provide tough ground cover anywhere with heart-shaped leaves and early blue flowers.

Campanula Bellflowers provide the best blues in the garden, unless you can grow gentians, and are good for bees. These are the only flowers specifically visited by Halictoides bees. The foliage of the wild species is eaten by the larvae of Lime-speck Pug and the flowers and seeds by the larvae of the Black-Banded moth. Seeds and capsules of *C. trachelium* is the sole known sustenance of larvae of the Campanula Pug.

Geranium Cranesbills make excellent ground cover and flourish almost anywhere. Foliage of wild species sustains larvae of Swallow-tailed Moth, Annulet, Fox Moth and, sadly, the Cabbage Moth.

Geum These tough plants make excellent ground cover with wiry clumps which flower in early summer, especially the cute red-headed 'Mrs J Bradshaw'. Foliage sustains larvae of Beautiful Golden Y and Riband Wave moths.

Helleborus The Christmas and Lent roses give winter and spring flowers for beneficial insects, while their handsome evergreen foliage is good ground cover. They are poisonous but rarely cause problems; I find they resent moving.

Iris Bearded irises are tough, beautiful and thrive even in dry spots. *I. unguicularis* is a scented winter gem and *I. foetidissima* a useful evergreen with magnificent orange berries. Foliage, flowers and seeds of wild species sustain larvae of Marbled Coronet, Lychnis, Tawny Shears, Campion, Marbled Clover, Sandy Carpet, Twin-spot Carpet and Netted Pug.

Lychnis *L. chalcedonica* is commonly grown, but I love the double-flowered catchfly, *L. viscaria* 'Splendens Plena'. Foliage, flowers and seeds of wild species sustain larvae of Marbled Coronet, Lychnis, Tawny Shears, Campion, Marbled Clover, Sandy Carpet, Twin-spot Carpet and Netted Pug.

Nepeta Catnip, *N. cataria*, is loved by feline herbivores. The less-loved *N. mussinii* is bigger with more pointed leaves; both are loved by bees.

Sedum spectabile Most of these are invasive; this one is controllable, but any bit roots or divides. It is loved by insects in autumn and has good shape and foliage. Native sedums make very good ground cover for poor dry soils. Foliage of wild sedums sustains Northern Rustic, Feathered Ranunculus, Yellow-ringed Carpet, Mullein Wave and Common Pug.

Tradescantia virginiana This has attractive, odd, rush-like foliage and pale blue or pink flowers all summer.

OPPOSITE FAR LEFT Alchemilla mollis *traps water on its leaves for birds and insects to drink so dot plants here and there.*

TOP LEFT *Columbines, Aquilegias, are so graceful in foliage and flower.* TOP RIGHT *The perennial wood Forget-me-not is pretty and sustains Crimson-speckled butterfly larvae.* BOTTOM LEFT *Sweet cicely is pretty enough with foamy white flowers and is deliciously sweet and aniseedy in every part.* BOTTOM RIGHT *Mint is a much underrated perennial for ground cover and supports numerous insects with its late flowers.*

MEDIUM- TO TALL-GROWING HERBACEOUS PERENNIALS

In windy areas, these taller plants may be broken or fall without support from string tied to canes, or to long stubs left when pruning.

Achillea Yarrows have feathery foliage and flat white flowers that attract beneficial insects for a long season. They are very tough and believed to be beneficial companions. Flowers are visited by at least 87 different insect species: 6 butterflies and moths, 30 species of bee, 21 species of diptera flies and 30 others. Foliage, flowers and seeds sustain larvae of Ruby, Cinnabar, Sussex Emerald, Lime-speck, Wormwood Pug, Ling Pug, Tawny-speckled Pug, Bordered Pug, V Pug, Black-veined Moth, Straw Belle, Portland Ribbon Wave, Mullein Wave and Belted Beauty.

Centranthus ruber This is often mistaken for valerian, but it is still good for insects. It self-seeds anywhere on any soil, even dry.

Coreopsis grandiflora Good for cutting and insects, tickseed must not be overfed or it becomes all foliage.

Eryngium Sea holly is loved by beneficial insects and has metallic blue flower-heads rising out of striking, spiky, bluey evergreen, holly-like foliage. Foliage of wild sea holly sustains larvae of Sand Dart.

Kniphofia Red-hot pokers make attractive, almost evergreen, grassy clumps which are surprisingly tough and excellent winter homes for insects, while the flowers are very melliferous; I drink the shaken-out nectar but in these litigious times cannot recommend this.

Lupinus polyphyllus Lupins are wonderful flowers and their foliage traps dew; they need dividing every third year or they fade away. Foliage sustains larvae of the Dot Moth.

Lysimachia punctata Yellow loosestrife will grow everywhere and benefit insects for many months. Foliage and flowers sustain larvae of the Water Ermine, Powdered Quaker, Plain Wave and V Pug, and is sole sustenance for the Dentated Pug.

Papaver orientale Oriental poppies produce brilliant orange-scarlet flowers and copious pollen for bees. These plants come back, no matter how often you dig them out.

Rudbeckia purpurea Coneflowers are loved by insects and come usefully late in the year.

ABOVE *Hogweed,* Heracleum, *a tall wild flower recorded as visited by 118 species of insect, is the sole sustainer for the Brindled Ochre and feeds the Swallow-tail, Plain Golden Y, Triple-spotted Pug, White-spotted Pug and sadly the less desirable Garden Dart.* OPPOSITE *Poppies, annual and perennial have no nectar but provide insects with lots of pollen and birds with seed.*

exudations against pests and diseases. *C. coccineum* is effective at killing soil nematodes. *C. cinerariifolium* and *C. roseum* flowers have been powdered for 2,000 years for use as an insect killer. The commercial version, pyrethrum, is used in massive amounts on account of its very low toxicity to mammals. Korean chrysanthemums come late, benefiting many insects. Shasta daisies are dependable, invasive, but provide a good dark foliage backdrop for other plantings. Ox-eye daisy flowers attract 72 different insect species: 5 butterflies and moths, 12 species of bee, 28 species of diptera flies and 27 others. Foliage and flowers sustain larvae of Gem, Satyr Pug, Cinnabar and Chamomile Shark.

Delphinium These wonderful spires of early summer are loved by both bees and slugs! Foliage, flowers and seeds sustain larvae of Pease Blossom and Golden Plusia.

Echinops Globe thistles are one of the best bee plants, statuesque and prickly with metallic blue heads. Foliage sustains larvae of Purple Marbled butterflies.

Eremurus Foxtail lilies have tall spikes of tightly packed flowers emerging from grass-like foliage and asparagus-like roots. They need sun and rich soil.

Helianthus These sunflowers are as attractive to bees and butterflies as the annuals.

Physalis alkekengi var. franchetii Chinese lanterns are invaluable for winter colour and decoration; they sprawl and I grow mine in front and up into a passion flower which has similar orange-coloured fruits.

Verbascum x hybridum Mulleins are beloved by insects and are another cottage-garden must with their woolly foliage and tall spires of yellow flowers. Foliage and flowers of wild species sustain larvae of Striped Lychnis, Mullein Shark, Satyr Pug, Cinnabar and Setaceous Hebrew Character, and in the stems, the Frosted Orange.

TALLER-GROWING HERBACEOUS PLANTS

Do not regiment a border with short plants at the front and high ones at the back. Instead, have it coming and going in waves with some of the following plants towards the front of a border to give more height and interest. These will probably need tying in to supports, but this is worth it as the masses of flowers they will produce benefit many insects.

Althaea rosea Hollyhocks are cottage-garden plants with prolific red and yellow flowers. They suffer from rust, so grow them in a rich soil at the back of the border in an open position, but masked by other plants. That way, the affected foliage (the oldest leaves) will be hidden. Foliage sustains larvae of the Mallow butterfly.

Chrysanthemum These are members of the Asteraceae family and many of them use

PARTICULARLY WELL-SCENTED HERBACEOUS PLANTS

Put these gems where you can get at them at the front of a border. Grow them around a seat or under an often-open window.

Convallaria majalis Lily-of-the-valley hates transplanting and needs a moist, rich soil, but then it romps and spreads; the scent is divine. Foliage sustains larvae of Grey Chi.

Dianthus All of these are delightfully clove- or sweet-scented, but the best of all are pinks. They need regular re-propagation from wee pipings pulled off the plant or they get straggly. Foliage of most species sustains larvae of Tawny Shears, and Deptford Pink foliage, the Mullein Wave.

Hemerocallis Day lilies only bloom for a day, but keep on producing more blooms for months. They grow anywhere in almost any conditions and the flowers are usually edible.

Hosta These are known for their foliage's susceptibility to slugs rather than their scent, which is similar to French soap, so 'Royal Standard' may surprise you.

Melissa officinalis Lemon-scented balm is admired by us and by bees; the golden-splashed version (*M. officinalis* 'Aurea') is lovely.

Paeonia Although they have a short season, peonies are exquisite, so soft and perfect with the dew on them, and they have good foliage.

Phlox A strange, spicy, musty scent, but these are long flowering on very upright stems.

Primula Wild primroses are sweet and easily established, as are cowslips. Also try the drumstick primula, *P. denticulata*. Foliage and sometimes the flowers of wild species sustain larvae of Northern Rustic, Lunar Yellow Underwing, Duke of Burgundy, Plain Clay, Clouded-Bordered Brindle, Ingrailed Clay, Dotted Clay, Triple-spotted Clay, Double Square-spot, Square-spotted Clay, Square-spot Rustic, Green Arches, Great Brocade, Lesser Broad-bordered (Yellow Underwing), Broad-bordered Yellow Underwing, Gothic, Feathered Ranunculus, Uncertain, Vine's Rustic, Riband Wave, Large Twin-spot Carpet, Silver-ground Carpet and Twin-spot Carpet.

Viola Not all violets are scented, but *V. odorata* is. Underplant roses with it as both like rich soil. Foliage sustains larvae of Ingrailed Clay, Plain Wave, Sub-angled Wave, Large Twin-spot Carpet, Red-headed Chestnut, High Brown Fritillary, Silver-Washed Fritillary, Dark Green Fritillary, Clouded Buff, Queen of Spain Fritillary, Small Pearl-Bordered Fritillary and Pearl-Bordered Fritillary.

OPPOSITE *True sunflowers are impressive, but in tough spots consider the perennial sunflower the Jerusalem artichoke, as the flowers are very sweetly scented.* ABOVE *Encourage violets as they sustain large numbers of butterflies.* LEFT *Dictamnus is a Mediterranean perennial which needs a sunny spot.*

TREES AND SHRUBS

I consider a plant to be a tree if it's shrubby with a single stem and can be used as a specimen. Most shrubs can be grown as small trees in the manner of standard roses and vice versa.

TREES FOR SPECIMEN FEATURES AND ADDING HEIGHT

I suggest some fruiting trees, as these are as beautiful as purely ornamental varieties, not too large for most gardens, and useful to us and wildlife. (See Chapter 6 for individual varieties of fruit trees, their needs and treatment.)

Betula pendula Silver birches look best in small informal groups; other birches have yellow foliage or attractive bark. Wine used to be made from silver birch spring sap and their presence is said to stimulate composting. Foliage and catkins sustain larvae of at least 114 different butterflies and moths and are the sole known sustenance for Lesser Swallow Prominent, White Prominent, Satin Lutestring, Yellow Horned, Scalloped Hook-Tip, Rannoch Sprawler, Orange Underwing, Birch Mocha and Argent and Sable.

Crataegus laevigata The common hawthorn, *C. monogyna*, has pink or white, fishy-scented flowers, is thorny and berries freely. *C. laevigata* 'Paul's Scarlet' is double-flowered, dark red, slightly less value to insects but very beautiful. Foliage sustains larvae of 75 different butterflies and moths and is sole known sustenance for Clay Fanfoot.

Cydonia vulgaris Quince makes the best specimen tree with a good framework, apple-like flowers, spring and autumn leaf colour, and edible, aromatic, long-lasting fruit.

Malus The fruiting apple varieties make excellent specimens and most ornamental apple varieties are good pollinators for the fruiters. Beautiful in flower, and with bright red or yellow crab fruits, try 'John Downie' or 'Golden Hornet'. Foliage sustains larvae of 30 different butterflies and moths.

Prunus Fruiting cherry trees in flower are beautiful and come on semi-dwarfing stocks, so plant these to benefit bees and other beneficial insects, as well as to fruit. Avoid the larger-growing flowering cherries; try 'Stella' on 'Colt' stock. Foliage sustains larvae of nine different butterflies and moths.

Sorbus aucuparia Rowans or mountain ashes are attractive in form and foliage and the prolific red berries are much loved by birds. I prefer the native to ornamental forms and there is a large-berried variety (*S. aucuparia edulis*). Foliage sustains larvae of at least a dozen different butterflies and moths.

EVERGREEN SHRUBS

As evergreen shrubs are never dormant, they are best planted in spring and kept well watered until established. Except for hedging plants, they should rarely be pruned heavily, but do this in spring or summer if necessary. Do not cut those with larger leaves or they brown.

Choisya ternata Mexican orange blossom needs shelter to protect its aromatic evergreen foliage, especially the yellow form. Often, the scented flowers come again in autumn.

Daphne All are poisonous, but have exquisitely scented flowers from early spring. They are often difficult to establish, needing well-drained, humus-rich soil, but they're very attractive, compact and most are evergreen. Most reliable is *D. odora* 'Aureomarginata'.

Elaeagnus Tough and mostly evergreen, these shrubs provide good shelter for wildlife. They have non-descript, scented flowers and some have edible berries. *E. pungens* 'Maculata' has a bright yellow leaf spot and is a cheery specimen.

Ilex Hollies are not just drab, plain, spiky bushes but also come in gloriously variegated yellow or silver forms. All are useful for shady positions and good for birds, providing shelter and berries. The foliage and flowers sustain larvae of Privet Hawkmoth, Dun-Bar, Double-striped Pug and Swallow-tailed Moth. The Yellow-barred Brindle eats the flowers first, then the green berries and the leaves, as does the Holly (Azure) Blue.

Juniperus Juniper is one of the better conifers, especially in dwarf forms. Foliage sustains larvae of Chestnut-coloured Carpet, Juniper Pug, Scalloped Hazel, and is sole sustenance for Juniper Carpet and Edinburgh Pug.

Leycesteria formosa This exotic, shrubby, bamboo-like plant has ferny foliage and jewel-like flowers with red bracts. It can be grown as a shrub or pruned to the ground each spring.

Mahonia Attractive holly-like leaves, black berries and yellow flowers are typical of this genus. *M. aquifolium* flowers in late winter, but *M. japonica* is sweeter scented.

Osmanthus These look like holly or privet but are more compact and have sweet-scented flowers.

Prunus laurocerasus Common or cherry laurel is a tough evergreen and makes a thick screen anywhere; the flowers are sweet-scented. The yellow-spotted laurel, *Aucuba japonica* 'Crotonifolia', is unrelated but similar with flashy red berries on the females.

Rhododendron These produce magnificent displays of flower and grand foliage. They must have lime-free soil, although can be confined in big pots. Most floriferous is *R. yunnanense*.

Skimmia These are neat, well scented and attractive, with red berries if a pollinating male is planted.

Sarcococca Winter box is a small, tough evergreen with lovely, but non-descript, pale, sweetly-scented flowers in mid-winter.

Ulex When gorse is out of flower, love is out of fashion; there is always a cheerful buttercup yellow flower or two on gorse (or furze); the dwarf form is better in small gardens. Foliage and flowers sustain larvae of Grass Emerald, Green Hairstreak, Long Tailed, Bordered Straw, Bloxworth Blue, Mazarine Blue, Dark Tussock, Silver-Studded Blue, Holly (Azure) Blue, Grass, Beautiful Brocade, Small Grass Emerald, Lead Belle, Double-striped, Grass Wave, Cream-spot Tiger and is sole sustenance for Scottish Belle.

OPPOSITE FROM LEFT *Apple blossom is often gorgeous pink in bud.* MIDDLE *Pear and plum blossom is always pristine white.* RIGHT *Wild and rugosa roses are better for wildlife than 'modern' garden varieties.* ABOVE *Mahonias have spiny leaves, sweet scented yellow blooms and edible berries; this one colours well in autumn too.* BELOW *This North American haw-thorn has huge thorns and larger more palatable haws.*

PARTICULARLY WELL-SCENTED SHRUBS

Scent is the glory of the garden and I revel in it, both flower and leaf. These are some of the best, but to each their own in taste.

Buddleja *B. globosa* is semi-evergreen and makes a quick screen with orange, ball-shaped flower clusters. *B. davidii*, the butterfly bush, has long, strongly-scented racemes in a wide choice of colours. Prune these back hard in spring. The cuttings root very readily, but established plants resent moving.

Cytisus Brooms like hot dry positions, are generally short-lived and small with yellowish, scented, pea flowers. I love the tall growing *C. battandieri* with silky, semi-evergreen leaves and pineapple-scented flowers. Foliage sustains larvae for 30 different butterflies and moths and is sole known sustenance for the June Belle, Streak, Broom-tip and Frosted Yellow.

Hamamelis Witch hazels are non-descript in leaf but, in winter, the flowers smell divine.

Lonicera fragrantissima Shrubby honeysuckles are straggly messes, but the flowers that come from December to March are gloriously sweet, so find a space for it. For the best summer scent, grow *L. syringantha*, which rivals (and is named after) lilac.

Magnolia These can get big, like the wonderful evergreen *M. grandiflora* which has enormous scented flowers. They prefer loamy, lime-free soil.

Philadelphus Mock oranges all have glorious scents but are a bit non-descript out of flower; they're good for filling borders.

Rosa The finest of scented flowers, there is such a choice, including old cabbage roses, the Damask, the vigorous 'Madame Isaac Pereire' ... but for its mossiness, try *R. x centifolia* 'Muscosa' or 'William Lobb'. Foliage of wild species sustains larvae of 30 different butterflies and moths; the flowers usually have no nectar but much pollen.

Spartium junceum Spanish broom has rush-like growths and pollen-laden, sweet-scented, pea-like flowers over a long season. Foliage sustains larvae of Long-tailed Blue butterfly.

Syringa There are many excellent lilacs from the common purple and whites to the divine Persian lilac, Canadian Preston hybrids and several dwarf forms. Foliage sustains larvae of Waved Umber, Privet Hawkmoth, Hebrew Character, Pale Pinion, Grey Chi, August Thorn and the Lilac Beauty.

Viburnum There are so many attractive scented varieties, yet the almost scentless *V. tinus* 'Eve Price' and *V. opulus*, the Guelder rose, are most common. Grow the compact *V. x juddii*, *V. carlcephalum* or *V. carlesii*. Foliage of some species sustains larvae of Common Quaker, Sprawler and Privet Hawkmoth, and the Yellow-barred Brindle eats flowers first, then the green berries before the leaves.

LEFT *Pink* Syringa microphylla *is not so huge a scrub, more like a small tree.* MIDDLE *The common* Philadelphus coronarius *is known as Mock orange for its powerful scent; others are almost peach or gardenia like.* RIGHT *Lilac,* Syringa, *may currently be 'old-fashioned' but is gloriously strongly scented.*

DROUGHT-TOLERANT SHRUBS FOR DRY PLACES AND BY WALLS

Although the following will grow in such spots, they need to be well established. Prepare the planting hole well and water often until they are making strong growth.

Artemisia abrotanum Southernwood has feathery ferny foliage and a delicious lemon-pine scent; plant lots. Foliage and flowers sustain larvae of Scarce Wormwood Shark and Feathered Footman on the seeds.

Erica The winter-flowering heathers are more tolerant of limy soils but none grow on chalk, no matter how much peat you add. These suppress weeds once established but will not stop existing infestations. Foliage, seeds and flowers of bell heathers sustain larvae of 27 different butterflies and moths, and cross-leaved heaths, 15.

Escallonia These are mostly not very hardy and many are evergreen or partly so; some have aromatic foliage. They're better grown by the sea and in very sheltered spots.

Fuchsia These are hardier than most imagine if the roots are well protected. They're easily propagated from cuttings and there are good foliage forms, such as *F. magellanica* 'Versicolor'. The foliage sustains larvae of Striped Hawkmoth, Elephant Hawkmoth and Silver-Striped Hawkmoth.

Hyssopus officinalis Please see the entry under Herbs, on page 168.

Lavatera maritima This is not very hardy, but is worth growing as it flowers long and late, benefiting many insects, and is easy to multiply by cuttings.

Lavandula Please see the entry under Herbs, on page 164

Rosmarinus Please see the entry under Herbs, on page 165.

Santolina chamaecyparissus Cotton lavender is a tough, low-growing, evergreen, aromatic and a lovely silver-grey.

ABOVE Poncirus trifoliate *is tough, thorny, slow growing and architectural with orange blossom flowers and small edible green orange-like fruits.*

TOUGHEST, MOST RELIABLE SHRUBS FOR MOST SITES

Berberis and the closely related *Mahonia* species An enormous number of varieties, these are thorny with brilliant autumn colour, prolific yellow flowers, and produce (usually edible) fruit freely. Many are evergreen or with coloured foliage. Foliage sustains larvae of Pale-shouldered Brocade and Mottled Pug and is sole sustenance for larvae of Barberry Carpet and Scarce Tissue.

Chaenomeles japonica Fiery red flowers appear very early in spring, followed by iron-hard, edible fruits on lax bushes; these are a bit thorny and best trained on walls, even shady ones. Foliage sustains larvae of Figure of Eight moth.

Cotoneaster All are loved by bees for the countless little flowers and by birds for the prolific red berries. The branches arch gracefully or can be trained on walls. They give good autumn colour, though some are evergreen. Foliage sustains larvae of Green-Brindled Crescent, Figure of Eight, and Purple Thorn.

Forsythia These are much grown for their wonderful mass of early flowers in early spring. Foliage sustains larvae of Privet Hawkmoth.

Potentilla These are very tough and long-flowering. However, avoid the 'red' versions because they are poor.

Pyracantha Firethorns have masses of flower and fruit for bees and birds, but mean thorns.

Ribes Flowering redcurrants come early, so are good for beneficial insects, but most smell like tom cats to us. They are easily propagated and flower in red, yellow or white. Foliage sustains larvae of Currant Clearwing, Spinach, Phoenix, Currant Pug, Waved Umber, Large Ranunculus, Grey Chi, Copper Underwing, Common Emerald, Garden Carpet, Comma, Mottled Pug, Magpie, V-moth and, sadly, the Cabbage Moth.

Sambucus Wild elder feeds the birds with copious berries. Variegated, cut-leaved and golden varieties are more ornamental, especially the lovely gold *S. nigra* 'Aurea'. Foliage sustains larvae of Swallow-tailed Moth, and occasionally Frosted Orange in the stems.

Spiraea Slender, graceful, small-leaved bushes, these flower profusely (especially *S. x arguta* 'Bridal Wreath').

Weigela These have foxglove-like flowers in great quantities, in reds through to yellow. *W. florida* 'Variegata' offers variegated foliage with slightly scented, pink flowers.

LEFT *Himalayan honeysuckle, Pheasant berry, Leycesteria Formosa, is a tough reliable shrub with decorative leaves and fantastic flowers and fruits loved by birds.*

CHOICEST CLIMBERS

Climbers need good establishment like any shrubby plant, and must also have support (apart from the self-clingers). They grow big and catch the wind, so make the supports strong, durable and renewable. If you give them enough space initially, most climbers can be left to ramble rather than being pruned, creating good nesting and shelter sites.

Buddleja alternifolia A lax shrub, this is easily trained up a pergola or wall for the long, hanging swathes of blue scented flowers.

Clematis These all need their roots in cool, rich, moist soil and their tops in sun. The large-flowered forms have good colour, are rarely scented and can be hard to establish. These can be cut nearly to the ground each year, except the early flowerers. There are many species with small flowers, which are well-scented and need no regular pruning. *C. armandii* is a barely hardy evergreen. *C. montana* cultivars are good for covering large areas. Foliage and flowers of *C. vitalba* sustain larvae of Sub-angled Wave, Fern, Lime-speck Pug, Wormwood Pug, V Pug, Double-striped Pug and Orange Moth, and are sole sustenance for Small Emerald, Pretty Chalk, Small Waved Umber and Haworth's Pug.

Hedera helix Ivy is a valuable self-clinger, providing late flowers for insects, berries and nest sites. Large-leaved variegated forms are not as hardy; plants rooted from fruiting bushes flower soonest. *H. helix* 'Goldheart' has cheery, yellow-splashed leaves and is good in dull places. Foliage, flowers and seeds sustain larvae of Holly (Azure) Blue, Fanfoot, Small Dusty Wave, Treble Brown-spot, Yellow-barred, Magpie, Swallow-tailed Moth, Willow Beauty and the Dot Moth.

Jasminum nudiflorum, barely a climber, has pale yellow flowers in winter and needs

TOP LEFT *A Montana clematis, an unknown red climbing rose and Goldheart ivy make a riot of colour by my front door.* TOP RIGHT *Close up of Clematis Montana Wilsonii which has the most wonderful vanilla perfume.* BOTTOM LEFT *This variegated jasmine is the only known hybrid, x stephanense, a cross between the common white and the rare carmine J. beesianum. Glorious in leaf and flower, it makes a dense head well suited to hiding bird nests.* BOTTOM RIGHT *Ivy is one of the best wall coverings and does far less harm than once feared.*

cutting to the ground afterwards. *J. officinale* is obligatory; no garden is complete without this sweet summer scent. It is a twining plant best left unpruned. Foliage sustains larvae of Death's-head Hawkmoth and Common Emerald.

Lonicera Honeysuckles are gorgeous, tough and easy, and nearly all have wonderful scent; I have over a dozen different varieties. They attract fewer aphids when grown in semi-shade and not overfed. Leave them unpruned to ramble. *L. caprifolium* blooms attract larger moths, while *L. periclymenum* ones are more accessible to bees. Foliage sustains larvae of over 20 different butterflies and moths and is sole sustenance for White Admiral and Early Grey.

Rosa Rambler roses are much more vigorous than climbing ones, perhaps too vigorous for most gardens; all need enriched soil and copious moisture. My favourites include 'Etoile de Hollande', 'Souvenir de Claudius Denoyel', 'Madame Isaac Pereire', 'Maigold', 'Handel' and, most of all, the long-flowering, thornless Bourbon rose, 'Zéphirine Drouhin'.

Vitis vinifera Vines give wonderful autumn colour with bunches of grapes. White grape leaves normally yellow in autumn, while red leaves redden. *V. coignetiae* has enormous leaves, but poor fruits. In the UK, we can root grapevine cuttings and grow them on their own roots as, so far, we have not suffered the Phylloxera root aphid infestation that devastated vines on the Continent. Foliage sustains larvae of Striped Hawkmoth, Silver Striped Hawkmoth and Elephant Hawkmoth.

OPPOSITE *Plant climbers, not ramblers, unless you have a huge space to fill.*

MARGINAL PLANTS

Many waterside plants like moist soil but cannot stand actual waterlogging. Real bog plants provide hidden wet habitats in and close to the water. This creates safe access, a nursery and a feeding area for many creatures, big and small. Bull rushes (Reed Mace), flag irises and other vertical shafted plants are necessary for dragonflies to successfully emerge from their larval stage.

Astilbe Goat's beards have attractive palmate foliage and feathery plumes in tones of red throughout the summer.

Caltha palustris Kingcup or the marsh marigold provides the most beautiful blaze of gold in late spring and grows a foot or so high.

Hosta will thrive in any cool, moist, shady spot and is fodder for snails, keeping them away from the salads.

Lobelia cardinalis will grow in shallow water and provide a yard-high show of brilliant red from summer till autumn; but take care the slugs don't get it.

Mimulus luteus is a foot high and provides yellow flowers all summer, but can be invasive.

PLANTS IN THE WATER

Oxygenating water plants are absolutely essential, though not very ornamental, as they oxygenate, feed and provide a habitat for many creatures and prevent algae taking over the pond. Have some flags, rushes or similar emergent foliage to provide perches for insects, especially dragonflies as they leave the water and transform into adults.

Elodea canadensis Canadian pondweed is invasive, but provides good composting material when dragged out, as well as being a good oxygenator.

Menyanthes trifoliata Bogbean has pretty, though small, flowers; the foliage sustains the larvae of Elephant Hawkmoth and Light Knot Grass.

Nymphaea Proverbially beautiful, the leaves of water lilies enable insects to gain access to the water. Preferring still pools, they thrive in plastic baskets with chopped turves, held down with a rock about a welly and a half deep.

Ranunculus aquatilis Water crowfoot has white flowers and is excellent in still or moving water.

BELOW *This blue water lily is sadly not hardy so needs careful over-wintering, but it is not as invasive as our hardier natives species.*

3 MAKING YOUR GARDEN NATURALLY BEAUTIFUL

The art and skill of planning your garden both to look beautiful and run efficiently throughout the year

The impending impact of climate change has altered the accepted view of gardens, with far more emphasis being given to plantings that need less input from the gardener. Garden designers now create schemes that require less water, work, fertiliser, and so on. Even that great arbiter of taste, the Chelsea Flower Show, has found vegetables and fruits returning once more, with 'wild' and allotment gardens appearing in place of manicured impressionist extravaganzas (well, at least some, anyway).

WHAT TO CONSIDER WHEN PLANNING

Before planning your garden, consider what you want from it. Is it to add value or interest, amaze your friends with your ecological or wild garden, or simply for the exercise? If you want to grow food crops, which ones do you want and when? Similarly, if you hanker after

flowers, do you want them for cutting or as outdoor beauty? All gardens need a place where you can sit, but is it to be an outdoor room or a vista from a window? If you want privacy, then effective screening may be more important than saving money or maximizing on self-sufficiency. Once you understand your parameters, then it is easier to plan around them. What you can have, as well as how much it costs in terms of time, effort and money, does not just depend on the size of your garden. All the factors are interchangeable, money being the most easily converted into the others!

ABOVE *Arches frame entrances making them more inviting and need be no more than bent down branches.*
LEFT *A warm brick wall is the perfect accompaniment to espaliered pears – though it may also be dryish there, so pay attention to watering.*
OPPOSITE *With forty individual beds it would be chaotic if I didn't first plan it all on paper.*

PLANNING ON PAPER

For an effective plan, make a map showing the boundaries, walls, pipelines, immovable objects, future building extensions, solid paths, trees, major shrubs and so on, which are very difficult to alter later on. Only pencil in current areas of grass, vegetable plot, beds and borders, as these can be moved around or changed. Choose which parts you want for vegetables or a fruit cage and so on, as these need the best (and sunniest) sites. Then add other areas as your space allows.

Do work out your plan on the map first before translating it onto the ground, as this saves much work and time later. Looking at the map also helps you to see and organise the garden as a whole. Try to get the maximum use out of each item. For example, use the storage shed to shelter a bed or the largest blank wall facing the sun for a trained fruit bush. The overflow from the shed's water butts can feed a pool, hedgehog nests put underneath the floor, and bird boxes under the eaves.

Flowerdew's Five Fs

1 Framework Because of its permanence through all seasons, the bare bones or framework of the garden is the most important part of the design. The outlines, shapes and views formed by the solid permanent features need to look good when there is little in leaf or flower to help decorate them (in the U.K. throughout half the year). The shapes and edges of beds and borders and paths are the most important features, but pergolas, walls, hedges, tree trunks and evergreens also create the solidity and endurance of any design. That's why care needs to be taken with their laying out and positioning. Plan carefully and use garden canes and string to try out different permutations before doing any work on the ground.

BELOW *In a healthy garden where the material is quickly by the garden where. In a healthy garden where the material is quickly by plus fill out little.*

- *Create a sense of mystery* A good idea is never to show all of the garden from any given point so that there is always a hint of more to discover. Create a hidden corner by extending the edge of a bed or border or plant an island bed, thus inviting the visitor to explore behind. Make long thin gardens more interesting by dividing them into a series of rooms with a meandering path giving glimpses of spaces beyond. Taper and curve paths to change perspective and make gardens seem larger or smaller in different directions. They should always lead to something, even if only to an urn of flowers, and then bend to disappear round a corner, inviting further exploration. Another trick is having *trompe l'œil* steps leading nowhere at a boundary, which gives an impression of size and of more garden to discover.

- *Arches, gateways and pergolas* These can be used to add vertical interest and heighten the sense of having 'rooms within rooms'. They allow for a smoother transition from one part of the garden to another with a different style, as well as blocking out unsightly objects and views. (Remember that the closer the screen, the less height is needed for it to work.)

- *Hard-landscaping materials* The colours and materials that make up the solid part of the framework will be more pleasing if they are compatible and consistent with their surroundings and with each other. Stain all wood and timberwork in the same hue and try to use local materials, preferably recycled ones, throughout the garden.

2 Foliage Although welcome in spring and appreciated in autumn, deciduous foliage is usually only noticed as a backdrop for flowers for most of the year. Yet the many different forms, textures, colours and scents of foliage bring new levels of interest to any planting. Carefully selecting these creates a more unified appearance than concentrating solely on flowers. You could even dispense with flowers altogether, as many plants have beautiful leaf colour at other times of year and not only in autumn. For instance, the admittedly somewhat invasive poplar, *Populus* x *jackii* 'Aurora', and *Jasminum* x *stephanense* both have brilliantly coloured new leaves in the spring.

There are also countless plants with variegated leaves in many patterns and shades. Many evergreens, such as *Elaeagnus*, *Euonymus* and *Ilex* (holly), have forms with white- and yellow-variegated or coloured leaves and these are useful for brightening up dull winter days and dark corners. Evergreens increase the feeling of permanence in a garden and should be included to give year-round interest,

3 Flowers A garden is incomplete without flowers, which provide nectar and pollen for beneficial insects, as well as being beautiful. The organic gardener must ensure a constant succession of flowers, using as many and as varied plants as possible, to nurture and sustain the maximum number and variety of creatures. Of course, flowers are often followed by seeds and berries, which then feed other beneficial insects and animals, so their value is increased further. These fruits may be even more attractive than the flowers, as with holly berries and Gladwyn iris. Naturally, few berries last for long, although those in unusual colours, such as yellow pyracanthas, last the longest.

Selecting flowers is a matter of personal taste. There are plenty of theories for composing colour schemes, with an emphasis on harmonising colours or promoting certain ones, such as single-shade borders or using only all-white flowers. However, some people seem to like violent discords and splattered, paint-box effects; others opt for pastel shades and gentle gradations, while many just want masses of colour. Make notes of what works in your situation, and what does not,

OPPOSITE I like this feeling of nature taking back over, but you may not.
ABOVE Not only flowers are colourful, autumn leaves rival them, even those of such utilitarian plants as blueberries. BELOW Paths are so important, visually and functionally – the diamond pattern here saves wearing the grass for minimal investment and looks inviting.

although you should take care when choosing them as too many can make the garden look rather sombre. The many shades and varieties of evergreens, as well as the golds, reds and blues of conifers and heathers, create colourful gardens that remain almost unchanged through the year. Once established, these gardens require little maintenance. Evergreens, especially ivy, also provide shelter, as well as nest and hibernation sites for beneficial insects and animals, so do include some in your garden.

The effect of foliage, particularly that of young herbaceous growth, is enhanced by multiple plantings. Single specimens can give a spotty appearance, which is then reinforced when the flowers come out; most look best when grouped in threes, fives and sevens. Repetition can become monotonous but using a favourite plant often in various areas can add much to the unity and ambience of the garden until it almost becomes a theme.

ABOVE LEFT *A forgotten favourite from long ago the Tuberose,* Polianthes tubberosa, *is a bit tender and needs care but then will grace your summer patio with one of the finest of all perfumes.* **ABOVE RIGHT** *You cannot have too many honeysuckles, most are gorgeously scented, and they breed up hosts of little critters too.* **BOTTOM** *Do pay attention to safety, bottle caps on top of canes and yogurt cartons over projections can save a poked eye or knocked head.*

and change the plants around as soon as possible. No garden is ever finished – it can always be improved! As with foliage, constant repetition throughout the garden and multiple plantings of the same flowering plant generally creates a stronger impression than assorted single specimens.

4 Features and themes These should not overwhelm or replace the main display. Features can be anything from classical statuary to a wheelbarrow full of gnomes. Water in any form, pergolas and timberwork, rustic arbours, urns and containers, special beds and specimen plants can all be featured. It is their setting and positioning that makes them effective. One main feature in each view, area or room is usually sufficient. Too many features, though, and the garden becomes a junkyard. Provide a seat for viewing attractive scenes and this will then create the centre-piece of yet another small scene, although it should not be in competition with the others.

Themes are subtle features in which certain areas, or the whole garden, have some commonality, either apparent or more theoretical. A water or a wild garden is a theme, as are scented gardens, historical gardens, Bible plants, silver borders and herb beds. The danger with themes is that they can become overpowering or constraining if followed too rigidly. Set the theme broadly and leave yourself room to manoeuvre. A wildlife garden that uses only native plants will omit such charming and useful ones as buddlejas and pyracanthas. A garden of all-black flowers is going to be harder to perfect than a border of silver foliage and black flowers. A bed can have more variation and colour if it attracts both bees and butterflies rather than just one or the other.

Some features and themes, such as ponds, wildflower gardens, native plants, beehives and bee gardens, are especially pertinent because they benefit life in the garden so much. Others may be worthy in their own right, such as wildlife sanctuaries and gardens of endangered plants, be they wildflowers, rare fruits or old varieties of vegetable.

Just using particular forms of plant can create a subtle theme. Spiky-leaved plants, such as yuccas and crocosmias, give a drier, more tropical appearance, as do Chusan palms, bamboos and large-leaved plants like figs. Conifers, heathers and silver birches produce a colder, heath-like effect. Most of all, I find that scent is my favourite theme and I have selected as many scented plants as possible so that my garden is an olfactory, as much as a visual, feast.

5 Finish Finishing touches and tidiness make for the most perfect gardens (with much labour). Ignoring them spoils the overall effect disproportionately. Most importantly, get rid of every bit of litter and junk and hide garden tools and equipment in the shed. The edging of turfed areas is also critical; little improves appearances as much as well-cut edges and the removal of tufts of grass against trunks and fences. Uniformity helps; one plastic cloche made from a lemonade bottle looks unsightly, three-dozen cut in the same way looks neat. When adding to anything in the garden or repairing, say, a fence, blend in the new with the old by painting them all the same colour. Most timberwork can be stained in a similar hue, while black bituminous paint gives an enduring, inexpensive and sympathetic black finish to metal.

ABOVE *Ooops – brilliant planning here as to harvest some of this fruit I have to stand in the water.*

What you can change, how and when, and what goes best where

Light Although all plants need light, they don't all need full sunlight; in fact, many ornamentals need partial shade to avoid leaf burn. In general, though, the problem is of insufficient light, especially because of the shade cast by trees and buildings. Judicious pruning can let in more light and dark places can be brightened up with white paint. Under cover, electric light can supplement weak winter sunlight, but all glass and plastic should be kept spotlessly clean to prevent light loss.

Warmth This works with light and shelter: the more light that reaches a garden and the more sheltered spots it has, the warmer it will be. The shelter provided by a good hedge or a piece of trellis, for example, protects the garden from buffeting and extracts heat from the wind. As the wind is filtered through hedging, twigs or trellis, the energy of the wind is given off as heat as it is slowed down. Thus, a good hedge can raise the temperature of a garden by several degrees. So, use hedges and windbreaks rather than fences and walls, although these can be

improved by mounting trellis and/or climbers on them. The temperature can also be increased by including brick walls, paths and other features to soak up and radiate heat. Brick rubble, dark stones and gravel all throw up heat and can be used to help ripen fruit sooner. Similarly, bare soil that's been blackened with soot will give off warmth to ripen fruit or protect flowers from frosts better than grass or mulch.

Air Although we need to guard against excessive winds, all plants need fresh air. Stagnant air encourages pests and diseases, especially mildews and botrytis. Good spacing and open pruning is required; this allows the plants to breathe. Plants breathe in carbon dioxide, so encourage more animal life into the garden and allow filtered winds to change the air.

Moisture More plants probably do badly through over- or under-watering than any other cause. In times of strong growth, it is almost impossible to overwater plants in open ground, while it is difficult to under-water plants in pots indoors in winter. The difficulty lies between these two extremes. In open ground, conserve winter rains with mulches. Unless you have drought conditions, only water newly emergent seedlings, new transplants and crops at a critical stage (usually when their flowers are setting) or before sowing. In times of drought, give your most valued plants one long soak rather than watering little and often. Never wet large areas of soil around each

ABOVE *Fleeces and fine nets make a sheltered as well as pest-proof growing space.*
BELOW *Enclosing one vine in the row with its own cold frame gives ripe grapes months earlier.*

plant as this mostly evaporates, but soak water down to the roots. Above all, keep down weed competition and hoe up a dust mulch or mulch well. Where lots of watering is needed, possibly install irrigation or at least a hose (see Chapter 5).

Shelter You can provide warmth-giving shelter on a smaller scale than that created by hedges and walls by planting tough evergreen plants, using sticks and twigs, and adding netting or cloches. All of these help tender and establishing plants through hard weather. Organic fruit, flowers and vegetables may need protecting from two-legged pests, as well as nature's trials. Fences, walls and hedges also provide privacy and security. Here are a few guidelines on making the most of these structural features:

- *Fences* are quick to erect and take up little depth, but need maintenance and rarely last longer than a decade or two. Panel fences that stop the wind tend to fail before open fences and trellis, but allow for borders in front; fruit or climbers can also be trained against them. Unfortunately, weeds come underneath very easily unless deep gravel boards are fitted. Open fences only act as boundary markers and are better in a garden if overgrown with climbers.

- *Walls* are more expensive but last for centuries, excluding weeds with deep foundations, retaining warmth, and blocking winds (but causing buffeting). Walls are harder to train on, as the fixings take more work, but are excellent for ripening fruit. However, they may be too hot and dry at the base for some plants' comfort if they face the sun, especially roses. Red brick is the best material as it retains most warmth, while dry-stone walls provide excellent niches for plant and animal life.

- *Hedges* are the cheapest of all, although they take longer to become effective. They establish more quickly given a temporary fence of windbreak material. Hedges provide wind-filtered warmth, a superb habitat for wildlife, and increase the variety of plants. Run a path rather than a border next to a hedge to make trimming easier and because the soil will be robbed of nutrients. (See page 70 for advice on different hedge varieties.)

- *Cloches and cold frames* can range from a simple jam jar to a large construction of brick and glass. They keep off the worst weather, provide a longer season of growth, and protect against pest attacks. The glass ones are the most expensive, but last longer and keep

warmer than plastic, which always degrades and becomes brittle. Larger ones are expensive and more difficult to move than smaller ones and none are cheap, though a home-made version is described in Chapter 7. Clear plastic bottles with their tops and bottoms cut off make for neat, tubular mini cloches (if you only cut off the bottoms, remove them sooner as the plant will lack air). These provide protection from birds and slugs and shelter from the weather for bedding plants, saladings, and transplants such as brassicas and sweet corn. Cover bigger plants, such as pelargoniums, fuchsias, marrows and tomatoes, with larger containers. Ensure that rows of cloches do not create a wind tunnel by blocking off the ends and pay attention to watering. Secure them in windy weather and harden the plants off first when removing them. Although low, plastic-film-covered hoops are the least costly, they use ecologically expensive plastic sheets that don't last long, so it might be worth investing in a longer-lasting, walk-in polytunnel (see Chapter 8).

BELOW *Plastic bell cloches are excellent for starting tender plants such as this watermelon.*

Choosing the garden's 'furniture'

As well as considering plants and natural ecosystems directly, use recycled and environmentally friendly products to minimise your impact elsewhere. The garden has furniture, both literally and figuratively. You will need seats and containers, if not classical statuary, but these should be ecologically acceptable as well as aesthetically harmonious. Well, that's where your ingenuity is called for.

BEDS AND BORDERS

When designing a border, by all means have shorter plants closer than taller ones, but do allow some tall plants to have forward positions. Taller, late-growing herbaceous plants can come in front of early flowerers like spring bulbs that look drab. Spring bulbs can also be grown under deciduous shrubs that come into leaf late, as they can use the winter light and be dormant in the dark, dry shade of summer. Remember to group three, five or seven of the same plant together in a bed.

Herbaceous borders With careful planning and choice plants, these can be less labour-intensive than you imagine; the only regular chores are tidying back withered growth in autumn and weed control. Spacing groups of plants well makes weeding easier, while heavy mulches are an immense benefit. Herbaceous plants combine well with bulbs with a similar habit but, obviously, climbers can only be added if a timber framework is provided. Many shrubs can be included with herbaceous plants to create a mixed bed, but will soon

ABOVE LEFT AND RIGHT *Two of my favourite fillers for colour, and all round benefits, are Crimson clover and cornflowers.*

predominate and can only be effectively combined if dwarf or given enough space. Herbaceous beds, even with bulbs and annual flowers, tend to be rather empty for much of the year and need positioning where they can be appreciated in summer, but are not so noticeable in winter. They can provide year-round interest if they are backed by winter- and early-spring-flowering shrubs.

Bedding plants, especially if bought in, are wasteful of resources as they are started off with heat, peat and plastic containers, so rate badly in ecological terms. They are an expensive way of filling a bed on their own because this will need replanting at least two or three times a year for continuous colour and interest. Some bedding plants, such as sweet alyssum, zonal pelargoniums, *Impatiens* and fuchsias, are ideal for creating small floral features throughout summer and will even survive confined in containers. Among the very best companion plants are French marigolds, which should be grown by everyone. As well as having a compact form and flowers over months, they attract beneficial insects, discourage many pests, and kill eelworms through root secretions. Never transplant them whilst in flower – simply nip out all the flowers and buds beforehand to ensure more success later.

Many bedding plants are not annuals, but are grown for only one season and discarded in the same way. True annuals may be used instead. Annuals offer some of the brightest blazes of colour, often growing well in very poor soil and sites, particularly when direct sown.

LEFT *Spring bulbs have given way to bluebells, Forget-me-nots and white comfrey (underneath a* Poncirus *and a hardy citrus hybrid).* OPPOSITE *No not a giant moth orchid but* Dictamnus, *dittany, fraxinella, whatever you call it, this is my favourite flowering plant – scent, foliage, flower and it's happy in any sunny spot.*

Shrub borders need the least maintenance, especially if they contain evergreens. The dense shade of large shrubs keeps most weeds under control and few ornamental shrubs need much pruning if well spaced. A general guide is to leave most plants unpruned unless they get too big. Timing is key: prune shrubs that flower early in the year immediately after flowering and prune those that flower later as soon as the leaves drop. Prune evergreens, more tender plants and those with hollow stems, such as buddlejas, in spring and the *Prunus* family in mid-summer. All shrubs benefit from soil enrichment and watering, but this is rarely necessary and they are mostly very tolerant of different soils. Climbers can add another layer, but herbaceous plants seldom flourish with them for long because of the competition.

ACCESS

Ease of access is important, as anywhere that is difficult to get to will be neglected. Paths, stepping stones and gates make the chores easier.

Patios made from a few humble slabs by the garden door provide the viewing points, as well as access for most gardens. Loggias and overhead timberwork combined with a patio help blend an unsympathetic building with the garden and cast a pleasing shade. A patio makes its own microclimate – hot and dry above with a cool, moist root run below, though it may be drier if sheltered from prevailing rains by the walls. This makes beds made in patios ideal for climbers such as clematis and roses, although the flowers do better climbing around posts than on hot walls, which are best used for grapes, pears or other fruit.

Some, such as sweet peas, night-scented stock, pot marigolds and *Limnanthes douglasii*, are outstanding value and should be included in every garden. One problem with annually replaced bedding plants is that they need starting off early in the year under cover, where they compete for space and time with vegetables. There are several ways to avoid this, other than having permanent herbaceous or shrub beds. Sowing annuals in situ saves space, but they need careful weeding and even the quickest do not flower until late spring. Hardy annuals sown in the autumn and overwintered flower earlier than spring-sown plants, though they may also finish sooner and then need replacing.

Biennials are the best solution; sow them in a seed bed in late spring and summer, after the brassicas are planted out and no longer need the space, and then plant them out in their flowering position in autumn or early the following spring. Sweet rocket, Sweet William, foxgloves, wallflowers and stocks can all be treated in this way.

Paths and drives As with patios, the hard standing creates a cool, moist root run with water run-off and throws up heat day and night, making areas nearby warmer and with better airflow. Beds nearby produce bigger and healthier plants and are ideal for less hardy shrubs. Grass paths wear badly in heavy traffic, but can be improved with the use of stepping stones. A slab path set on sand is low-maintenance, very durable and can be moved. Gravel with board edging and hardcore underneath makes an attractive path. If the gravel is deep enough, it can be kept tidy and weed-free with raking. However, if you want a gravel path anywhere that muck or mud is often dropped or that weeds seed, then it will be difficult to keep clean. This is also the

ABOVE LEFT *Don't forget that little will grow in the deep dry shade on the sunless side of a tall hedge. White comfrey (Symphytum orientale) gives winter foliage and spring blooms good for early humble bees.*

case with brick paths, crazy paving and badly laid cobbles with lots of gaps. Point the gaps well and fill all niches with creeping thymes or chamomile before they become a weed problem! Concrete paths are fine, but are permanent and utilitarian in appearance. Shredded bark or pine-needle paths work well if laid over hardcore; otherwise they can be churned to mud. They look best in woodland or shrub settings, but are also useful in vegetable areas as they repel slugs.

LAWN AND HEDGE CARE AND IMPROVEMENT NATURALLY

Lawns and grass paths are a major part of the garden's framework, so keeping them well maintained is critical. If they are in a poor condition, then they draw attention to themselves rather than enhancing the garden. Their shape and positioning needs careful planning along with a good start to reduce or ease maintenance work later.

Lawns and grass paths Emerald-green grass shows off plants to perfection, but lawned areas involve a tremendous amount of work, cash and resources. In very small gardens, consider dispensing with grass altogether, saving on the need for a grass cutter and liberating ground space. Areas for sitting could be hard-surfaced or gravelled and surrounded or patch-planted with low-growing plants like chamomile and thymes. In the largest gardens, grass is a sensible ground cover, as it is relatively easy to keep tidy. Grassed areas compete with plants growing in them, but you can use the clippings as a mulch and suppress the grass immediately around favourite specimens. Grassed areas can be established in three ways: seeding, turfing and cutting the natural cover regularly, as follows:

- *Seeding* gives the choice of grasses, which companion plants you include, and is inexpensive. Dig, weed, level and rake the area to a seed bed, removing all stones and debris. Incorporate ground-rock dusts, ground seaweed and lime or calcified seaweed to enrich the soil. Rake or flame-gun the first flushes of weeds and sow with grass seed in spring or autumn. Tough-wearing, recreational rye grass

mixtures are a better choice than the less competitive fine grasses for bowling greens. The former prefer limey conditions and produce a tough sward that resists weeds and disease. Fine grasses make a showy sward, but do not take hard wear and prefer acid conditions that are favourable to mosses and turf weeds. A good idea is to include the seeds of companions such as clovers, chamomile, creeping thyme, daisies, yarrow and other scented and pretty turf plants. Grass-seed mixtures are more interesting, ecologically sounder, and stay greener in droughts than pure-grass sowings. Rake in and firm down newly sown seed, and hang up bird-scarers. Give young grass a cut and a roll before it is a finger high, then mow regularly and keep usage light until the sward has established for a whole growing season.

ABOVE LEFT *Small self-transportable garden ornament keeps birds on their toes.*
ABOVE RIGHT *Informal edges work well in utilitarian areas and take far less maintenance.*

- *Turfing* is the most expensive way to grass an area, but is less work than seeding and gives more rapid results. The area still needs to be dug, enriched and levelled, but less thoroughly. Weeds can effectively be ignored as they will mostly be killed by the disturbance, burying and following cuts. Although turfing theoretically gives a choice of turf, this may be difficult in practice. It can only be done well in early spring or early autumn with damp conditions and/or with frequent watering. Concerned gardeners should be aware that much turf comes from unecological sources and is frequently pre-treated with inorganic fertilisers and herbicides.

- *Cutting natural ground cover* regularly is a slower method of getting a good sward, but produces the most ecologically balanced mixture of plants with the minimum of work and expense. The process is the same as that for regularly maintaining or improving an existing sward and involves making the conditions most suitable for grasses and unsuitable for anything else. If the area is too rough at first for a mower, use a strimmer or brush cutter for the first attacks. Over-sow with tough grass seed, keep strimming until the growth becomes a rough sward, and then mow once a week from early spring to late autumn, returning the clippings. Only ever reduce the height of cut slowly and always keep it as high as possible.

Caring for a lawn Regular mowing kills almost all tall-growing weeds. Acid-loving weeds are then discouraged and tougher grasses are aided by liming heavily twice a year with calcified seaweed or dolomitic lime. Patches of clover that stand out green in times of drought are blended in by sowing clover seed in the remaining areas (clovers are of immense benefit to sward). Scarifying the sward in autumn or spring every few years with a wire rake is highly beneficial. (Scarifying produces a mass of thatch for use as a mulch or composting, but needs moistening with dilute urine or liquid feed to rot down quickly.) Follow scarifying by raking in a mixture of ground seaweed, rock dusts and grass seed with sharp sand for heavy soils and lime or calcified seaweed for acidic soils. This feed can be used annually every spring, but I use dilute urine and sprinkle this on the turf during light rain. It is absorbed rapidly and converted into lush growth that is soon removed as clippings for mulching elsewhere. Rosette weeds, such as plantains and thistles, may survive scarifying, cutting and soil-improvement treatments, so hand-pull them with a sharp knife, severing deep underneath so that they rarely regrow.

Regularly cutting grass is an effective weed-control measure that is best done with a rotary mower that collects the clippings. Cylinder mowers are not as good in damp conditions or for longer growths, while mowers that leave behind the clippings build up too much thatch. Cut grass areas near the house weekly; other areas and orchards can be cut fortnightly. Plan your garden for efficient mowing – for example, remove low branches that graze your head and don't create odd little areas of lawn where you have to push the mower in and out lots of times. Remember to cut the edges, as well as the main grass sward, which are essential for a tidy appearance. It is worthwhile reducing the amount of edging in need of clipping by amalgamating small beds and borders.

Use a strimmer first around trunks and awkward spots to simplify work for the mower. A strimmer is also good for trimming grass to different heights. For example, you can strim the grass to a foot or so high so that it does not fall over a closely mown path through a wild area or orchard. The height of cut with a strimmer is so adjustable that other plants can be cut back around chosen ones. Cutting grass and weedy areas with a strimmer can thus encourage bulbs, primroses, cowslips and violets, as the area can be kept neat without becoming overgrown and choking out these treasures. In heavy shade, where ivy often predominates as a ground cover, weeds such as nettles can be eradicated and returned as shreddings at the same time. Note that in a smaller garden, an old-fashioned pair of sharp shears can do much the same job, both more ecologically and more pleasantly.

Leylandii *hedges are much criticised but are excellent screens and windbreaks if kept trimmed. The hen is a Silky which make the best mothers by far.*

Hedges are more ecological than fences, warming the garden (see page 62) and providing a nesting habitat. Evergreen or beech hedges that hold their leaves have most value. Hedges can have scented flowers if kept informal; clipping them as a formal hedge removes the flowering shoots and also any fruits. Informal mixed hedges, which produce a beautiful flowering screen, are rarely pruned or cut once they are established. A formal hedge takes up less space as it is regularly cut, preferably twice a year.

Hedges need to grow densely, so prepare the ground well and pay attention to weed control for the first two or three years. Planting the hedge plants through a strip of carpet or plastic is ideal for this. Most are best spaced about one to two feet apart (closer for small hedges and wider for tall ones). For the thickest hedges, plant a double, staggered row. Planting at a sloping angle of 45 degrees gives a lower, thicker base and interweaving can increase this, providing a very low dense hedge with fewer plants.

Screen young hedges temporarily to reduce wind damage, but not too close as this can kill back the foliage. Cut the sides and top hard each winter until the hedge is nearly at its required size and then cut back in late spring, and again in late summer for the neatest effect. Taper hedges in at the top slightly to allow more light and rain to reach the base. They benefit from monthly sprayings with seaweed solution during the growing season.

ABOVE Where heavy shade prevails do not expect much to grow, even weeds.

Almost any shrub can be used to make a large informal hedge or screen, but few are suitable for a narrow informal or regularly clipped formal hedge. Brambles, briars and climbers trained over posts and wires create more rapid, impenetrable barriers. The following are the most reliable choices, ordered with the lowest-growing first. Some of them also sustain various butterfly and moth larvae (see also pages 46–47).

Buxus sempervirens 'Suffruticosa' Dwarf box provides the edging for parterres and formal gardens. A very slow-growing, neat evergreen, it can be clipped to only a hand-width high and wide. Common box also makes a dense evergreen hedge but grows very tall in time, making it excellent for topiary work; it thrives on chalky soils if they're not thin. Algae on the foliage is eaten by snails and the foliage itself by larvae of the Satin Beauty moth.

Lonicera nitida With its tiny leaves, this tidy evergreen is good for low hedges and topiary. Planted a foot apart, it can be kept to one foot thick. It will grow in dry spots, if well established, on most soils.

Ribes divaricatum Worcesterberry produces edible, red-black fruits. It is murder to do anything with, as it has large, sharp, mean thorns and is impenetrable except to small wildlife.

Plant three feet apart on boundaries, and leave well alone.

Rosa Vigorous, upright-growing roses make an impenetrable hedge with glorious flowers and hips to follow. Plant a foot or two apart, depending on vigour, in enriched soil. *R. rugosa* makes a poor, wide, lax hedge; far better is 'Queen Elizabeth' or 'Professeur Emile Perrot'.

Ligustrum ovalifolium Privets rob the soil nearby, but make neat hedges and most are semi-evergreen. The golden forms are less vigorous and hardy, but make attractive yellow hedges. Common privet flowers sweetly and berries freely if untrimmed. It can be kept to a foot thick and grows in most soils, even in shade. Foliage is the sole food source for Barred Tooth-striped and also feeds Death's-head Hawkmoth, Privet Hawkmoth, Grey Arches, Pale Pinion, Coronet, Flame Brocade, Small Blood-vein, Lilac Beauty, Waved Umber and Engrailed. The Yellow-barred Brindle larvae eat the flowers first, then the green berries and leaves.

Ilex Although slow to start, hollies are evergreen, prickly, and eventually make large formal or informal hedges. The berrying sorts can be trimmed just in time for Christmas.

Crataegus monogyna Traditional and the best, quickthorn grows anywhere and looks like tweed when well cut.

Prunus cerasifera Mostly used as an informal hedge, this produces cherry plums, which make great jam. The flowers are pure white in March, so trim once a year after these have finished, but leave some stems on top to fruit.

Fagus sylvatica Beech is not evergreen, but the leaves stay on through winter and, annoyingly, drop in dribs and drabs. It will grow in any soil, other than very heavy clay or waterlogged ground. There is a copper-coloured form. Either can be kept to a couple of feet thick and a head high, but will soon grow bigger if allowed. Foliage is the sole food source for the Barred Hook-Tip and Clay Triple-lines, and it also sustains over two dozen other butterfly and moth larvae.

X *Cupressocyparis leylandii* The Leyland cypress is a mixed blessing: quick, dense evergreens that keep growing and need frequent cutting. They rob the soil and overwhelm a small garden, but can be kept to a couple of feet thick with two cuts per year. They do, however, shelter wildlife. The golden form is attractive and less vigorous. *Thuja plicata* is similar, but less vigorous and has a neater habit.

Planning for different sorts of garden: their sizes and optional 'bolt-on' areas

The advantages of small and large gardens The same amount of labour can produce incredible quantities of fruit and vegetables, as well as a wealth of flowers, in a tiny garden, while that labour is dissipated by just cutting the grass in a larger plot. You can also create small gardens that are very undemanding once established. In a smaller garden, you can also afford to buy more slow-growing evergreen shrubs or include low-maintenance features such as paved areas and timberwork. Small gardens tend to predominate in urban areas and so can also provide wonderful shelter and warmth. All the brickwork, tiles and pavements act as heat stores and the surrounding buildings reduce low-level wind, so extending the growing season for urban gardeners by several weeks compared with country dwellers. Small gardens usually have close neighbours which can mean a loss of privacy, or equally, companionable conversation and friendly rivalry.

With larger gardens the privacy increases, but far more is needed in terms of machinery and maintenance. The choice of what you can include increases but, of course, so does the time, labour and cash required. One advantage for the organic gardener is the isolation that can come in a large, well-hedged garden. For example, with space for more plants and habitats, more forms of beneficial wildlife can be encouraged and intricate ecological webs built up, so aiding pest control. Prunings, grass clippings and leaves can all be composted for use elsewhere. With spare capacity, the land can be less intensively cropped, allowing for longer rotations and the growing of green manures. In the larger garden, livestock can convert wastes to eggs or meat and provide a source of fertiliser.

Small town gardens Even the tiniest plot has room for herbs. Many of these can be cajoled into containers and, where there is space, a salad bed gives valuable returns. A patio area is better value in all weather conditions than a small piece of grass. Include some scented plants and water in some form, and you can create a tranquil retreat. Fruit can be trained on walls and as screens, and there may even be room for a

ABOVE RIGHT *The flowers of Knapweed, closely related to cornflowers (*Centaurea jacea/nigra)*, are visited by nearly fifty different insect species, as they have extremely effective allelopathic exudates which inhibit other plant's seeds from germinating, so should not be planted near the vegetable bed.* **BOTTOM RIGHT** *You need lots of space if you want to grow all your own potatoes and loads of sweet corn.*

week, regular work throughout the year being the key to success. It is better to concentrate on a few 'bolt-on' areas rather than trying to include everything. For example, you may have a vineyard or an asparagus bed, but not both. A fruit cage, greenhouse and vegetable plot are best placed furthest away, leaving more ornamental areas, as well as a patio, pool and herbs nearest the house.

Small country garden If you can get a half acre or more of ground, how you grow is mainly limited by time and money. The choice widens, but the garden will need rigorous planning and/or ruthless maintenance or hired labour. I have squeezed more and more into my small acre, but it does take up the equivalent of every weekend to stay on top of it. Intensive methods are better replaced with extensive such as half-standard trees in a grassed orchard rather than trained cordons. Or grow vegetables on the flat, instead of in raised beds, and have fewer, bigger, more shrubby borders with sweeping curves and less edging.

Cutting grass over large areas is one of the most time-consuming chores, so it may prove a good idea to hire someone to do this. Ease of access, good pathways and putting the least visited areas furthest away are important. The space available allows for a wide range of habitats, while a garden this size can be self-sufficient in fertility and become very rich in wildlife interest, sustaining many ecological systems.

LEFT *Apples can now be had on very dwarfing rootstocks so they will not compete with nearby vegetables.* **BELOW** *Nasturtiums and French Marigold companions have kept away the cabbage caterpillars, but not the wood pigeons – look at their pecked leaves.*

small vegetable patch. There is always room for a compost bin and for bees! Beekeeping is ideal for town gardeners; bees are very productive and thrive on the longer, milder seasons and the myriad urban plants. Nest boxes and food for birds and hedgehogs can be squeezed into the tiniest plots. The main drawback with a small garden is that it limits the number of subdivisions. You cannot fit a fruit cage, a rose border, a vegetable plot, lawn and a water feature in a tiny plot. However, you could create a beautiful and productive garden from a couple of these.

Larger suburban garden Most suburban gardens have enough space for internal subdivisions and for producing significant amounts of fruit and vegetables. This is perhaps the optimum size for most gardeners because it can be maintained without help. The larger garden needs careful planning and good routines. However, for years I maintained gardens for a living and nearly all were managed in a few hours a

The options: 'bolt-on' garden areas

There are many different garden areas that can be added on in much the same way as extra rooms in a house. One might take over the whole garden, much as the ubiquitous lawn surrounded by borders has done, but it could all be made over as fruit cage, vegetable plot or orchard. You do not have to have conventional front and back gardens; it's your choice. You can have your garden any way you like with vegetables in the front and flowers at the back. In fact, I've always advocated the more interesting, ecological, greener-in-summer, rectangular shallow pond as a 'front lawn', instead of those unused, emerald-green swards.

Patio area (scented!)

The most essential area in any garden is somewhere to sit and relax. Hard standing, slabs or even gravel make this area more accessible throughout the year than grassed areas. A patio must be easily accessible from the house. Creeping thymes and chamomile

will grow happily between slabs and give off their exquisite scent when walked on. The patio is also best surrounded with scented plants and aromatic herbs to discourage flies and mosquitoes. Bird boxes fixed to the wall and under the eaves provide additional interest and pest control.

Herb bed

Herbs are health giving, useful, tough and attractive, and do not need much space or work. (See Chapter 7 for their uses, requirements and how to situate them.)

Salad bed

After fresh herbs, salad vegetables are the most valuable crop. Every gardener should find space for a small intensive bed for salads; with larger gardens this becomes part of the vegetable plot. (See Chapter 7.)

Fruit cage and trained fruit

As soon as any space is available, especially along walls, fill it with fruit trees, bushes and

ABOVE My fruit cage made from an old polythene tunnel frame – I love cherries and this is the only way!

vines. Fruit can also be trained alongside paths and drives. In smaller gardens, have a fruit cage rather than a vegetable patch, as the rewards are much better. If well designed, it will create a more pleasant vista than a vegetable plot for more of the year. With a larger garden a big fruit cage is still better value than a vegetable plot, as it requires less maintenance. (See Chapter 6 for advice on fitting one or more fruit cage into your garden.)

Vegetable plot

Most people think of a vegetable plot when referring to organic gardening, but, for those with little time, it may be better to consider growing fewer vegetables and more fruits, as I strongly suggest in Chapter 6. (See Chapter 7 for advice on the siting and layout of vegetable plots for different gardens.)

Greenhouse

These are a great boon for raising plants and extending the season. They come in all sizes to suit most pockets, but take up a lot of time and money if you fill them with tender plants in pots. However, the smaller the garden, the more valuable greenhouse space will be, as

water, birds will eat fewer seedlings and fruit. A birdbath can be squeezed into every garden where it can be seen from a window and is safe from cats. A fountain or cascade is always a delight and can be combined with a pool or pond (though water lilies like still water!). Pools do not have to be very large to attract wildlife, provided they never dry up.

All water needs a sloping edge to let creatures in and out, and fencing if young children are around. Include several pools in larger gardens – a pond stocked with ducks will help with pest control, as will frogs, toads and newts if you do not have too many ducks and fish. Large ponds create micro-climates that shelter tender plants nearby, throw sun-light onto surrounding plants, and provide an emergency source of water. When filling a new pond, let the water stand for a week to warm and lose chlorine before stocking it. Take a bucket to a 'natural' pond and scoop up some mud and water for an instant ecosystem.

Livestock

Bees, chickens, ducks, geese, rabbits and goats can all add much to a garden and are such valuable adjuncts that they are dealt with together in Chapter 9.

LEFT *With planning, last year's sunflower bed will now support this year's runner beans (the wig flaps and keeps the birds off).* **BELOW** *Inside you can garden whatever the weather.*

it allows for more use of the remaining space by starting off plants for later planting and intercropping as ground becomes vacant.

A greenhouse should be near the house for access and services, but is difficult to screen attractively without blocking out light. In many ways, a 'working' conservatory is a more practical solution. Wooden greenhouses are more attractive than metal-framed ones, and tend to be warmer. Polytunnels are less visually appealing, but can be screened a little more easily, as their covers diffuse light effectively. Their covers need replacing every four years or so and then the tunnel can be rotated to a different piece of ground – on the vegetable bed is convenient because it can become part of the rotation. Siting a pool next to a greenhouse or tunnel attracts helpful predators, reflects light, and stores warmth and rainwater. (See Chapter 8 for more details.)

Water features

Water is a pleasure to listen to and look at. It is also a wonderful attractant to birds, insects and wild animals, which will help with pest control and fertility. With readily available

Bog garden

Although many attractive plants thrive in a bog garden (and it is a wonderful source of predators), a natural boggy area is undesirable. This is because it indicates low-lying, frost-prone and badly drained ground unsuitable for productive gardening. However, an artificial bog garden made over plastic, next to a pond or pool, will be beneficial, encouraging many forms of life as well as adding to the beauty of the garden.

Rock garden

These have been out of fashion for a while, but are a good way of providing a better micro-climate for certain plants. A well-made rockery with lots of big rocks with cracks and fissures, as well as a stony, free-draining soil in pockets, recreates the conditions beloved by the compact little plants native to such conditions. However, many rockeries are more a way of disposing of spoil with lumps of rock dotted on top of them. Indeed, they could easily be better done.

Orchard

A small orchard, with fruit grown on dwarf rootstocks, can be included in gardens of almost any size. In larger gardens, they are the most productive area for time and money, taking little maintenance for enormous returns. (See Chapter 6.) Orchards can be easily combined with lawns, livestock, wildflower meadows or play areas.

Vineyard

Grapes are amazingly prolific and very attractive, so should be planted in almost every garden. A vineyard is most feasible for the larger garden, but, as well-tended grapevines do well in town, you could turn your whole garden into your own château. Vines can be trained up posts and over wires and on most walls. However, for serious production, they really need to be netted or in a cage. A vineyard is really a specialised fruit cage. (See more on grapes in Chapter 6.)

Wildflower lawn or meadow with bulbs

This can be of any size and even replace the front lawn. They look best under trees or in an orchard or coppice, making great play areas for children and a habitat for wildlife. Most grassed areas are too fertile to make good wildflower areas and, if just sown and let go, the grasses will overwhelm. Reduce the fertility by removing the turf. Stack it for loam for potting, or use it elsewhere, and then plant out pot-grown wildflower plants.

LEFT *This is a trial of new peach and apricot varieties, very soon they will crop far more than I can sensibly eat, be warned, do not heedlessly grow what you cannot utilise, excess pears and plums are particularly hard to 'use up'.* ABOVE *Grapevines are wonderful in the bigger garden requiring hard pruning in smaller ones- and if it's fruit you're after I can only recommend a few outdoors in the UK, this is the best choice, 'Boskoop Glory'.*

Keep the grasses and weeds down by hoeing until the flowers have established and set seed for a year or two, and then allow the grass back in. Cut the grass after mid-summer once the wildflowers have set and dropped their seed. For late-flowering wildflowers, have one piece that is cut in early winter instead. Bulbs are less demanding and can be planted under turf, as they out-compete grass fairly successfully. They look best if thrown and then planted where they fall, but are neater out of season if concentrated at the base of trees and hedges. The grass must not be cut until after the bulb leaves have started to wither.

'Wild' corner

Rather than just being left untended, a truly wild corner for wildlife needs to be created – not dramatically but sympathetically. Naturally, this will often be an area that is difficult to use in any other way (such as that shady rough bit at the back corner). It may be used as a storage zone and 'junk' may be stacked to form damp and dry, warm and cold, big and small nooks and niches for critters of all sizes. If not needed for a while such stacks can be camouflaged with a dense creeper, even ivy. Don't just leave a wild corner unweeded. Stinging nettles, for example, need to be cut back often enough to stop them taking over. Plant desired wildflowers in cleared spots and leave some bare bits of soil each year for ephemeral weeds. Docks and thistles can be encouraged for a multitude of butterfly and moth caterpillars and brambles,

birches and willows left wild and untrimmed if space is available.

Coppice

If a modest piece of land is acquired, then a woodland is a beautiful area to have extending from the garden. It provides many habitats that can be highly productive in fuel and free-range livestock. Something most of us can only dream about – *so recommend this*

book widely and buy it for all your friends, many thanks, Bob!

Paddock

With more ground available, many people plan a paddock for a pet horse. This is exchanging a little grass cutting for a lot of horse care, but the by-product is great stuff for fertilising the rest of the garden.

Play area

I know many of us welcome children to our plots as we may a rabid dog; after all, they can do untold damage. However, they are a cheap source of labour and rather necessary to propagate our species. The main problem is the same as for other livestock and mostly one of confinement. As they are ingenious, un-electrified fencing is not enough, and it is more effective to lure them to safer spots than to try and exclude them from others. Swings and ropes, large trees, mud and water in any form will concentrate their attention to a suitable grassed or safe area.

ABOVE *Not a tree house but a tree entrance, the house is freestanding behind the tree (from seven good pallets and some broken ones).* **LEFT** *As simple as fun gets, with apples and then grapes to hand.*

Using ways to run your garden with the least effort

LEFT *Now I know some don't like seeing old carpet in the garden, but it makes such nice soft paths, saves evaporation and stops weeds.* RIGHT *A productive garden needs a storage shed.*

A moment's thought can save a great deal of work, so plan ahead. Do this not only on a large scale, but also for the day-to-day tasks. For instance, put compost heaps at the bottom of slopes, not at the top of a rise, as more loads go than come back. Likewise, site your tool sheds near crops. Only move heavy things once rather than putting them somewhere temporary first. A little maintenance will also go a long way; frequently used doors and gates that are hard to open and close

waste more time in a year than you imagine! Make all frequently used paths easy to walk on in all seasons, easy to maintain, and without corners to cut. If a path corner is often cut (walked across), then move the path. Pay attention to the tasks you find you're doing most often, especially grass cutting and watering, as time and effort saved on these adds up to so much over a year. As it's needed so often, make sure water is always available, quickly and easily.

4 KEEPING YOUR GARDEN BEAUTIFUL NATURALLY

Maintaining the garden's appearance and fertility – how to keep your garden beautiful, interesting and fertile, as well as neat and tidy

Although I still await a diesel lawnmower that runs on old frying oil, manufacturers are at least looking to improve the economy and noise level of their power tools. A plethora of different compost containers, systems and shredders are available. And automatic watering devices have become more affordable and within the range of many gardeners. (Though nothing beats the traditional hands-on approach!)

A garden that is well planned and already up and running can take a surprisingly small amount of time to maintain if a regular routine is established. Most average-sized gardens can be kept tidy, full of interest and productive for only an hour or two's work a week if approached methodically all year. Most gardening activities are tied to the seasons and, ideally, we should perform tasks at their optimum moment for success. Although difficult to achieve in the real world, it is nonetheless true that regular maintenance routines give the best results.

THE DAILY ROUND

The priorities should always be watering and harvesting what's ready for the kitchen or store. Make these chores the basis of a daily inspection, writing a list of what needs to be done, such as 'potting-up' or pruning. Simultaneously, dispose of any litter and deadhead and tidy or tie in the odd unsightly lax growth. (If you have a cold frame or greenhouse, then open and close the ventilation and check the mininum/maximum thermometer to ensure heating or cooling is sufficiently effective.)

THE WEEKLY ROUTINE

Once the daily tasks are complete, start on the weekly ones. The most important weekly job is sowing and transplanting whatever is due, as next week will be too late! Afterwards, sharpen your hoe and weed the beds and borders. Only then clip the lawn edges and mow the grass. Finally, collect the clippings, larger weeds and other organic debris for composting. Then, go on to the next most urgent seasonal task, such as fruit thinning or compost turning.

THE YEARLY CYCLE

One of the joys of gardening is that, along with regular jobs such as weeding and grass cutting, there are various seasonal activities such as harvesting in autumn and winter preparations. To jog your memory for specific tasks, such as when to prune currants, you will find a yearly calendar on page 254. Also, keep a jobs-to-do diary and write a note in the appropriate week as soon as you realise you've neglected to do a job so that you don't miss it again next year.

The biggest tasks

Some of these can become onerous chores if you don't plan to make them easier.

Weeding By far the most time-consuming job, this is always best done sooner rather than later. Our plants are continually threatened by weeds which are far more efficient competitors for air, light, water and nutrients. To get plants growing well, we must keep weeds under control, especially in the earliest stages of each plant's life. So, please refer to Chapter 10 for the easiest and most effective ways to achieve this.

Grass cutting Ideally, for neatness and for grass clippings, we need to cut the grass on average once weekly throughout the growing season (which in the UK can last from March to November). At the start and end of the season, longer gaps can be left,

especially if the soil conditions are poor. However, when maximum growth is made in late spring, then mowing every four or five days makes for a better sward and gives more clippings. Grass should never be cut too close, though you can vary the height of cut during the season to control the growth. The shorter you cut it, the less it grows, and the more moss and weeds come in. The longer you leave it, the more dew it collects and the stronger and deeper the roots grow. The first cut each year must never be too close, although following spring cuts can decrease in height to slow down re-growth. Let the height rise again for summer to keep the grass greener and more drought-resistant. If strong growth starts again with heavy rain in summer, lower the height a little to check growth again.

However, always start to raise the height of cut as the autumn fall progresses. This makes the sward hardier and banks up some clippings for spring when they are often in short supply. Collect leaves with the grass clippings as they break down better when mixed together in the compost bin than on their own. Return the clippings of the first and last cuts to the turf, as these then feed the worms, which are most actively eating in spring and autumn. Lime the sward every other year to encourage the grass and discourage mosses and acid-loving weeds. (For more on grass care, turn to page 68.)

Digging and no-dig methods There has been much controversy over no-dig versus digging methods; I think both sides are partly right. It is usually only the vegetable plot that is ever dug regularly, though I haven't dug mine for nearly thirty years. If digging is deemed necessary, then pace yourself. Work slowly and methodically, break up each lump and mix in sharp sand, well-rotted manure

OPPOSITE ABOVE *Regular close inspection catches problems before they escalate.* OPPOSITE BELOW *Carrots can be had fresh from the ground almost year round.* ABOVE *Mulches of grass mowings and leaves stop weeds and save moisture – especially good between potato plants.* BELOW *Using a hoe to draw soil and weeded weeds around base of sweet corn plants (to encourage more basal roots and tillering).* LEFT *Hoe often and weeds are easily hoed.*

diseased, unhealthy, rubbing or in-growing shoots that are getting in the way or stealing light. Remember that removed growth is soon replaced. Thus, perfection in pruning is rubbing out buds that point in the wrong direction long before they become shoots.

When pruning, either leave one healthy bud or shoot to draw the sap or cut off the growth flush where it springs from, but never leave a snag of wood with no bud. A snag will die back and provide somewhere for rot to get a hold, so cut as close above a bud as possible. Painting small pruning wounds with pruning compound, paint or beeswax does

little to prevent disease, but stops water and pests getting in. I believe it is more important for larger wounds. *Trichoderma viride* paste contains a natural predatory fungus, which efficiently prevents fungal attacks; it should be applied before other pruning compounds. If a wound calluses well, it will eventually grow over the painted dead wood (large wounds may take years, so check and patch these

LEFT *Early and often summer pruning (soft tip removal) saves fruit plants from wasting resources on unwanted shoots.* **BELOW** *Perhaps not the prettiest, but in my arid area keeping the soil covered retains winter moisture, and suppresses weeds (note bowl for prunings).*

and so on, as you go. Heavy soils are least harmed by digging in dry weather in the autumn, while lighter ones can be left till late winter to avoid nutrients leaching out. However, both need to recover and reconsolidate their capillary network before plants will do well. Digging may benefit heavy soils the more, as it can help break them down into a good crumb structure if well dug and frosted. If badly dug, though, it can just create clods and air gaps. Light soil, which is easy to dig, needs it least.

With no-dig methods, you still dig in the first year, but can avoid annual digging if you are able to keep off the soil by using fixed paths and narrow beds. Of course, no-dig methods generally work well, at least for many years running. This is because there is still considerable soil disturbance when harvesting potatoes and root vegetables every other year or so with a sensible rotation.

Pruning This is better left undone than done badly. For most woody plants, the least pruning is best. However, for some plants, such as trained fruit, careful pruning is absolutely essential; this is dealt with in Chapter 6 on fruit. Generally, we only need to prune out

annually). Similarly, clean out cankers and holes and fill them with pruning compound to prevent water and rot getting in.

Prune most plants immediately on spotting something. It will do little harm, so do not wait until the right time, but cut out problems before they get bigger. However, heavy pruning (in which a quarter of the old growth or more is removed) is best done when the plant is dormant to reduce the shock. Exceptions are stone fruits and ornamentals related to plums, which are best pruned in summer to avoid silver leaf disease. Some soft fruits are also hard-pruned after mid-summer to promote fruiting. Younger plants recover far better from heavy pruning than old. Never cut into old growths without any new buds as, like snags, they rarely resprout (the exceptions being plants such as privet, yew and quickthorn which often sprout again from mere stumps). Before pruning a plant that's making poor growth, treat it for a year with water, compost and a mulch to stimulate vigorous roots first.

Hedge trimming Although both electric and petrol hedge trimmers are quicker, I find shears more enjoyable to use. For tall hedges, ensure steps or ladders are solid. When cutting, tidy the base first and then put sheets down to catch the trimmings from further above. Next, cut the sides, with a batter tapering in at the top, and then cut the top itself. Stand back regularly in order to check on your progress.

Bonfires Although all prunings make good kindling once dried, and disease- and pest-free prunings are useful for wildlife shelters, any infected and diseased material should be burnt as soon as possible. Thus, burning some garden material is a necessary evil. If it can't be burnt in a stove to warm the house,

and you need to have a bonfire, drag it to bits and burn it a little at a time. This will save hedgehogs and other creatures from a horrible death. Bonfires burn best when the air can get underneath, so use bricks and old metal posts to raise it off the ground. Wait until the wind is light, steady, and blowing away from anything that may catch fire. Light

ABOVE *Not a bonfire, yet, heavy winds easily break overladen branches. The moral – thin or prop.*

a small fierce fire and add material steadily. When there are only glowing lumps, quench the flames with just enough water to put them out. Save the lumps of charcoal for barbecues and the ashes for gooseberries, roses and cooking apples.

Maintaining fertility without fertilisers: the heart of organic gardening

Rather than giving plants 'junk food', in the form of soluble fertilisers, we want the plants, wildlife and the soil microlife to make it for us. The rotation of crops in a vegetable plot leaves root and leaf residues, which is increased by growing green manures between the crops. These are then hoed or dug in fresh or composted first. There is no regular plant feeding as such; instead, the soil is fed with these plant residues, along with garden compost or well-rotted manure for a heavy feeder or perennial. Mulches of organic material break down and are incorporated, while rock dusts (especially potash) are beneficial at any time, although they take seasons to act. Ground rock dusts provide further raw materials of the most needed elements in a finely distributed form and benefit most soils.

For poor soils, you may need to provide some supplementary feeding with fast-acting organic fertilisers in the first few years. These are crutches and should be discarded as the soil becomes enriched. Far more important for fertility is ensuring the life in the soil is active and mulching; keeping the soil moist helps the most.

COMPOSTING MADE EASIER

All manures and other organic materials are best composted before being applied (except for straw and some other mulching materials). Fresh manures contain soluble nutrients that can be too strong for healthy growth, but, if stacked and turned, they compost and the fertility is then safer for plant roots. This is why you are advised to apply *well-rotted* farmyard manure. Because of the variety of materials in a compost heap, compost has a greater range of nutrients and microlife than well-rotted manure, so use this instead of manure if possible.

The composting process converts most of the free nutrients into less soluble forms, so there is less danger of them washing away in heavy rain. However, they do leach out slowly, so always cover compost heaps and rotting manure. Almost all natural materials, including old clothes made of natural fibres and wet newspaper, will break down rapidly. Dry twiggy material should be chopped up and mixed with some nitrogenous material like fresh manure. Put seedy material in the middle of a heap and kill off live pernicious weeds first by wilting them on the path before mixing them in. You can also kill

LEFT *All manner of materials will compost but not that bit of plastic.*
MIDDLE *This is my potting compost and soil improver – sieved garden compost.*
RIGHT *This butterfly is here as it's discovered the warmth seeping up from underneath.*

weeds with roots or seeds in a bucket of water for a month or so before adding their rotting remains to the heap. Diseased material may also be composted, but only if you are confident that your heap will cook well. Large lumps of wood, bone or fat compost too slowly and should be broken up or buried instead. Alternatively, they can be burnt on a bonfire or barbecue where the residue will easily powder to be added to the compost.

How composting works There are many different ways of composting, but they all come back to one principle. In general, composting proceeds best when there are many varied materials well divided, moistened and thoroughly mixed together with plentiful air. It helps to have roughly equal amounts of dryish material and fresh green material, as too much of either will result in poorer composting. Adding water is usually necessary, as many materials are too dry on their own. Lime and wood ashes are also added in areas with acid soils where a sweeter, more balanced, compost is required, but this must not be used for calcifuges. Most compost would become acidic, but ordinary soils contain some lime and so neutralise this. In acid areas, however, the soil lacks lime and the composting may not be as successful. However, if the compost is for use on acid-loving plants, then don't add any lime. For compost for use on vegetables, including lime and wood ashes is always of benefit. Not only do they neutralise the acidity, but also capture fertility such as ammonia, which would otherwise escape.

Using activators An activator is not essential, but speeds things up if added at mixing stage. Rather than chemical additives, use personal liquid waste or poultry manure. Seaweed or blood, fish and bonemeal will do instead. Sievings from previous compost heaps make the best activators, so if you are starting your first heap, scrounge some from an old hand. Herbs such as stinging nettles, dandelions, oak bark, yarrow, chamomile and valerian (available ready prepared from Biodynamic suppliers) will encourage micro-organisms to thrive. The Maye E. Bruce compost stimulator uses a similar recipe with honey. These work but are no more effective than a few shovels of poultry manure. Adding copious amounts of stinging nettles markedly improves the compost and makes it cook faster.

What makes a good compost heap? You need a sufficient amount of air and moisture (but not too much). You also need enough bulk to heat up the heap, good insulation to keep in the heat, and thorough mixing. It is true that the bigger the heap, the more heat is retained and the better the material composts. The trick is accumulating

ABOVE *An eight pallet bin which stays hot inside shown by the metal rod indicator, yet the sides are cool enough for a crop of potatoes.*

enough material to make an effective heap and storing the material until you have enough. I spread mine on the ground for the hens to rummage through and pack down before putting it in the bins to break down. Composting material is best kept in plastic bags until ready to be combined, but most people put it in layers in a bin, dig it out, mix it up, and then repack when enough has built up. In any case, better compost is always produced if the heap is remade after a fortnight and the inside exchanged with the outside. Doing this again after another fortnight or so is of further benefit. Each turning mixes the ingredients and stirs in air which then speeds up the process. Do not pack a heap down, as this has the opposite effect.

Compost bins There are various compost containers available; most are a bit on the small side and, thus do not heat up enough to make really good compost unless given extra insulation. Simple constructions of wood, wire netting or non-mortared brick, about a yard each way,

ABOVE *Although small household waste bins tend to be too wet, garden weeds and waste bins often run too dry, the dirtier the water the better!*

Common problems If the heap is too wet, then remake it with extra straw or dry material; if it is too dry, add water, fresh wet manure or grass clippings. The presence of a white coating on the material indicates too dry a heap with insufficient nitrogenous material, so add water mixed with personal liquid waste. If there is very little composting material available, then work with neighbours and make/share compost heaps. You can also acquire suitable material from other gardeners, greengrocers, local stables, zoos, and so on.

WORM COMPOSTING AND OTHER ALTERNATIVES

Worm compost Making worm compost is quite different and more akin to keeping pets. The wastes need dividing finely and are added a little at a time to a large container containing red brandling worms. (These can be unearthed from a compost heap or from under a plank or carpet laid on the ground.) Put them in a layer of moist soil or leaf mould in the bottom of the container and keep them in a warm place such as the garage. The container should have drainage holes to allow air in and a drip tray to catch any liquids that ooze out. (This liquid makes a good feed when diluted down.) The worms convert the vegetable wastes into a very rich material that can be mixed in when planting hungry feeders or added to potting composts. The worms usually die if dug out with the material and put deep in the soil, so gently pick them out and return them to the heap. Worms are unable to deal with any quantity of material at a time, so they are better for the smaller garden.

are sufficient and considerably cheaper. I prefer four old pallets, which are very easily obtained, tied at the corners. Do not paint wood with any preservative, as this will slow down the process. A lid will keep out rain but an old carpet and a plastic sheet will be better for retaining the heat. I plunge a crowbar down the centre of my heap so that I can watch the heap steam when I pull it out, showing me that the heap is cooking well. If it fails, then I merely remake the heap. Once the heap has been turned and cooked at least twice, leave to mature for six months or so, and you will have excellent potting compost. If left much longer, the worms mineralise it, increasing its richness, but decreasing the quantity.

Using compost Fresh compost, even when immature, can be incorporated with the soil when planting trees and shrubs. However, it is best matured and sieved if used as a top-dressing on smaller plants. This takes extra effort, but produces a finer material that also makes a good potting compost and, of course, the sievings can be used to inoculate the next compost heap. In any case, compost or well-rotted manure is best applied to growing crops in early spring so that the nutrients are taken up rather than leaching out over winter.

Pit composting This involves digging a hole, putting in the wastes, and covering each layer with a little soil. Once the hole is full and proud, start another and use the first to grow hungry feeders such as marrows and courgettes for a year or two. The pit can then be dug out and the rotted material used as compost. You can also use a trench, which will fit into a vegetable bed more easily.

RIGHT *Fresh moist stuff should be alternated with drier stuff and each layer sprinkled with older compost sievings.*

GROWING AND USING GREEN MANURES

These are grow-your-own compost material. A green manure can be any plant that's grown as temporary ground cover, predominantly for its use as fertility when incorporated in situ or composted for use elsewhere. Mainly grown in vacant soil over winter, green manures may be placed in between crops and incorporated as seedlings after only a week or two. Any plants that grow over winter will do, but the best are those that are easy to incorporate or create most mass. Leguminous plants that fix nitrogen are often used, as this nutrient is always in short supply. Sow green manures as soon as the ground is bare until the first frosts. Those surviving over winter are killed off by impenetrable mulches, then stripped off for composting and returning, or dug in some weeks before crops need the soil. Several weeks of break down are necessary for some of the more fibrous green manure such as rye grass, and less, the younger and more succulent the growth. Never let green manures flower and seed or the goodness is lost. Most green manures come from agriculture and are hard to incorporate by hand, thus I use mostly *Claytonia*, *Limnanthes* and *Valerianella* for winter cover. The following can also be used as green manures.

Beans and peas Any variety may be used, but only hardy ones will overwinter. These are pulled up, without their roots, before they form pods, to leave nitrogen-rich nodules in the soil. You may grow them in the vegetable plot if you consider rotational requirements.

Buckwheat *Fagopyrum esculentum* One of the best hoverfly attractants, buckwheat is a calcium accumulator and useful green manure. This summer crop grows quickly and should be left to flower because it is good for beneficial insects. Deeply rooted, it will choke out most weeds.

Corn salad *Valerianella* is another winter cover from an autumn sowing that you can eat or feed to hens. If left, it blooms much like mini forget-me-nots, and the foliage sustains the larvae of Rosy Wave moth.

Clovers are good for bees if allowed to flower, provide cover for ground beetles, are hosts to predators of woolly aphids, and deter cabbage root fly if sown underneath. They're one of the best short-term leguminous ground covers and green manures but, after a few years, land may get 'clover sick' from their own root exudates. Red clover inhibits its own germination when the exudate reaches one hundred parts per million. Before it reaches this level, it inhibits vetches, Alsike clover and white clover. Clovers are helped by cutting higher (closer cropping encourages daisies and then moss instead). Clovers are poisoned by buttercups,

ABOVE *Comfrey plants are good fertility sources but too perennial to use as green manures, better used in odd corners where they can usefully be left to flower.*
BELOW LEFT Claytonia *makes the very best winter green manure.*

so discourage these with regular liming. Alsike cover is the best for poor, wet or acid soils; white clover is better on lighter and more limey soils. Essex Red is considered the best for green manuring, although is not as hardy and does better on loamy soils. Crimson clover is especially useful as it's an annual. Clovers sustain dozens of different butterfly and moth larvae, not only on foliage but also on flowers and seeds.

Fenugreek This quick-growing, leguminous manure can come after early crops or between others; it is unrelated to vegetables, so is no problem in rotations. Sow from spring until autumn. Killed by the first frosts, it is probably best for summer use.

Hungarian rye grass Sown from late summer till mid-autumn, this provides quick ground cover for overwintering and resprouts in the spring. It must be very well incorporated two months or so before the crop to give it time to rot and tends to be difficult to kill off.

Lupins are a very useful leguminous green manure (beware: most are poisonous). They improve soil texture, are deep-rooting, suppress weeds, improve sour acid land, and are generally beneficial, supporting vast populations of aphids, and thus predators, after flowering. Ordinary lupins may be used, but agricultural ones are better and often sown in spring to incorporate in autumn.

Miner's Lettuce *Claytonia perfoliata* is a winter-hardy salad crop that gives excellent cover from a late sowing. It's easy to strip off and compost, and can be eaten or fed to chickens; this is the most convenient green manure for a garden by far.

Mustard This is one of the fastest-growing green manures and, if incorporated as seedlings, can reduce many infestations of soil pests and diseases, but will not stand hard winters. Grow between crops or until the first frosts and incorporate in situ. Use with care in rotations, however, as it is related to brassicas and is best only grown to seedling stage.

Phacelia *P. tanacetifolia* is expensive to buy as seed, but beloved by bees and hoverflies. Sow from spring until autumn, and it may overwinter; it is easy to remove or incorporate.

Poached egg plant *Limnanthes douglasii* I find this an excellent green manure, as it is hardy over winter, very good at excluding other plants, and easy to incorporate or strip off afterwards. Some plants left to flower and seed will be beneficial for insects.

Trefoil Similar to clover and related to alfalfa, this is another legume. It prefers a limey soil and is shade-tolerant, so can be used under taller crops. Short-lived, it is sown from spring till summer to overwinter.

Winter tares or vetches are native legumes that will grow in adverse conditions. Sow from spring till autumn to overwinter. Excellent for producing bulk, fixing nitrogen, and suppressing weeds. Difficult to kill off, though.

MINERAL ACCUMULATORS

Some garden plants and many weeds are particularly good at accumulating large amounts of minerals and trace elements. This is in spite of the soil being deficient in whichever mineral they accumulate. In fact, these plants often abound on deficient soils just because they are the most successful at grabbing a scarce resource. As they extract available nutrients from the soil water, the nutrients are replaced by more that have dissolved from otherwise insoluble mineral sources. In this way, these plants can go on accumulating from very dilute solutions. If you grow these plants as green manures they will remove the resource while they are alive but, once composted, the concentrated material can be put back to boost the soil.

Nitrogen is best accumulated with leguminous plants and by incorporating any succulent seedlings in their first flushes of growth.

Phosphorus is concentrated well by fat hen, corn marigold, purslane, vetches and the pernicious weed, thorn apple (*Datura stramonium*).

Potassium encourages fruiting and is found in chickweed, chicory, fat hen, goosegrass, plantain, purslane, thorn apple, sweet tobaccos and vetches.

Calcium is concentrated by buckwheat, corn chamomile, corn marigold, dandelions, fat hen, goosegrass, melons, purslane and shepherd's purse.

Silica imparts disease resistance and is made active by plantains, couch grass, stinging nettles and the most perfidious weed, *Equisetum*.

Sulphur aids disease resistance and accumulates in the *Allium* or onion family, brassicas, fat hen and purslane. Other minerals are accumulated by many plants and especially by weeds, some of which are worth tolerating for this and other reasons.

OPPOSITE LEFT Claytonia *is one of the few plants to grow through winter.* OPPOSITE RIGHT Limnanthes *– a green manure and useful companion.* BELOW LEFT *Let alliums flower for the insects then collect heads and stems before they ripen their seed.* BELOW RIGHT *Ten minutes with an old knife and I've a bucket full of minerals (plantains).*

BOUGHT-IN MANURES

Conventional fertilisers are ranked according to their N:P:K (nitrogen, phosphorus and potassium) ratio and content. They are regarded as direct plant foods, replacing those elements taken away by the crop. Nitrogen stimulates growth and leaves; phosphorus, the roots; and potassium, fruiting and disease resistance. Although these same elements exist as salts in the soil solution naturally, it is not natural to have them in very high concentrations, as occurs when they are applied as conventional soluble fertilisers.

Organic gardeners protect soil micro-organisms by avoiding substances that can damage them and applying fertilisers that are effectively insoluble and cannot become too concentrated. These have to be broken down and incorporated by micro-organisms before they can increase the nutrient supply in the soil solution and become available to plants. Thus, they do not leach away as readily and are longer lasting. Regard them as soil stimulators rather than plant fertilisers because they promote increases in soil life, and the by-products from this increased population then feed the plants. You don't need to apply them heavily; on average, a handful per square yard every other year is sufficient.

ANIMAL MANURES

All animal manures contribute directly and indirectly to soil fertility, but should always be well composted first (including raw poultry droppings). In order of preference, choose horse, sheep and goat, which are all sweet to handle; cow muck is less pleasant, while pig muck is vile and often contains contaminants. Rabbit and other pet droppings can be added to the compost heap, but cat and dog litter is best pit-buried under trees. Poultry manures are very strong, highly nitrogenous and a good source of potash. They make a compost heap cook!

Human liquid waste is not a health hazard in temperate climates and it is wasteful to use water to flush away such a rich source of fertility. Saved in a bucket,

it can get whiffy, but then makes a superb compost activator; the whiffiness is much reduced if you add some sugar to the bucket. Alternatively, apply each day's quota directly to the heap. Sewage sludge may be contaminated, so is only recommended for ornamental plantings as a slow-release source of phosphate. Commercially processed cow manure and, more commonly, pelleted composted chicken manure are becoming widely available. Both are effective, relatively pleasant to handle (compared to the real thing) and much more expensive. Still, if it's all you can get.

Traditional organically based balanced fertiliser – blood, fish and bonemeal – is very effective and long lasting, but not so good on ecological and compassionate grounds. Use in moderation, raking in immediately before planting hungry feeders. Beware: cheap brands are often adulterated with chemical fertilisers and sand. Bonemeal is an excellent source of phosphates, containing about a third; the finer ground the bone, the faster it acts. It is expensive but good when planting woody plants and strawberries. Hoof and horn is equally expensive, but an effective, slow-release source of nitrogen for hungry and woody plants. These fertilisers are likely to be pinched by animals or birds unless mixed in well with the soil, so store the bags in a safe, dry place.

GROUND ROCK DUSTS

These are very slow-acting sources of fertility, the most natural and long lasting, and good at revitalising worked-out soil. Clay soils contain plenty of these ingredients in an already finely divided form, so rock dusts are more useful for poor sandy soils. Although rock dust is almost insoluble, if it is ground very finely water can act on an immense surface area to dissolve a little. The plants can remove this from the soil solution, which then allows more to dissolve. This same area is also available for colonisation by microscopic soil life, which eats the rock dust and converts the surface material into biological mass. Thus, by adding rock dusts rich in, say, potassium, we make more available to the plants, but only if our soils are moist and teeming with the microlife that can make use of it. So, add some rock dust to the compost heap to make it bulk up the right microbes. These will then inoculate the soil and make it more able to utilise the bulk of the dusts when applied more directly later. Most rock dusts can be applied at any time of year, but winter is convenient. Choose a still day so that it doesn't blow away and let light rain wash it in or rake it in by hand. Never inhale rock dust. Some rock dusts are now supplied compounded to make them temporarily more granular and easier to handle.

Lime is commonly used on grass swards and vegetable patches. In a rotation, it is applied before peas and beans or with brassicas, but never just before potatoes. It is the main source of calcium and in a form that reacts chemically with acids and stronger alkalis in the soil; thus it is said to 'sweeten' most soils. Garden lime is ground chalk – builders' and slaked lime is not for garden use. Dolomitic lime comes from rocks that also contain magnesium and so is doubly useful and most recommended. Calcified seaweed is the most beneficial form of lime because it contains all the trace elements and so encourages microlife populations. It is also valuable added to compost heaps and as a general-purpose fertiliser where the lime fraction is no disadvantage, being especially beneficial for tough turf, brassicas, legumes and stone fruits. However, much of it comes from non-sustainable sources and these are not recommended.

Ground rock potash is rich in potassium, which promotes flowering, fruiting and disease resistance. Especially needed on light soils and in wet areas, it is appreciated by gooseberries and culinary apples. Apply at any time.

Ground rock phosphate is rich in phosphorus, which encourages healthy roots. It is useful for restoring healthy life to abused, over-acid soils and soils in wet areas. Mix into composts or soil at any time. It is good for strawberries.

Ground rock basalt and granite may also be added to any soil. These are rocks containing a spread of minerals, so encouraging many micro-organisms, and they are thought to almost single-handedly revitalise worn-out soils. Most beneficial on light sandy soils; heavy clays already have sufficient finely ground minerals.

OPPOSITE LEFT *Compost de-seeding and pre-processing in action.*
OPPOSITE RIGHT *Soiled bedding from the bunnies' cage is excellent compost fodder.*
ABOVE *Lime is best added before or with the brassicas in the rotation.*

OTHER DUSTS AND MEALS

Wood ashes are a very rich source of potash, but this is soluble and leaches out, so only apply to soil around growing crops, especially fruits and onions, for ripening and disease protection. Sprinkle the ashes on the surface and rake or mix in with the compost or soil.

Soot from fires that have burnt no plastic contains some value as a fertiliser once mellowed with age, but is especially useful for darkening the soil surface and thus improving its warmth-giving properties (see page 95). Dust aged soot (shake it in an old stocking foot) onto the soil surface after rain around early crops, such as asparagus, and do not disturb.

Cocoa husks are a nitrogenous waste that have impressed me. They make an expensive mulch, but this acts as a good binding agent with others. I've also found it useful in potting composts.

Seaweed meal contains a wide spread of trace elements and significant nitrogen and potassium, but is a bit short of phosphate, needing some bonemeal or ground rock phosphate for balance. Organically and ecologically, this is the best nitrogenous fertiliser and soil stimulator, and also a very good compost activator. Made from a very renewable resource, seaweed meal is pleasanter to handle than blood, fish and bone-meal as a general-purpose feed, and is best raked in during spring. Highly recommended.

FOLIAR SPRAYS

These are highly diluted solutions sprayed onto leaves and bark, and then absorbed directly. Only use clean water and never spray in very sunny or windy conditions as the foliage may scorch.

ABOVE *Mulches around fruit keep in moisture and suppress weeds, but never cover the graft (that bulge near ground level).*

Seaweed solution This is not so much a fertiliser as a catalyst or 'vitamin injection'. Although only applied as a foliar feed in very dilute solution, the effect on plants is rapid and marked; they take on a darker, healthier colour and better resist pests and diseases. Seaweed solution also stimulates soil microlife and is probably the most effective way of improving their variety and number. I spray the soil and every living thing in sight once a month from early spring. It can be diluted down and watered on as a liquid feed, but is then better combined with a cheaper source of nitrogen such as comfrey or borage liquid.

Equisetum tea This is made from the dried plant and boiling water, then sprayed as a foliar feed, having been cooled and diluted. High in silica, it is said to make plants more resistant to pests and diseases. Stinging nettles, alliums, chamomile and many other herb teas are used by organic gardeners; there is much potential to be discovered.

ABOVE *Compost tea – compost in a stocking soaked in water for the plants, not the gardener, of course.*

LIQUID FEEDS

Plants in containers cannot reach further afield for nutrients after they have used up those around their rootball. Top-dressing and repotting are possible solutions, but often we resort to giving them nutrients in their water (which is at odds with the organic desire to avoid soluble fertilisers). However, we are not applying the feed directly to the soil and only in very dilute solutions – in fact, the weaker, the better. Feed little and often, and never if the plants are not in strong growth or are under stress. They can also be used in moderation on hungry plants in the open, such as tomatoes or sweet corn, and for bringing on spring greens in cold years.

Comfrey liquid Collect the comfrey leaves, pack them in a container, and activate with a little personal liquid waste, weighed down, and cover with water. The leaves soon rot to form a black soup that smells horrible, but watered down to a pale straw colour, it makes a well-balanced plant feed with considerable potassium and nitrogen. The concentrated soup can also be added for fertility in potting mixes. Too much may cause some plants to turn yellow from excess potassium, locking up other nutrients, so use nettle or borage liquid instead.

Stinging nettle liquid is made and used in the same way as comfrey liquid. It also possibly makes plants more resistant to disease and pests, especially if diluted and sprayed on.

Borage liquid Made like comfrey liquid, I have found this produces a highly nitrogenous concentrate that is worth trying for the hungriest feeders like melons and brassicas. It makes a better general-purpose feed than comfrey, as it also contains magnesium, and is less likely to turn plants yellow.

BELOW *Strong solutions kill – I dilute down such extracts to, say, a cupful to a watering can, better weak and often than once too strong.*

Dung bag tea Bags of manure are hung in sacks, socks or stockings in water butts for the same purpose. The resultant soup is obviously variable, depending on the dung used.

Fish emulsion This very rich source of nutrients is effective mixed with seaweed solution as a liquid feed. Obviously, this may come from unsustainable fishing sources. I have made my own by boiling down fish wastes (aided with some wood ashes), and cannot recommend the experience.

Personal liquid waste Call it what you will, this is sterile at source, rich in nitrogen and contains significant potassium and other nutrients. When fresh, it can be diluted down twenty or forty to one and used as an excellent feed. Save it all up and use on the compost heap. (Those taking antibiotics or suffering from hepatitis should refrain.)

ABOVE *Borage leaves make the best general purpose feed, take them before the plants flower (here seen with yellow Evening primrose).*

The importance of correct watering

Bigger yields and more vigour can be gained by one generous application of water at the right stage than by almost any other improvement you can make, although poor conditions such as low light or compacted soil need improving beforehand. Without sufficient water, no life processes take place; add some water and plants grow, add plentiful water at the right time and they flourish. Potatoes, for example, respond best to water when in flower, as this indicates that the tubers are beginning to swell.

More plants probably do badly through over- or under-watering than almost any other cause (see page 62). Do not wet large areas of soil around each plant, as this mostly evaporates, but soak water down to the roots. A hole, half-buried pot or trench beside plants that need copious watering speeds up the task. A neat idea is to cut the bottoms off clear plastic bottles, invert and then push one in beside each plant. A litre or two can be poured rapidly into the funnel to soak in slowly.

In pots and containers, keeping the soil or potting compost moist, but not waterlogged, is difficult and more so with many peat-substitute composts. Daily checking with your thumb is essential and more often in very hot dry weather. In winter, err on the side of caution; water rarely but thoroughly, and drain well. In summer, water frequently, but still drain well. For large numbers of pots on benches, stand them on capillary matting fed from a simple reservoir.

Water control Many of the fungus problems, especially mildews, are aggravated, if not actually caused by, bushes getting too dry at the roots or by stagnant air around overcrowded tops. Sprinkling or spraying plants with a little water is worse than leaving them alone, as it increases the stress and makes them more vulnerable to disease.

Wet gardens are best enjoyed from afar because a lot of damage is done by moving about in them – young growths snap more easily, while packing the soil underfoot breaks fine roots and excludes air. Later, during dry periods, the footprint marks evaporate water more rapidly than loose soil and their hard surface forms clods and cracks. Touching plants in wet gardens also spreads and lets in diseases. Many of these wait for wet periods to release spores, so that they can be carried in drops of water. Bacteria can also travel protected from the danger of desiccation. Research on the ways viruses enter leaves has shown that they can most easily attack healthy leaves if they are wet with contaminated water and lightly rubbed. The moral is clear, walking amongst and touching wet plants is probably doing them much harm.

ABOVE LEFT *How NOT to water – this splashes the compost up out of the pots. Use a rose or watering saucers.* **ABOVE RIGHT** *A bevy of strategically placed dustbins connected by hose siphons act as watering points, saving walking.* **OPPPOSITE** *Having fixed pathways saves packing down the soil in the beds, so they seldom need digging.*

Irrigation Drip irrigation is preferable to sprinklers, which waste too much water. Even better are underground hoses that seep water to the roots. Where plentiful water is available, you'll find trench irrigation effective and cheap to install. When I could legally use as much water as I wanted, I flooded trenches around particular beds and achieved fantastic yields. When a hosepipe can be used, water all parts of the garden from a short length of hose connected to another hose at several hidden points. This saves dragging long lengths of hosepipe around the garden and decapitating plants. This permanent pipe layout can be made from ordinary hosepipes buried in the ground or run along fences and hedges.

Storage As we experience more droughts, we need to guard water as a precious resource. Rainwater is more valuable than tap water, so capture every drop. Old deep freezers make neat water butts. (If gnats and mosquitoes are a problem, then put goldfish in the butt from spring till autumn.) Water butts can be connected to one another with permanent siphons if they are all stood at the same level. This increases your storage capacity and moves water to where you want it. Any excess is best run into soakaways, rather than down the drain, so it can benefit trees and deep rooters. Indeed, far more can be stored in the ground and in plants. Increasing the amount of humus in the soil increases the water-holding capacity enormously. Green manures, compost, mulches and minimal cultivation improve the ability of the soil to store winter rains until the following summer.

'Grey water' Local laws permitting, grey water from sinks, showers and baths can be diverted from the drains and run or siphoned down a hose to valued plants in times of drought. Water from clothes- and dish-washing machines may carry too many chemicals for safe use on plants, though.

Mulching Dust mulches used to be advocated as a water-conserving measure, but are mostly effective because of the simultaneous weed control. A proper mulch on top of the soil is more effective at stopping water evaporating away. The mulch itself will hold about an inch of rain for every few inches depth, depending on the type of mulch. This can be a disadvantage if rain falls only a little at a time because the mulch will absorb each shower and it will not reach the soil. Only heavy precipitation will penetrate through to the roots, which is why mulches are best put on after rainy spells, not before, and even raked aside temporarily. (For the types of mulch and their use as weed control, please see page 247 in Chapter 10.)

Using the plants as their own mulch Well-mulched bare soil loses water at the least possible rate with no plants taking any moisture out. Grow only a few plants widely spaced out in hot, dry conditions and they will start to take out a lot of water to compensate, particularly on an exposed site. Thus, a few weeds lose much water, and so will over-spaced crop plants. To minimise water loss from crops, grow them closer together with companion plants. The microclimate formed by the mixed layers of leaves traps moisture-laden air, and the leaves thus keep themselves and the soil moister and cooler. Then, at night, more dew condenses. The same occurs with deeper swards of grass and clover mixtures – these attract more dew than closely cropped grass. If the sward is allowed to grow up and tumble over, it then loses less water than when it is regularly cut, but there is less material being returned for fertility. In the fruit cage, mulches are nearly essential because soft fruits need plenty of moisture as they are swelling during the dry days of early summer.

Drainage Waterlogging kills by driving out the air, so is more of a problem on heavy soils which hold much more water than sandy or silty soils. Obviously, drainage is needed in the very worst cases but, more often, reducing compaction, encouraging earthworms, adding organic material or using raised beds will utilise that water rather than just draining it all away. If drainage is needed, then ditches may work, or herringbone patterns of drainage pipes leading to a soakaway will need laying.

Aeration The real benefit of drainage is that it prevents waterlogging excluding the air. Plant roots and almost all soil microlife breathe in oxygen and breathe out carbon dioxide. Waterlogging kills by removing this oxygen supply. So, drainage is not as important as good aeration. A better soil texture with more granulation and pore spaces, and plentiful worm tunnels, breathes more deeply, thus becoming more fertile. Too claggy mulches, plastic sheets and impermeable layers can also cause air-deficiency problems. Those with really sticky soils considering installing drainage should perhaps consider burying perforated plastic drainage pipes a foot or so down, open at one end and connected to a chimney at the other. This will promote air flow to dry and warm their soil, as well as aerating it.

5 SEEDS WANT TO COME UP, PLANTS WANT TO GROW

Much of being a successful organic gardener is just tending our plants well

Seed companies have been looking to the expanding organic market and now offer ranges of organically raised seeds and plants. They have selected and bred many with more disease resistance and even some not so troubled by pests. For example, we now have carrots unattractive to root flies, lettuces less susceptible to root aphids, gooseberries without mildew, and peaches that do not suffer as much from leaf curl disease.

Seeds want to come up: place them in a suitable place at the right time and they will do their job. Plants want to grow, flourish, flower and fruit. All we have to do is both ensure seeds and plants have the things they need and avoid anything that hinders them. If we get it right, so will they! Sowing and growing methods vary with every plant, but certain basics must be adhered to.

SOWING AND GROWING METHODS

Seeds are better sown thinly than too thick, shallow rather than too deep, and late rather than too early. Remember, seeds are living things and need cool dry conditions to stay alive. Store them in a sealable box, ideally with desiccant bags of silica gel. Do not leave seeds in full sun or in a greenhouse or kitchen, or buy them from sun-exposed racks or heated rooms at garden centres. Instead, buy from seed catalogues, which are also usually packed with information. If you get good-quality seeds and keep them well, then almost all will still be viable after three or four years. Larger seeds, such as courgettes, may germinate after a decade, while smaller seeds expire sooner.

Saving seed This is remarkably easy with many vegetables. Large seeds, such as peas and beans, are expensive to buy and the easiest to save, especially as they tend to come true year after year. Let them ripen on the plants and store the dried pods in paper bags until required. Carrots, parsnips, celery, onions, tomatoes, leeks and lettuce are all fairly easy, but then their seed is not so expensive.

ABOVE *Trays of tomato side shoots being rooted for more plants.*

The marrow family are very promiscuous, so if you have different ones flowering together, the seed will not come true. Most F1 hybrids do not come true and so we are told they cannot be saved. However, I have often had excellent results from seeds saved from them, so they may be worth trying. Potatoes, garlic and shallots are all expensive to buy and very easy to save 'seed' (offsets) from. You could potentially build up diseases and get poorer yields, but you can also save a lot of money.

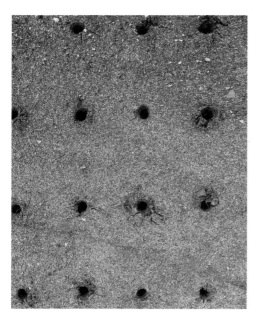

Sowing seed in the open When sowing seeds in rows, a drill is usually drawn out with a hoe, but it is more accurate to press a thick straight cane or rod into the soil. For those plants that need a wide spacing, such as parsnips, sow a few seeds at each station and thin out to the best seedling as soon as they emerge (rather than sow evenly along the drill). If seeds are sown as a block, use a cane to make a hatch pattern and get equidistant spacing. For deeper holes, mark with a cane and use a blunt dibber to make a hole at each station. In any case, water the drill or holes, preferably with rainwater plus a dash of seaweed solution, let it soak in and then sow the seed. (Larger seeds, such as peas and beans, can be soaked for an hour or so beforehand.) Ensure there is sufficient moisture under the seed when it is sown and keep weed competition down during the earliest stages of growth. Never let young seedlings dry out and do not forget that drying winds in early spring can dry out the topmost layer of soil when your seedlings have only made a few shallow roots. Cover the seed with dry soil or, preferably, any weed-seed-free material such as sharp sand and leaf mould or old potting compost. This ensures few weeds come up next to the crop. Big seeds can be filled in with ordinary soil, then covered with a thin layer of grass clippings which will keep them well mulched and suppress most weeds. Firm down well, then label with the date and variety.

Sowing seed in pots and trays When sowing in pots and multi-cell packs, all the same rules apply, except that you should only use a sterile sowing compost. Soak the pots from underneath after sowing and don't water them on top. Some fine seeds may need to be surface-sown and then need dark, not light, to germinate; read the packet!

Generally, more seeds fail because they were sown too deep than too shallow, both indoors and out. Sowing under cover in pots is usually more successful because of the warmth, but plants soon become drawn from the dimmer light and often outgrow their pots.

OPPOSITE LEFT *Tray of sowing compost dibbed with well spaced holes.* OPPOSITE MIDDLE *Onions are pricked out as tiny plants, one per hole.* OPPOSITE RIGHT *The same is done again outdoors later, with bigger holes and wider spacing.* **ABOVE** *It's no good just growing the plants well – here onions are being dried off well otherwise they'll never store long.*

Potting up If you don't pot on plants as soon as they fill their pots, you get poor bonsai specimens. Try to pot up just before it becomes necessary. Watch the rate of growth: if it slows for no other obvious reason, then the plant needs more root room (check by knocking out the plant to see if the roots run around the rootball multiple times). I often position the rootball to one side of the new pot. More importantly, keep the plant aligned as it was when it germinated; having the label in the pot at the north point acts as a reference.

Never grossly over-pot, as the compost stales, and never use garden soil for potting, but choose a reliable potting compost. Mix well-made, sieved garden compost with some sharp sand and, ideally, some leaf mould. For slow-growing and ornamental plants, I top off with bought-in compost or just sand or gravel, as these are weed-seed-free and keep the surface clean (see page 101.)

Seed beds Although the best plants come from seed sown in situ, they can get eaten by pests or damaged by the weather, so start them off under cover in pots or in a seed bed where they can be given special attention. Nursery beds are simply seed beds in use for a longer time. They are used for growing slower plants and for propagating from cuttings, which take at least a year until they are ready for planting out. Most often, a seed bed is used to grow crops to a small size for transplanting into the main vegetable area. This keeps the main beds available for a prior crop and allows for easier weeding and intercropping.

For success, there needs to be a nearby source of water and, ideally, a stack of cloches and bird protectors. Seed beds do not need the high fertility of salad or vegetable beds, but need copious watering. If possible, slope them to face the sun and

ABOVE *If it's just the plants you're after any container may do – this doesn't look so pretty does it, but it will soon be sat inside a larger patio planter.* **OPPOSITE LEFT** *A simple plastic bottle tubular 'cloche' keeps off the weather and most ground dwelling pests and most importantly those pesky wood pigeons.* **OPPOSITE RIGHT** *Economise on bought composts by first half filling containers with sieved garden compost or home made mixes.*

are growing they will cope (but not flourish) in almost any half-decent potting compost. Thus, try several until you find a good, non-peat-based compost that suits your type of plants. There are now many peat-free composts available, but, if you grow ericaceous or difficult plants, you may prefer to consider peat as a renewable resource that we should be encouraging the sustained use of.

When sowing, use a freshly sieved (not to remove lumps but to re-introduce air) seed compost, such as a John Innes No 1, or a diluted mixture of multi-purpose compost with one-third sharp sand. Or, if desperate,

use a home-made mix of one-third each of heat-sterilised garden soil, steamed leaf mould and sharp sand. For rooting cuttings, use a mixture of any sterile sowing compost with its own volume of sharp sand. For small, tender and valuable seedlings, pot up into a reputable brand of potting compost, such as John Innes No 2. Stronger and bigger plants may prefer the richer No 3. For robustly growing plants, pot up into either a fresh organic compost or sieved garden compost. I use the latter for almost all my potting, making it extra strong for courgettes, melons and cucumbers by mixing in grass clippings.

shelter them from cold winds. Seed beds are mostly used for brassicas and leeks, bedding plants and biennial flowers before moving these to their final sites. Parsnips and other roots (and usually the legumes) have to be sown in situ where they are to finish.

Choosing composts Most sowing and potting composts are based on peat, sand and chemical fertilisers. John Innes formula composts, based on sterilised loamy soil, are potentially the best, but may still contain a little peat. Organic versions may duplicate these or be based on composted or worm-worked wastes. Sadly, in trials, many conventional and most peat-free and organic composts have proved inferior to the best peat or John Innes loam-based composts. Any sort of compost will deteriorate with age, so never buy old, wet, or end-of-season cheapies! Organic ones go off most quickly, so only buy a well-known, fast-moving line from a reputable supplier with large, well-stored stocks.

When growing in any container, always use sterilised commercial compost. Do not compromise on sowing compost, but get the best you can. However, once the plants

HOME-MADE POTTING COMPOST RECIPE

Use peat (if you dare be lumped in with smokers, fox hunters and meat eaters) or a good substitute like coir, leaf mould or composted barks.

Mix three buckets of whatever with one of sharp sand. This mix will aerate and drain freely, but contains little plant food. Add to this one bucket of worm compost or casts or three buckets of sieved garden compost and/or just a measure of a balanced organic fertiliser. The last alone is better if you need a weed-seed-free mix. A balanced mixture I used successfully for years was: for every four two-gallon buckets of the 'peat' and sand mix, I added 3oz (75g) of calcified seaweed, 4oz (110g) of blood, fish and bonemeal, 4oz (110g) of hoof and horn meal, and 3oz (75g) of wood ash. Those who wish to spurn animal by-products can replace those ingredients with the same amount of seaweed meal, but it is not quite as good, so pot up generously. However, I've started making

my garden compost with even more stinging nettles as I've found this makes the most excellent potting compost once sieved, needing only the addition of some sharp sand (and sometimes some lime) to suit most plants.

Light, temperature and water control for sowing, seedlings and young plants Seed is usually easier to germinate in warmth and under cover, and success is more certain with plants started in little pots or multi-celled trays and planted out when they and the site are ready. Indeed, tender plants, such as tomatoes, MUST be started this way and in the warm or they never have time to crop in our short growing season. However, the transplanting almost always checks the plant and it rarely does as well as one sown in situ if it survives! So, when growing in pots, we must take as much care as we can.

Multi-celled trays give each plant its own little space with minimal root interference or disturbance. Also, the insulated trays are easy to fit in a propagator and move around. In pots or cells, never risk letting seedlings crowd each other. The commonest mistake is sowing thickly in one pot, intending to prick out later – and leaving this for a day or two too long causes severe losses of yield. A few annual and bedding flowers, beetroot and onions can be allowed to have two or three seedlings growing together to produce clumps of smaller plants. For other plants, sow two or three seeds in each cell or pot and thin *as soon as they emerge*.

When sowing in pots or cells, take care not to waterlog the seeds or let them dry out. Fill pots with damp compost and then stand them in a tray of water till the top is wet. Remove and drain well, and do not re-water until the seedlings appear (unless the compost starts to dry out badly). Never use stale rainwater for seeds or seedlings in pots, as this can cause damping-off disease. Once the plants are growing strongly, then rainwater is preferable to tap water as it contains no added chlorine and fewer pollutants.

A greenhouse is not needed for starting off hardy plants in cells or pots. They will be more than happy in a cold frame or a sheltered spot until they are ready to go out. However, it is easier to provide better conditions earlier, especially enough light and warmth, in a greenhouse. Cloches are nearly as good, but do not provide as much space and are difficult to use. Polytunnels give the best value for money, but are not very nice to look at. Whatever you can afford, keep the glass or plastic clean as light is more important than heat for most plants, especially hardy vegetables. Ventilation is necessary, as it is easy to cook small seedlings in full sun while they are tightly sealed up. Either be vigilant or invest in an automatic vent opener.

Hardening off Once hardy plants have started growing well in pots, then they can be planted out in the main plot; however, they MUST be hardened off first by standing them outside each day and putting them back under cover at night for three or four days. If you use cloches or clear plastic bottles to protect them, then they can be planted out with a little less hardening off. If the main plot or the weather is not ready when the plants are big enough, put them into larger containers or they will stop growing.

Planting out When planting out hardened-off or seed-bed-grown seedlings, water well the day before and, ideally, water the planting holes too. Certainly, water the holes long enough to allow the water, with a dash of seaweed solution, to percolate away; do not plant in mud! Make the holes bigger than necessary and, for hungry feeders such as brassicas, sweet corn, tomatoes and cucurbits, mix a handful of sieved garden compost into the soil before backfilling around the rootball. Protect your seedlings from bird damage with wire guards or cloche tubes cut from plastic bottles.

LEFT She can do this, you can't. This huge homemade cold frame is not 'child friendly.' Construct and place similar with care! **RIGHT** *Peas (and most climbing crops) prefer rigid to flimsy supports, plastic netting is poor compared to this recycled chocolate bar conveyor belting.*

Tender plants Growing tender plants from seed is more difficult, as most of them need starting off in warmth early when light levels are low and they easily get leggy. They need repotting several times, since they cannot be planted out, even under cover, before summer without extra heat. In fact, the main problem is finding somewhere in the warm as they get bigger and bigger in larger and larger pots. Heating the greenhouse is an excellent, if expensive, option (constructing a heated cold frame in the greenhouse is cheaper).

ABOVE *Yes I know it looks as if the alien attack has started, but these covers keep the weather and pests off so effectively.* LEFT *The more carefully you transplant, the better the result.* RIGHT *Lift a cover occasionally to weed, or your crop may get choked unnoticed.*

Planting out bought-in and larger plants

Transplanting and planting are effectively the same, except transplanting is taken as moving plants growing in the soil from one place to the other. Planting usually involves putting plants into the soil from pots, or with bare roots, as they arrive from a nursery. Only vegetables and bedding plants are usually transplanted whilst growing strongly, whereas most other plants are better moved while dormant. In either case, the bigger the rootball and associated soil, the better; that is, unless the plant is root-bound. Plants get root-bound by being confined for too long in a small container. If this is the case, tease out the roots and plant them spread out in the soil, as for bare-rooted plants. If plants have been out of the soil for a long time or have dried out, then the roots need a quick soak before planting. Always keep them covered to prevent sun scorch and drying, especially in strong winds. If they have been under cover or in a protected environment, they need to be hardened off. Check the plants over and remove any badly damaged roots or shoots.

Water the planting hole well beforehand, but always let the water drain away before planting. If drainage is slow, then break up the subsoil in the bottom of the planting hole. Note that soil that is too wet is just as bad as soil that is too dry or frosted; it should be friable and moist. Always dig a generous hole to give the roots a free run. This also breaks up existing root systems and aerates the soil, thus stimulating the microlife. Although this encourages the plant to re-root quickly, the microlife needs raw materials to convert, so mix in well-rotted compost and rock dusts with the planting soil. Do this generously for annuals and modestly for perennials, which will do better having more applied later as top dressings and mulches.

The hole for a tree or bush needs to be as big and as deep as possible; not just large enough to squeeze the roots in. Do not mix together the different soil layers, though breaking them up is useful. Mix enriching materials into the topmost layer. Never put in large amounts of anything without mixing it in well, especially peat-like materials. I used to see many promising trees killed by too much peat packed around them from gardeners enthused by adverts. A surrounding layer of peat isolates the rootball, so the tree fails the first dry summer when no rain or capillary moisture can reach it. Equally as important is firming in each root, so that it is in direct capillary contact with an unbroken soil network. Always firm in each root in the same respective position it originally occupied, at the same depth and in the same direction. So, always pack in the refill carefully, and firm and then refirm as each layer is completed.

Watering is the next most important part of establishing transplanted plants. Fast-growing annuals sown in situ with enough initial soil moisture fend for themselves, but a large, newly transplanted woody subject will need watering through the first season of growth while it builds up a root system. Herbaceous plants fall somewhere in between and, provided they are moved when dormant, usually look after themselves. Even so, they will benefit from watering during early dry periods. Generally, unless you live in a wet or waterlogged area, water all woody transplants during their first season of growth and herbaceous plants during any dry period early in their first season. Mulches will help retain moisture, suppress weeds, and aid quick establishment.

LEFT *Each courgette plant has its own watering funnel – they can be given a gallon each quickly, which can slowly soak down.* BELOW *Growing in containers has many advantages, in return for daily watering without fail.*

Replenishing your own plant stocks

Although you can buy plants from garden centres, it is advisable to obtain them from reputable nurseries or mail-order catalogues. Better still is propagating your own plants from scratch. There are a number of ways in which to do this, as follows:

Sowing seed This always gives the best, most vigorous plants especially if you are sowing in situ, although this can be inconvenient if the plants are slow growing. For this reason, most plants are started off in pots or a nursery bed and then planted out when they are big enough to survive in their final position. Growing from seed has one major drawback, however, which is that the best varieties of perennial plants normally cannot be propagated from seed, but need to be propagated vegetatively from cuttings, layers, grafts, buds or root division in order to come true.

Taking ripe or hardwood cuttings For many woody plants, the simplest way is to take ripe or hardwood cuttings in autumn. These have the summer's energy stored away and cleanly cut young shoots, a foot or less long, root easily. Firm them in a slit trench with sharp sand in the bottom. Keep them moist and shelter them from the worst of the weather, and they will be ready for planting out the next autumn. Cuttings are usually best able to heal and root from the nodes in the stem, so are cut close below one at the bottom. However, for a few plants, such as *Clematis*, they are best cut between nodes. Lower buds are removed unless many shoots are wanted from the ground to form a stool, as for blackcurrants. Autumn cuttings root well, but have to endure the winter. In hard

areas, keep them in moist sand, in a frost-free place, and plant them in the spring. Cuttings of some less hardy plants, such as rosemary and lavender, will not stand a hard winter or storage as cuttings, but they can be rooted successfully if taken and firmed in during early spring. Lazy cuttings are best for this, which is when small shoots are pulled off with a tiny heel of old wood.

Taking summer cuttings Summer cuttings (also known as unripe or soft cuttings) come from fresh young growth and would wither before rooting unless given the special conditions that a propagator can provide. They need warmth underneath, high air moisture, and shading with a sheet of paper to prevent them scalding in strong sunlight. Soft cuttings are shoots of current growth; usually, a pair of leaves is left and two or three pairs removed to give a short bare stem to firm into a sterile medium. Sharp sand in pots is excellent, as it is well aerated and the grittiness helps rooting, but the cuttings must be potted on into richer potting compost to grow on. The cuttings form smaller plants than autumn cuttings, but more readily and, after overwintering, can be planted out into a nursery bed or potted up.

Layering is used for plants that do not take from either sort of cuttings easily and is simply rooting the cutting while it is still attached to the parent. If a branch cannot be pegged down into the soil, then a pot can be held up to it. In either case, a wound is made in the bark and held in moist, sharp-sand-enriched soil until it roots. It can then be detached and planted. Hormone rooting powder may encourage rooting of difficult subjects, though it is not generally organically acceptable.

Root division is used for most herbaceous plants. As herbaceous clumps grow big, they become poor in the middle. At this stage, they can be dug up and the vigorous perimeter divided into chunks for replanting, while the worn-out middle is discarded. Often the clumps just need splitting into a couple. Rather than cutting them up, tease them out or pull them apart by hand. The tightly entwined roots are more easily pulled apart if the rootball is immersed in water. This is best done in early spring, after dormancy, but before the plants really get going, but you can divide most of them in the autumn.

ABOVE *Grafting your own is not as easy as you may think – approach grafting (or inarching) is the most likely way to be successful. The rootstock in a pot is lifted up to the scion while it is still on the parent, grafted together and left until 'glued'.*

Recognising your soil type and improving it organically

We rarely have the opportunity to choose the site or soil for our gardens. Most gardens are on old sites and may be exhausted and pest-ridden. Those in towns are likely to be polluted, especially if many chemicals have been used. Derelict sites that are full of rampant weeds will probably have better soil. In general, most soils will produce flowers, shrubs or tree fruit without much improvement, but need to be better for vegetables and soft fruit. Almost all soils can be easily improved, but it is worthwhile just putting on extra topsoil if it is very poor. You can improve most types of soil by adding copious quantities of organic material. Anything else is almost inconsequential in comparison. Soils can be divided into types in many ways, but what concerns the gardener most are their effects on plant growth and ease of labour.

Loamy soils are produced when old meadow or grass sward is dug up or by heavily enriching most soils with organic material. This is the best type of soil for most plants. The best loams have a rich, brown, sugary texture, made mostly of earthworm droppings, which encourages plants to produce masses of fine root hairs that pull up granular soil particles with every root. A supply of loam-like soil can be made for favoured plants by stacking and rotting down turves of grass.

OPPOSITE Two batches have just been pricked out into this multi-celled tray to grow on – in a month or two the smaller, unchecked ones on the left, will surpass the older.

ABOVE No variety of soil is much good for germinating seed in pots; use a proper sowing compost for this.
BELOW My soil is light so needs feeding, borage mulches are experimental but look promising.

Heavy clay soils are hard to dig, stick to every tool and boot, drain poorly, and pool with water in heavy rain. They are, however, the richest soils, rarely suffer mineral deficiency, and resist drought well, though they eventually set like concrete. Clay soils must never be compacted when wet, so DO NOT STAND ON THEM. They need copious amounts of coarse organic material and sharp sand or grit; they also benefit from liming and fixed-bed gardening. Heavy soils encourage slugs, but also produce the best cauliflowers and roses.

Sandy soils are a joy to dig, wash off tools and shoes easily, and never pool with water, even in downpours. They need more organic material, rock dusts (especially ground rock potash) and organic fertilisers than other soils as their wonderful aeration burns off humus

quickly. They warm up rapidly in spring for early crops, but dry out badly. If not too stony, they produce super carrots.

Silty soils are more like sandy soils than clays because they do not retain water and are fairly easy to work. Often built up on old river beds, they benefit from ground rock dusts. They are good for most crops if well fed, but tend to splash and cap badly in the wet.

Lime-rich or, worse, thin chalky soil causes chlorosis (yellowing leaves with green veins) in lime-hating plants by locking up iron and other nutrients. Slightly lime-rich soils suit most plants, though (especially brassicas), if they are also rich and moist. Good for many trees, figs and grapes, these soils need feeding and mulching. Thin ones over chalk or limestone are then hot and hungry, so raised beds will significantly improve them.

Stony soils tend to be freer draining. The stones are of little cons-equence to most plants but frustrate cultivation, especially hoeing. These soils are better with perm-anent plantings and mulches rather than for growing annuals and vegetables, though these can thrive on cleaned beds. Mulches of sharp sand make hoeing and sowing easier.

Peaty soils are not always advantageous. Although very high in organic material, they can be short of nutrients, dry out, and are not stable enough for large trees. They will grow good salads and soft fruits, though, and will be naturally suited to lime-haters such as rhododendrons. With the addition of lime, many other plants can be grown, but weeds thrive.

Wet soils tend to be sour or acidic, may need to be limed and drained, especially if low lying, but be careful not to overdo it. Water gives life; only waterlogging is a problem. Adding copious amounts of organic material improves drainage and water dispersion, and also increases moisture retention.

Testing your soil For most gardens, having your garden soil analysed for nutrient content is unnecessary. You'd be better off simply applying a bag of seaweed meal. Instead, aim to incorporate some broad-spectrum organic fertilisers and as much organic material as possible, and most soils will be productive.

The only thing worth checking is the pH – the acidity or alkalinity (lime content) of the soil. Don't bother with cheap meters, which are invariably inaccurate. Instead, use a simple chemical test kit with an accurate colour chart. The basic pH may vary between ground level and deeper if the soil layers have built up a rich surface mould, so take several samples from a typical worked soil. The pH may change as the soil is enriched, particularly as more organic material is added, so most soils tend to become more acid. Thus, liming the soil every few years will be beneficial, especially for vegetables and grassed areas. Lime can be plain chalk or, better still, Dolomitic lime which contains more magnesium and other nutrients. Best of all is calcified seaweed, which contains all

the trace elements too. Never apply lime at the same time as manures or compost. Apply it before rain on top of the soil or grass and rake, brush or allow to leach in during late autumn or winter.

Improving soils Although most soils can be improved and thereby made suitable for a wider range of plants, there is a difference between improvement and change. Various materials are proffered as soil improvers and some flocculating agents based on lime or gypsum do help clay form lighter textures. But for most soils, applying generous amounts of well-rotted organic material will give the greatest benefit.

What will affect plants most is not the nutrient levels of a soil, but the physical texture, aeration and moisture retention. All these are improved by adding more organic material, especially when combined

ABOVE LEFT *You can see how sandy my soil is – I've even got pit spiders!* **BELOW** *Sacks of sieved garden compost ready for use as potting compost and soil improvement.*

ABOVE *Trials of weed seed survival from waterlogged compost, (note serious Nitrogen deficiency in older left hand batch.)* BELOW *This was the lid off a chest freezer on three racing slicks, with a wire bread tray mezzanine for growing on above, vernalising seed below.*

with a mulch. Introducing organic material adds to the nutrient level directly and also increases the soil microlife. This then attacks the fresh resource, as well as the soil's mineral content. This almost limitless resource is then made available to the plants. There is sufficient in the soil of almost every element to last for millennia of heavy cropping if the microlife has other materials to enable it to break the particles down.

As we have seen, soil microlife needs water first and foremost. Air is the next most important component of soil, as almost all microlife and plant roots need oxygen and give off carbon dioxide. Much of the latter is reabsorbed by the soil, but fresh air has to replace the former. Organic particles in

various stages of decomposition keep soils open and allow for aeration. This is augmented by earthworm burrows, which descend for several metres. So, it is the earthworms that are most effective at bringing the greatest depth of soil into use – gardeners cannot dig this deep. The soil composition also varies with depth and only the top few inches throb with life. A foot deep is subsoil containing almost nothing but worms and roots. Initially, digging may be necessary but this disrupts the soil layers; you should never mix sterile subsoil with fertile topsoil. So, optimise these precious few inches of soil with several more inches of organic mulch, keeping them warm, well fed and moist.

Growing in containers

You can grow many different plants in containers in even the smallest of gardens. Choose the largest containers you can manage (even plastic dustbins can be used if you put drainage holes in the bottom). Container growing cramps the plants' root systems, prevents them getting too big, and brings them into flower earlier. However, pot-grown plants are prone to dropping their leaves and even dying unless regularly watered (up to three or four times a day in summer). You also need to prevent the roots freezing in the winter. Fortunately, pots can be taken under cover to protect against frost or to bring on earlier growth.

Plants in containers need an enriched growing medium. For most plants, opt for John Innes No 3 potting compost, which is based on soil. It is heavy, so it keeps plants upright in plastic pots. Peat- and peat-substitute-based composts are good but lightweight, making the pots unstable. They can also be hard to re-wet if they get dry. These are mostly based on chemical fertilisers, but organically formulated versions are available. I use sieved garden compost for the bulk of my potting, adjusting it for strength and openness with sharp sand or mole-hill soil but, otherwise, it is used as it comes for the bottom four-fifths of each fill. Each container is then topped off with a sieved, sterile potting compost or heat-treated soil, so I do not suffer a plague of weeds. This works well for me, but I only recommend it if you make good compost!

If you can, choose a dwarfing rootstock and arrange some form of automatic watering system. Wherever possible, try not to use very small pots, baskets, containers or organic growing bags. Plants have amazingly extensive root systems, so to confine them in a small amount of soil or compost makes their life very difficult. Narrow borders in greenhouses or against walls are much the same, though they usually give a cooler root run than a pot. Any very restricted root run provides too little fertility and risks the soil or compost drying out or waterlogging. Thus, any plant may be checked and will never do as well as it would in the open ground.

Watering Either constant attention or an automatic system is needed. Sprinklers activated by a timer or sensor, drip feeds or capillary matting

can all be used in a greenhouse, but become more difficult when containers are spread about a patio, for example. Keeping the soil or potting compost moist but not waterlogged is difficult, particularly with the new peat-substitute composts. Check all pots regularly to see if they need watering. In winter, err on the side of caution by watering rarely, but thoroughly, and let the pots drain well. Overwatering is a serious risk at this time of year, so good drainage is essential. In summer, water frequently, but still drain well. If you have large numbers of pots on benches, stand them on capillary matting fed from a simple reservoir. Standing the pots on drained gravel is best and also creates a beneficial humid atmosphere around the plants.

Feeding All plants growing in containers or small borders soon use up the goodness in the rootball and require supplementary feeding. Liquid feeds can be added to the water at regular intervals, but take care to dilute this well so that it does not burn. Never feed when growth is slow or the plant is under stress. Foliar feeding with seaweed sprays at monthly intervals will help all plants in containers.

Selecting plants To save effort indoors and in summer, confine your choice of plants for containers to those that will stand water stress, such as pelargoniums, aspidistras, spider plants, succulents and cacti. For outdoor containers all year round, grow the tougher herbs and, best of all, houseleeks. Unless you wish to check their growth, always regularly pot up plants as they fill their pots; repot permanent pot plants every spring. Where several are grown together, use fewer and they will all do better. This applies to growing bags too. For example, three tomato plants in an organic growing bag do no better than two – and one would probably produce nearly as much fruit.

OPPOSITE LEFT *In my arid East Anglian garden, celery (self blanching) and leeks are much easier to grow in containers than the ground.* OPPOSITE RIGHT *Undercover containers are almost essential, for example, here in the black tub I'm forcing a crop of raspberries.* BELOW LEFT *Watering via 'saucers' suits some plants, especially melons which must never get their necks wet.* BELOW RIGHT *Peaches in tubs can be moved undercover for flowering and cropping, safe from weather, and birds.*

6 FRUITS ARE FANTASTIC

Easy, tasty, productive, nutritious, little work, aesthetic, flexible and ecological

Many new 'wonder' fruits have been introduced in recent years and some are not that tasty. Goji berries are a good example; they're not that great when compared with most soft fruits, while the plants have a somewhat scrambling, scruffy appearance with small purplish flowers. The berries are red and pointed like a mini-pepper and, even if they're high in vitamins and anthocyanins, they're about as fine a nibble as a rose-hip. However, the blueberry has become very popular, and rightly so. Despite needing tub cultivation in ericaceous compost and rainwater, it's tasty, highly productive and has a long season. Likewise, now widely available is the edible honeysuckle berry or honeyberry (the most common species are poisonous, so beware), which is very similar to a blueberry but easier to grow. The chokeberry (*Aronia*) has incredible, vitamin-rich fruits that make good jams with apple purée added to help them set.

The best grapes for outdoor use, 'Boskoop Glory' and 'Siegerrebe', are also more widely sold, as well as several other 'new' and improved ones, such as 'Regent', 'Muscat Bleu' and 'Phoenix' – these are far superior to those sold in the past. Cherries now have more dwarfing rootstocks, making these practical for a fruit cage or in a tub on the patio.

BELOW *I strongly recommend you get a 'Boskoop Glory' vine, 'nuff said.*

EASY

As a form of gardening, fruit culture is not only rewarding but also easily successful, especially when compared with vegetables. Fruit is also simple to grow organically, as the plants tolerate poorer soils and conditions and, being perennial, their pests and diseases are more easily controlled by the natural ecology. Because the majority of fruiting plants are perennials, they need no annual digging or seed-bed preparation, and no sowing and planting out. Harvesting and storage is easier for fruits than vegetables, with less bending and no mud. Thus, growing fruit is ideal for the lazy or hard-pressed gardener. Most fruit trees will crop for years with no care or attention, as nearly all the work is done when planting.

TASTY

The delicious taste of a good fruit is a subtle blend of flavours and aromas with the acidity balanced by sweetness. Shop-bought fruit can rarely be as fresh or well ripened, especially as the varieties in shops are invariably commercial ones chosen predominantly for their high yields. You can choose to grow old-fashioned varieties with exceptional flavour. Furthermore, as you are growing organically, you can eat your fruit without peeling or washing.

ABOVE *This trained pear is a visual delight even without the fruit.*

PRODUCTIVE

Economically, fruit can give better returns in weight or cash value than most vegetables from the same area. One gooseberry bush can yield a baby's weight in fruit and yet occupy little more space than a cauliflower. Although the initial cost may be higher for trees and bushes, it is a one-off outlay and you recover it in the first years of fruiting, while seed bills for vegetables are annual. Vegetables will be cropping immediately the first season, but many fruits are not lagging far behind; strawberries can be cropped a year after planting, for example. All the currants and berries give good crops the second year after planting and often top fruit, such as apples, peaches and pears, will start to crop in their second or third year. Yields increase every year for the majority of fruits, reaching peak production after five to ten years.

LEFT Redcurrants crop really regularly, reliably and abundantly. RIGHT Cherries actually crop well, it's just birds will steal them before we can pick them.

NUTRITIOUS

Although some fruits may contain fewer vitamins and minerals by weight than some vegetables, it is more pleasant and easier to consume much more fruit. It is certainly easier to get children to eat more fruit than more vegetables! Fruits are most valuable nutritionally when picked fresh, ripened naturally and kept uncontaminated. That's why home-grown fruit can be more health-giving than commercial fruit that is grown with chemicals and picked under-ripe so that it can be transported over great distances.

LITTLE WORK

Care is needed to establish fruit plants well but, thereafter, little work is needed for top fruit and not much for the soft. Fruit-bearing plants benefit from soil enrichment, but this is not as essential as for vegetables. Pruning is required most by soft fruits and, even then, it is not arduous. Trees or bushes of top fruits can be left unpruned for years and still give excellent crops. Some, such as stone fruits, are best

left well alone anyway. Another point to consider as our climate changes is that, although fruit benefits from careful watering, it tends to withstand droughts better and still produce good crops in seasons when vegetables fail.

AESTHETIC

It is easier to make an attractive and productive garden using fruit trees, vines and bushes, than it is with vegetables and, of course, the length of their season of interest is longer. The bare branches of fruit trees look attractive silhouetted against a winter sky. The changing months bring the green shoots of spring, the billowy masses of blossom, the ripening fruits and the leaf colours of autumn. Trained fruit forms can be used as dividing screens or to block unsightly views, while climbing vines can be encouraged over pergolas or used to cover sheds.

LEFT *Kumquats and other citrus are attractive and productive and can live out all summer.* **RIGHT** *This old Golden Transparent gage is a gourmet treat beyond comparison.*

FLEXIBLE

Many fruiting trees, such as pears and cherries, are very floriferous and can be planted instead of ornamental trees. Fruit trees and bushes are also good competitors and may still produce crops when grown among vigorous plants in overcrowded borders or in wild gardens where vegetables would be overwhelmed. Fruit trees planted as standards with a clean trunk will shade the pram the first summer, can be grassed underneath to leave a play area, will be fruiting before the kids reach school, be robust enough for a goal post, and soon of a size for a swing for the grandchildren. And, if you only have little space, grow fruit trees in containers. More dwarfing rootstocks enable most fruits to be grown in movable tubs; they fruit early and need little pruning. Of course, they do need careful watering, but you can take them with you if you move.

ECOLOGICAL

The permanent nature of most common fruiting plants means that they make fewer demands on peat, heat and consumables than ornamental bedding schemes or vegetable patches. Once established,

most tree fruits can be grassed or mulched around, leaving no bare soil to erode or leach. Their long season in leaf fixes much carbon dioxide and their root systems go deep enough to utilise more of the soil's nutrients than do other plants. The quantities of flowers with fruiting plants are valuable for pollinating, parasitising and predatory beneficial insects when in adult form. Their permanence makes it easier to build up a beneficial ecosystem and they also provide wildlife with nest sites, shelter and, of course, food (if we leave the fruit unprotected). Indeed, if we do not utilise and protect our crops, then wildlife will take advantage of it, whereas rows of surplus vegetables are mostly only good for composting.

We can, therefore, make a fruit garden partly for wildlife and still have sufficient fruit for ourselves and our garden friends. Although birds may try to steal our fruit crops, they are also valuable allies in our war against smaller pests so, with cunning and nets, we can prevent them stealing more than a modicum. Nature intends them to spread her fruits, so we should not take their depredations too personally. Thus, it is with a clear conscience that we consume fruit – the plants give it freely, providing food so that we can travel on and spread their seeds as we go.

CULTIVATING THE VERY FINEST FRUITS, NUTS AND BERRIES

'If you want strawberries, don't plant turnips', or so the Chinese saying goes. Currants vary little in flavour; apples, gooseberries and grapes vary tremendously. Without trying every sort, it is difficult to know which are going to be the best. A guide is to look at the year of introduction, as an old variety must have some good attributes if it is still around. Naturally, some new varieties are higher yielding and many offer some resistance to disease. But where flavour is concerned, it is a matter of taste and many of the old varieties were grown solely for that quality. The best way to choose varieties is to go somewhere with a wide selection of fruit on trial, such as Brogdale Garden, in Kent, or a pick-your-own farm. Carefully gleaning around local shops and supermarkets may produce several varieties for you to taste. Otherwise, read the catalogues with a sceptical mind as to the nurserymen's claims.

Also, extend the season for each class of fruit by choosing early, mid- and late-fruiting varieties. This spreads the picking and preserving workload and also means there is less likelihood of all of a single crop being lost for any reason. Where space is available, choose several varieties just for such safety in numbers. Even if space is limited, you'll find that many varieties of growing trained forms will fit into a small garden. For favourite fruits, consider extending the season of a particular variety by planting two – one in a warm sheltered spot and one in a cool shady place – which spreads the cropping period by a week or two.

Successful harvesting and storage will affect both the quality of your fruit and its shelf life. Always handle all fruits as gently as possible, as the slightest bruise will start decay. Please also note that fruit picked wet rapidly rots and that fruit kept with other strong-smelling items may become tainted. But, if a little care is taken, then your home-grown fruit harvested at the right moment and lovingly ripened will be beyond compare. See Chapter 9 for more on harvesting.

LEFT *You do not know what a strawberry can taste like till you grow 'Gariguette'.* **RIGHT** *Gooseberries can get so large, sweet and succulent that they seem like another fruit.*

The fruit cage, the backyard orchard and the nut patch

Fruit cages Fruit-cage fruits are predominantly the soft fruits, currants and berries, or bush and cane fruits, because they are so popular with marauding birds. Sensibly, these, the most prone, are kept in a netted cage. Netting draped over bushes can help protect fruit, but is not that effective. Although commercial cages are expensive, they do work one hundred per cent. However, it is easy and less expensive to build your own cage. Once built, the roof net can be taken off in winter to prevent snow build-up breaking the cage. Storing the net away reduces weathering, so it will last longer and the birds can then eat pests during the winter. Cherries are sometimes included in a fruit cage, but can make too much growth to be contained (although newer dwarfing stocks should make this possible now). Most soft fruits like the dappled and mulched conditions of their native woodland's edge and can be happily housed together in a cage.

Orchards Although several fruit trees on dwarfing stocks could be dispersed about in any garden, where there is space they are better grown in an orchard. If planted as a half standard or standard with strong roots, then the orchard can also serve as a play area, paddock or wildlife meadow. For the best fruit, a fruit cage for each tree or the

ABOVE *The props may look excessive, but this 'Charles Ross' crops heavily and will need it.* **BELOW LEFT** *To keep cherries within the cage I'm experimenting with in-weaving rather than pruning.* **OPPOSITE** *They make fantastic macaroons.*

whole orchard is desirable, but rarely practical. Still, there are fewer losses when more are grown. When planning an orchard, put the tallest trees on the shady and windy sides, and the more tender peaches and pears on the sunny and sheltered side. And, although planting in neat straight lines may seem formal, this does allow for easier grass cutting. Small orchards, with dwarf trees or cordons, will be more productive and easier to manage if the area is heavily mulched and grass is dispensed with.

Nut patches Nuts are big seeds that are exhausting for the plant to make, as they are rich in oils and nutrients. The trade-off is that the plant 'hopes' that by producing a lot of tasty nuts, some will be carried elsewhere, stashed by squirrels, rodents and birds and then never recovered, thus starting new colonies. Most nut trees are wind-pollinated and bear catkins so, generally, do not have scented flowers and give little nectar to insects but, of course, they are a rich source of pollen. Unfortunately, nut trees can grow very large, making it harder to protect or grow them under nets or cover. Chestnuts and almonds are unreliable in Britain; susceptible to frost damage they prefer two good years running, the first to ripen the wood, the second the nuts.

Cultural requirements and calendrical instructions

Soil and site As for almost any plant, better results come from a deep, rich, moist soil full of organic material, so every effort should be made to improve it before planting. Equally important, the ground MUST be cleared of weeds! (Consult Chapter 10 for reliable methods.) Top fruits need soils that are neither extremely acidic nor alkaline, with apples preferring a slightly acid soil and stone fruits, such as cherries and plums, preferring it more alkaline. Soft fruits generally prefer acid conditions, especially blueberries and cranberries that thrive in peat bogs. Thin dry soils, especially over chalk, will be unfavourable, particularly to pears. Grapes, hazels and figs will grow in gravelly or chalky conditions if established well initially where other fruits would not survive.

Few plants will thrive in soil that is prone to waterlogging, so consider installing drainage or planting in raised beds or mounds as a cunning alternative. No fruits will do superbly in heavy shade, especially from large trees, and the root competition from these will also make establishment and cropping poor. Light shade will not severely handicap most soft fruits, but they will make sweeter fruits with more sun. On windy exposed sites, plants will often suffer from poor pollination, slow growth, early and excessive loss of blossom and leaves, and premature fruit drop, so windbreaks are worthwhile. But don't go to the other extreme; stagnant air pockets, especially in hollows, encourage moulds and mildews. Productive windbreaks can be made from hazels, damsons and cherry plums.

Frost damage probably causes more loss of fruit than every other problem, apart from birds, put together. Frost pockets are low-lying places that collect the coldest air. They are unsuited to strawberries, early-flowering fruits and low bushes. Instead, grow taller forms such as half standards to keep the flowers up out of the cold. Grow early-flowering fruits against walls where they are less likely to be damaged and, if they are further protected by a cloth or fine net, will probably escape unharmed. Tree and bush crops can also be saved by throwing some form of cloth over them to stop the heat escaping to the night sky. Warm sunny spots on walls and patios should be saved for the most susceptible fruits such as pears, peaches and apricots. Soft fruit in a cage is often protected by a roof net and this can be augmented by an old sheet or wet newspaper on top. Frost will also damage young fruitlets for a fortnight or so after pollination, so protect these whenever a frost is predicted.

Pollination In order to set and form fruit, most plants need to be pollinated. Where there are different varieties of the same fruit nearby, say within fifty paces, you can get away without ever considering pollination. But, if you wish to have certain sorts, you will be wise to plant their suitable partners. Most widely grown varieties of bush and cane fruit are self-fertile, so problems rarely arise, but heavier crops usually result where several varieties are grown together. However, more care is needed with top fruit. Some popular tree fruits, such as Victoria plums, are self-fertile but, as with the soft fruit, they give better quality and heavier crops if cross-pollinated.

Of course, the pollinator may not be pollinated in return, necessitating a third partner, as happens with what are called triploid

LEFT *Old baths make good containers for plants such as blueberries.*

apples. For example, planting a Cox, or a Cox and a Bramley which are not compatible, means no crop, but add a James Grieve and all will be pollinated and fruit. Family trees partly solve this pollination problem by having compatible varieties grafted on the same roots, but these then tend to grow lopsidedly. Pollinating partners have to be compatible but, obviously, they also have to be in flower at the same time, so the biggest problems arise with very early- or late-flowering varieties. Don't panic, a good garden centre or nursery will indicate suitable pollinators for any variety. Where a pollinator is required and no space is available, graft a branch of a pollinator onto an existing tree. Alternatively, the wild forms of a fruit, such as crab apples, are usually excellent pollinators for the cultivated forms and can be grown in a hedgerow where they will also act as sacrificial crops for birds.

Rootstocks The type of root a plant grows on can alter the results more than your cultural methods. The majority of cane and berry fruits are usually no problem, as they are grown on their own roots propagated from cuttings. Fruit trees are generally harder to root, so most are grafted onto special rootstocks. Normally, these are dwarfing rootstocks that prevent the tree growing as large as it would on its own roots or those from a seedling, and this brings on earlier cropping. Such trees need staking throughout their life and, inevitably, produce less in total per tree than those that grow bigger.

For bigger trees and larger crops or to cope with difficult soils, different stronger rootstocks may be better, and most trees sold for specific purposes, such as full standards for growing in orchards, are normally supplied with a suitable rootstock by the nursery. At the other end of the scale, rootstocks for cordon training or growing in containers are even more dwarfing. Trees on the following rootstocks will make more compact growth than on any others: M9, M26 or M27 for apples; Quince A or C for pears; Pixy, Colt or Gisela 5 for cherries; Montclair/Mont Clare for apricots and peaches; and St Julien A for plums. The plums will still not stay compact, regardless.

Container growing It is possible to grow fruit trees, soft fruit and even vines in containers. (See Chapter 5, page 96 for advice on growing in containers.) Remember to use generously sized containers of John Innes No3 compost, or ideally a good organic potting compost, as well as the most dwarfing rootstock. Also, arrange some form of automatic watering system. Don't forget to pot up every couple of years. Rather than increase the size of container, I start with only the bottom half full, then lift the lot up and add a layer underneath and repack around. Eventually, any container gets full and too big to move. At this stage, propagate and start again, planting the old one out if you have space. Two people, a sack barrow, trolley or similar makes it easier to move big tubs, prolonging their life. Do not be put off; I have cropped most fruit trees in much smaller tubs – it's just that they don't do as well or live as long.

Orchard-house method You can get longer cropping seasons with pot-grown plants if you have a greenhouse or cool conservatory (they do not need to be heated). Your favourite fruits grown in tubs are brought under well-ventilated, light, frost-free cover from mid-winter. They're brought in all at once or a few of each variety at a time for a succession of cropping. They come into leaf, bloom and crop months sooner than outdoors but, of course, need assiduous watering and hand-pollination. Then, after harvest, they go outdoors again. This way, most fruits are also under little threat from outdoor pests and diseases. This is especially good for grapes, allowing for the cultivation of choicer varieties and reducing pruning to a simple hacking back.

Spacing and staking Spacing is most critical with fruit culture, affecting the quality by allowing more nutrients, light and sun to each fruit; do not skimp. Give each plant more space than you think it needs and you'll be surprisingly successful. Obviously, a rich soil and a good site will affect growth, but a rough guide for planting distance is given

in paces for the average-sized person (adjust for yourself accordingly). With fruit trees, you need to give each tree the spacing it requires according to the rootstock. This applies particularly to trained fruits and principally to apples, which vary the most. Standard trees on the vigorous apple stocks M2, M25 and MM111 will need to be seven to ten paces apart and need staking only in the first year. Cordons or those on the very dwarfing M27 and M9 need only be a pace or so apart and need permanent staking or wire supports. For medium-sized gardens, M26 and MM106 stocks are probably best. They do not need staking once established; these need to be four or five paces apart. Stakes should support trees as low down as possible to ensure the development of a strong trunk. The tie should be wide, padded, firm but with some give, adjustable and removable. Plastic string and wire are not acceptable alternatives to proprietary ties, but old tights and bicycle inner tubes are.

Propagation: replacement and replenishment Successfully growing your own replacement plants is simple for most of the soft fruits, using cuttings from healthy bushes. Unfortunately, your own plants will probably need replacing because they have picked up diseases and are thus unsuitable propagation material. This is particularly true with blackcurrants, raspberries and strawberries and, because of this inherent tendency to virus diseases, it is a good idea to replace old with new periodically. Replace strawberries every third or fourth year, although I find you can replant with your own newly grown runner plants for eight to a dozen more years before buying in completely new stock. Blackcurrants and raspberries need replacing after ten to fifteen years. The other currants and gooseberries last a couple of decades and most of the tree fruits will still be producing crops long after we are pushing up daisies.

If you want multiple plants of any one variety of soft fruit, then buy one good, certified, virus-free plant and take twice as many cuttings as you need. Hardwood cuttings of about a foot long, taken in the autumn from healthy, strong, new growth, usually produce excellent fruiting plants in under two years. Rub off the buds from the lower half and push the cuttings a hand's breadth deep and a foot

apart into clean gritty soil in the open ground on a seed, vegetable or nursery bed. On heavy soils, force sharp sand into the bottom of a slit trench and plant the cuttings in this, but be careful to firm them in well. Shelter the cuttings from the worst winds, cloche them during hard winters, keep the soil weeded and moist, and new plants will be ready to be moved out the following autumn.

Blackcurrants are the easiest and, as these are unusually stooled with many growths from ground level, all the buds can be left on their cuttings. Other currants are very easy, gooseberries and grapes fairly so, but these benefit more from cloching. All the blackberry family and hybrids can be grown from the tips of the canes allowed to root into pots in late summer. In addition, most shrubby plants can be rooted by bending a branch down, making a wound in the bark and burying it in the ground or a pot of moist gritty potting compost.

Raspberries produce suckers all over the place. Choose strong ones with fat underground buds and a mass of fibrous roots and transplant these in autumn, cutting them back to knee high at that time. Strawberry runners coming from clean, deflowered, vigorous plants are easily rooted into pots in early summer and then planted out in late summer to fruit well the following year. Top fruit cuttings do not root easily and, if they did, would not be controlled by a suitable rootstock! It's also hardly worthwhile growing most common fruits from seed, as they take a long time for you to find that the offspring are not very good.

I repeat myself, it is essential to use healthy plants for propagating, so avoid obviously dubious specimens and especially old blackcurrants, raspberries and strawberries. Remember, when replacing, always move to a different site to avoid replant disease.

OPPOSITE ABOVE *A recycled radiator path throws light and warmth up onto the crops on either side.* OPPOSITE BELOW *Tubs of grapevines for early grapes have bonus crops of first Claytonia then strawberries.* ABOVE LEFT *Some strawberry plants have their early flower trusses removed to give bigger later crops.* ABOVE RIGHT *Fruit trees combine well with herbs underneath.*

Companion plants It is essential to keep a circle of at least a pace or two around a tree or bush for the first few years, so it can establish without competition. The bigger the mulched or weeded area, the quicker the tree establishes. If you have other plants growing nearby, this inevitably leads to poorer growth and lower, later yields. So, growing companion plants around them would compete initially but, later, can be of immense benefit for bringing in and maintaining larger populations of predators and pollinators. Rosemary, thyme, sage, lavender, chives, garlic, *Limnanthes douglasii*, *Convolvulus tricolor* and nasturtiums are all of particular benefit to fruit trees and bushes. Also good are red-, dead- and stinging nettles, docks and thistles.

Traditionally, orchards were furnished with grass, alfalfa and clover as companion crops, though most soft fruits should not be grassed down. Pears, in particular, are more affected than most trees and only grassed under if over-vigorous. Grassing down must never be done

until the trees are well established anyway. The grass competes with the trees but, if the clippings are returned, their fertility returns and the sward prevents soil erosion. Orchards need cutting at least once a year to prevent shrubby weeds taking over and grassing down increases the danger from spring frosts, as bare soil keeps the air above warmer at night.

Planting See the section on page 104 in the previous chapter for general advice. Sprays of seaweed solution will be of immense benefit to new plants during the first year and they should be applied routinely at monthly intervals. Never let trees or bushes fruit in their first year, as this diverts too much of their energy from growth while they are too young. Deflower them as soon as the petals fade, though it is permissible to allow one fruit only per tree or bush for identification purposes.

Training methods For the least effort, grow all fruits as trees; either standards, half standards or bushes. Pruning is minimal, with only ingrown, rubbing and diseased growths needing removal. Trees take up a lot of space and are slightly slow to start producing so, for small areas or where many varieties are desired, go for dwarfed and trained forms of fruit. Although these require more work and permanent supports, they give large early returns and better-quality fruit. But they cannot be neglected without dire results.

Forming the initial framework of trained fruit is not difficult and, if left to the nurseryman, will cost you more than buying unformed maiden trees. It is more satisfying to do it yourself, but takes time and thought. Generally, once the shape has been established, only maintenance pruning is needed, except for trained stone fruits which need serious reworking almost every year.

- *Cordons* are one branch of a fruit tree grafted onto a dwarfing rootstock. These are conventionally grown at an angle to make them as long as possible and need posts and wires to support them. They can be planted at close intervals, allowing different varieties in a short run, perhaps along the side of a path. Though each cordon produces much less than a bush or tree, they produce more per acre and the quality can be better. Apples and pears are very suitable for cordon training, as are red- and whitecurrants and gooseberries.

- *Espaliers* have several horizontal tiers and are an attractive way of enhancing a wall. Step-over espaliers are designed for small gardens, having one low tier, a foot or so high, running parallel to the ground. Espalier treatment is suitable for most apples and pears, but many other tree fruits are more difficult to train this way and are easier as fans.

- *Fans* have all the branches radiating from the top of a short trunk. They are most suited to the stone fruits, which are difficult to train as espaliers.

Winter pruning This is usually done initially to form the shape of a tree, as it stimulates replacement growth. However, too much winter pruning is often done in place of summer pruning. Naturally interfering, rubbing and dangerous, dead and unhealthy growths should be removed when they are spotted (which is usually when the branches are bare). However, winter pruning is best avoided for the stone fruits as these may then be attacked by silver leaf disease. Winter pruning is required when the major removal of several boughs is necessary because, otherwise, the tree may die of shock. Also, when vigour has been lost, winter pruning and feeding may stimulate new growth. Excessive winter pruning may cause ill-placed replacement growths, such as the 'hedgehog look' of water sprouts.

OPPOSITE LEFT *This vine in a tub has* Claytonia *underneath for salads and a dock for nettle stings.* OPPOSITE RIGHT *Dead and even stinging nettles do little harm to this raspberry crop.* BELOW *This pear, 'Souvenir du Congres', with little attention has cropped well every summer for decades.*

Summer pruning Often ignored, this is a more important method for looking after trained trees and soft fruit than winter pruning. It does not stimulate growth, but fruiting. Summer pruning is removing half to three-quarters of each new shoot once mid-summer is past. This allows air and light access and checks growth, so encouraging the formation of fruit buds. Of course, where the plant is still being allowed to expand, then shoots going in the desired directions are not cut off. These may be shortened in winter, which both encourages them to continue and more sideshoots to develop.

Soft fruit pruning is easier than for top fruit and the plants are much quicker to respond to training. Those grown as stools are simplest. Blackcurrants are grown as stools with many shoots from ground level and the oldest third of all the branches are cut out each year immediately after fruiting. Raspberries, blackberries and their hybrids are also normally grown as stools, with young growths being encouraged from ground level to replace the old on an annual basis. The old are cut away after fruiting to leave the new; this simultaneously removes most pest and disease problems. Tying the fruiting canes down on either, or to one, side then allows the next year's new flush to grow straight up and keeps them clean of disease spores dropping from the old. Red- and whitecurrants are forgiving and can be grown in almost any form imaginable, as can gooseberries. All of these need the young growths cutting back by half to three-quarters in summer and then again by a bit more in winter. These are all best grown as open goblets or, failing that, as bushes on short legs so that the sun can penetrate and air can circulate, which helps keep them disease-free. If you want prize berries, grow them as cordons and feed the soil heavily.

Inducing regular fruiting If your trees are established and growing well, but not flowering and fruiting, then attach lines near the tips of any strongly growing vertical branches and pull them gently down from the vertical. This checks the sap flow and induces fruiting more effectively than pruning. The branches can be kept bent by tying on weights; a plastic bottle of water is adjustable. If flowers are prolific, but none set, suspect the lack of a suitable pollinator. 'Borrow' some sprays in bloom from friends' trees and try pollinating with these. If any of the

OPPOSITE LEFT *This is my own pear grown from seed, and is a good storer until Easter.* OPPOSITE MIDDLE *So a few have Codling moth damage; they're for the birds.* OPPOSITE RIGHT *Figs just don't suffer from pest and diseases (other than birds).* OPPOSITE BELOW *Blackberries are now a 'new' superfruit, wouldn't my Gran have been surprised.* RIGHT *Two baths for blueberries and (sorry) an apt container for Myrica gale (Bog Myrtle).*

trials set fruit, then graft a branch on. Some fruit, especially apples, will biennial bear where they only crop in alternate years. They require thinning in the fruiting year, when we remove half or more of the fruits so that the tree is not exhausted, and then it does not need a year off. Indeed, almost all the tree fruits, gooseberries and grapes will give bigger and better fruit if thinned every year. Thinning is best done early and often, and well before fruits have started to swell significantly, and it should be done ruthlessly. The plants can afford to give us plenty of fruit to eat; it is the seeds inside that exhaust the plant, taking proteins, fats and minerals. Reducing the numbers of fruits reduces the numbers of seeds. This relieves the tree which still gives the same weight of fruit but with each remaining fruit being bigger. Thinning twice is better still, with the second following a month later, leaving only perfect, well-positioned fruits. Three times thinning is worth the effort, with the last thinning being of fruits big enough to use in cooking.

Annual maintenance Check the tie regularly (at least twice a year) on every staked tree. Also, firm the ground around new trees after hard frosts. Hygiene is essential, so remove all diseased material, especially diseased fruits as soon as they are spotted and preferably burn or bury, or even compost, as few problems survive proper composting. Regularly top up sticky bands; all fruit trees and bushes benefit from banding with sticky tree bands because only pests climb trunks (and band the stakes, posts and wires as well). Top up mulches, as fruit trees and bushes benefit immensely from these, and give them sieved garden compost every third year or so. During winter, occasionally rake mulches and compost aside for a day or two so that birds can get at pests overwintering underneath. I find a monthly spraying of the orchard and fruit cage with seaweed solution from early spring to mid-summer is beneficial, as it promotes vigour and disease resistance.

Watering This is vital for fruits growing in containers – they need watering three times daily in hot summers. Fruits growing next to walls or in dry corners will benefit from watering, as rain does not reach them very often. Water every plant before it suffers or wilts.

Fruitlets often drop in late spring as the soil dries out, so apply mulches early and water well before the plant shows any distress. (Warm water will soak into dry soil better than cold, while ice cubes melt so slowly that they will wet even really dried-out compost.) Take care not to waterlog plants, especially when growth is slow, as this can kill them by starving their roots of air. Water well before the fruits start to swell; do not leave it too late or the skins harden as growth slows and then split when it resumes again. Given the choice, water earlier in the day rather than later and use rainwater, which is much better than tap.

Feeding As well as an appropriate top dressing to each plant in a container in spring, it is a good idea to add a very dilute feed to each and every watering until ripening approaches. Usually, it is then best to reduce watering and stop feeding altogether. Do not feed plants in containers or the ground in autumn, as this promotes soft growth.

Cultivation for perfection

Here is my fruit-by-fruit guide to producing perfect crops, including advice on any significant pests, diseases and treatments; the best methods of harvesting and storage; and my recommended, tastiest, most luscious gourmet choices.

FRUIT-CAGE FRUITS

Blackcurrants These are one of the easiest fruits to grow successfully. They have dark purple, almost black, berries with an unforgettable aroma. Blackcurrants are self-fertile, but it is worth having several varieties to spread the flowering and miss the frosts. This also spreads the cropping and picking through summer and autumn. Although closely related to redcurrants, blackcurrants need a much richer, moister, heavier soil.

ABOVE RIGHT Whitecurrants – sweeter than red, indeed quite unique, and nice. BELOW Redcurrants – let them hang long and they're sweeter. OPPOSITE With blackcurrants the ripening fruits, even the very leaves and stems, all smell so distinctly of their jam.

Nonetheless, they will crop in even quite adverse conditions and in moderate to heavy shade, and even as bog plants.

Blackcurrants are unique in that they must be planted deep. They are grown as a stool, as they fruit best on young wood. Plant them at least two paces apart. Pruning consists of cutting out the wood that has fruited, leaving the younger shoots. This can be done brutally, with one-third to half of each bush being razed to the ground each year, providing they are being well mulched with copious amounts of compost or well-rotted farmyard manure. Seaweed sprays are also beneficial and help ward off mildew attacks (although many of the newer varieties are almost completely resistant to this).

Blackcurrants need to be protected with nets from birds. Aphids curl the tips in early summer, but are little problem. Big bud is a common problem so, around about mid-winter, pick off big buds which are much bigger and not pointy. Then burn them to reduce re-infection by the microscopic mites. Reversion is a virus infection spread by these mites; if yields drop unexplainedly and will not return after heavy feeding, then grub up all the bushes and grow new ones. Stinging nettles grown nearby may benefit blackcurrants which, incidentally, must not be grown in parts of the USA, as they are host to white pine blister rust.

Epicurean attentions Blackcurrants make tasty jam, especially mixed with redcurrant juice, and freeze well. Spread newspapers under the bushes before the currants drop as these do not hang on long once fully ripe. As you remove the oldest third of the stems each year and these will be cropping, you can prune very early and then pick the fruit off at leisure.

Bob's gourmet choices New varieties are well worth getting: 'Ebony' is especially sweet, 'Ben Connan' (early), 'Ben Hope' (mid-season), 'Ben Sarek' (mid-season) and 'Ben Alder' (late) will spread the cropping , while 'Big Ben 'will give you the biggest berries. The Jostaberry is a much larger hybrid, more like a thornless gooseberry, with large, blackcurrant-flavoured berries (see Gooseberries, page 130).

Red and whitecurrants These are very productive and easy fruits to grow. Redcurrants respond best to a cool, well-mulched soil and don't need such rich conditions as blackcurrants or raspberries. They grow in partial shade and quite happily on cold walls, even cropping well on a north wall. Although highly productive, birds love

them so they must be netted. They often get apparently disastrous attacks of leaf blistering aphis, which puckers and colours the shoot tips and leaves, but this never affects the yields and is cleared away with summer pruning. Fortunately, these currants are amenable to pruning and training and can be fitted in anywhere, though, as bushes, they need to be at least two paces apart. Redcurrants may benefit from stinging nettles grown nearby, while *Limnanthes douglasii* makes a beneficial ground cover once the bushes are established.

Epicurean attentions Raw redcurrants are delicious cooked with other fruits and the juice makes other jams and jellies set. Their jelly is often preferred, as these fruits are pippy, and with jelly-making you don't need to desprig the berries. They ripen early in summer but, if protected from pests and wet weather, will hang on and remain usable and become sweeter until late autumn.

Bob's gourmet choices 'Earliest of Four Lands' (now an heirloom variety) was my favourite but all redcurrants are amenable, productive and vary little in taste, acidity or season – though this may cover three months in a good year. 'Raby Castle' is most hardy, while 'Jonkheer van Tets' (early) and 'Rovada' (late) are modern choices. 'White Grape', 'Blanka' and 'White Versailles' are whitecurrants which are sweeter, but, generally, poorer croppers than the reds.

Gooseberries If well grown, the gooseberries can be as big and sweet as plums, and eaten as dessert. It is said, 'God gave us gooseberries for where grapes will not grow', and it is true. A good gooseberry, well ripened, is a huge drop of nectar in a skin, and available in red, green, white or yellow, each with a different flavour. A forgiving crop, gooseberries can be trained in any form imaginable, but are easiest as goblet-shaped bushes on a short

leg. They need moisture and a rich soil and will tolerate some shade, but detest hot, dry spots. Tomatoes and broad beans nearby are reputed to aid them (I grow them with *Limnanthes douglasii* as ground cover).

Gooseberries can get American mildew on the tips, in dry conditions, which may spread onto the berries, leaving these only suitable for jamming, so keep the plants well pruned, mulched and watered. Sodium bicarbonate sprays and sulphur-based ones (which burn some varieties) are available for organic growers. Occasionally, often in the third or so year after planting, gooseberries suffer damage from sawfly caterpillars. First appearing as a host of wee holes in a leaf, they move on to stripping the bush; vigilance and early action prevents serious damage. The caterpillars were once killed with a spray of derris, though, better still is to put a sheet underneath the bush and shake it so that they fall off and can be collected. Ripe gooseberries are eaten by birds, mice and wasps, so need to be protected. Birds also attack the buds in winter, so their pruning is often left until near last.

ABOVE *'Langley Gage' gooseberries, so sweet they're better than grapes.* **BELOW LEFT AND RIGHT** *You cannot have too many strawberries, grow them in the ground and many more in pots under cover – the rain, slugs and birds can't get them there.*

Epicurean attentions The protected ripe fruits mellow and hang on until late summer, becoming sweeter and fruitier, but only if the weather stays dry. Green gooseberry jam is exceptionally good. Use young green fruits (not of red varieties), thinning them at the same time in early summer, and cook them at a low temperature or the jam will turn red. Gooseberries freeze well and are easier to top, tail and de-whisker once frozen.

Bob's gourmet choices Try these as cordons: 'London', a large, old, late-season red; 'Early Sulphur', an early yellow; and the long-cropping 'Langley Gage', a superbly sweet white. 'Leveller' (mid-season) is a legendary culinary and dessert fruit and the new varieties, 'Pax' (mid-season, also thornless) and 'Invicta' (early) are mildew-resistant, as are 'Hinnonmaki Red' (mid-season) and 'Hinnonmaki Yellow' (late-season); 'Xenia' (mid-season) is claimed to be the sweetest and almost thorn-free. Jostaberries and Worcesterberries are both very similar to gooseberries, but larger, needing to be three paces apart, with fruits that resemble a cross with blackcurrants. Jostas have a drooping habit, crop heavily and are thornless, so are a good choice. Worcesterberries are very mildew-resistant, but viciously thorned, so the fruit is unpickable, though it would make delicious jams and pies.

Strawberries These are probably the most rewarding of all fruits. Strawberries need a very rich soil, full of humus, and benefit from slow-release sources of phosphorus, such as bonemeal. The site must be free of weeds. Also, good preparation, with additions of well-rotted manure or compost, and/or seaweed meal dressings, will be result in much heavier cropping. The more space you give strawberries, the better they will do and the less work they will be! A stride each way is ideal, but a couple of feet is a sensible distance.

Strawberries must have bird protection, so use nets or jam jars if a cage is not available. Slugs and ground beetles can also eat quite a few fruits. The worst problem, though, is wet weather when the fruit is ripening, which not only causes mould (botrytis) but also reduces their sweetness. By growing several varieties, you can spread the cropping and minimise this risk. Cloching once the fruits are green is an alternative or, if used from late winter, will bring the crop forward by some weeks. Strawing up once the fruits are swelling helps keep the fruit clean and infections to a minimum, as does removing and destroying any mouldy fruits that develop, preferably before the mould goes 'fluffy'. Regular spraying with seaweed up until flowering will make them sturdy and help prevent infections.

After fruiting has finished, tidy the plants, shearing back surplus runners and dead leaves and, in winter, tidy them again, removing old straw as well. Aphid attacks can be controlled with soft soap sprays. Any

sickly, mottled or odd-looking plants should be pulled up and burnt to prevent virus problems building up. It is necessary to replace a third of the bed every year with new plants on new ground, as this ensures continuous, consistent cropping. Ideally, grow replacements from your own stock for, say, five to ten years and then buy new stock and start again.

Do not carry on with old beds; new crowns produce few but big fruits, in the next year, more but smaller fruits, and in the third, fewer much smaller fruits, while the fourth year is rarely productive. Runners are the obvious replacements, usually available to excess. Choose those from quality plants reserved for propagation and deflowered; half a dozen good ones, or many more poor ones, can thus be had. The first plantlets on early runners are best. Start new beds in late summer or early autumn to allow them to establish and then they will crop well the next summer. Late autumn or spring plantings should be deflowered the first

summer to build up their strength for a massive crop the next.

I do not like those vertical growing containers with many holes; these have too little compost and need far too much watering to be worthwhile. Strawberries can be grown in walls built of hollow concrete blocks or car tyres filled with compost. Given sufficient watering, this works well for early crops if facing the sun. Seedling-grown strawberries are generally poor fruiters, though some varieties can be grown from seed. Alpine strawberries do not form runners, but are easy from seed, although they only live for a few years and have tiny fruits. Alpines are very tolerant of soils and sites and will grow almost anywhere. Birds do not eat them as readily and, when ripe, the flavour is divine. They give only a few fruits at a time, but carry on fruiting from early summer until late autumn.

Epicurean attentions Strawberries freeze easily but the texture is lost on thawing; however, if they are partially thawed they are delicious! Of course, they make wonderful jam. To make the jam set, add redcurrant, whitecurrant or lemon juice. If you want strawberries to keep fresh for longer, pick them early in the morning with a bit of stem, without touching the fruit.

Bob's gourmet choices Many modern varieties have fair flavour, but avoid those whose main claim is they freeze or jam well, though 'Cambridge Favourite' is still oddly popular! 'Royal Sovereign' was the standard by which others were judged but is a poor cropper, likewise 'Late Pine'. 'Gariguette' has been voted the tastiest but is small, 'Malwina'

ABOVE, BELOW AND OPPOSITE *I've grown raspberries, blackberries and hybrids from seedlings just for the curiosity. They mostly do fairly well and taste pretty good (as do currants but seedling strawberries and grapes are seldom brilliant).*

is dark red, large and phenomenal. I like 'Sweetheart', 'Redgauntlet' and 'Marsh Marvel' for earlies, 'Pegasus', 'Alice' and 'Amelia' mid-season, and 'Symphony', 'Florence' and 'Sophie' for late varieties. 'Fenella' is most reliable. However, most still fruit at much the same time in early summer, but the autumn-fruiting strawberries continue to the first frost. Their fruits tend to be less sweet from lack of sun, but are delicious anyway. The best for flavour are 'Aromel' and 'Mara des Bois', while 'Finesse' and 'Flamenco' are other good ones. All will fruit more heavily in autumn if early flower trusses are removed.

Raspberries Strangely, these are little grown as garden fruits when they are the easiest to grow and care for. Raspberries vary considerably in size and are usually red, with yellow ones now on sale again. In good varieties, the conical fruit pulls off the plug easily, leaving a hole. Some are less easy and the berries may be damaged, as they are soft and thin-skinned. Raspberries are very productive and the flowers are also loved by bees. Preferring cool, moist conditions, raspberries do wonderfully in Scotland, doing considerably better given plentiful moisture, a rich neutral or acidic soil or at least copious quantities of compost and very thick mulches. They do not like dry conditions against walls, but can be grown on cool shady ones with a moist root run.

The autumn-fruiting varieties tend to be more productive than the common summer fruiters, especially on drier sites. Summer raspberries are pruned after fruiting by cutting out the old canes, leaving the new to grow on. It helps to have thinned these by mid-summer to a hand's-breadth or so apart. Autumn raspberry pruning is simpler still; all canes are cut to the ground in late winter and, again, the young canes benefit from thinning before mid-summer, leaving the strongest to fruit later. Raspberries produce canes only a metre or two long, which can be trained almost horizontally, so they do not need tall posts and wires to support them. Weeding must be done carefully because of their shallow roots, so thick mulching is almost essential.

Birds are the major cause of lost crops. The raspberry beetle can be controlled with mulches raked aside in winter to allow birds to eat the pupae. These maggots are rarely a problem with autumn fruiters. Virus diseases may appear, mottling the leaves with yellow, and the plants become less productive. Replacing the stock and moving the site is the only practical solution, but wait until the yields have dropped. Inter-veinal yellowing is caused by alkaline soils, so get rid of this by using monthly seaweed solution sprays with added magnesium sulphate. Also, use more compost and deeper mulches. Raspberries reputedly benefit from tansy, garlic, marigolds and strawberries grown close by, but not underneath them.

Epicurean attentions Pick gently, leaving the plug. Raspberries do not keep for long if wet and less still if warm. If you want to keep them longest, cut the fruiting stalks with scissors and do not touch the fruits. They must be processed or eaten within a matter of hours, as they are one of the least durable or transportable fruits. They make tasty jam, especially mixed with redcurrant juice, and freeze well. When you think you've picked them all, look up into the canes!

Bob's gourmet choices New varieties of raspberry are almost the only ones available and soon replaced by others at a great rate. I still like the almost forgotten, but tasty, 'Malling Jewel' (early), though 'Malling Minerva' (early) is admittedly better. 'Glen Moy' (early) is also tasty. 'Glen Ample' (mid)

is a reliable cropper but 'Glen Fyne' (mid) is better flavoured. 'Glen Coe' is dark and luscious for conserves. I also love yellow raspberries. Less vigorous and with paler leaves, these naturally tend towards autumn fruiting. 'Golden Everest' is superb, with richly flavoured soft, sweet berries that lack the sharpness of many reds. 'Fallgold' is another yellow and 'Autumn Bliss' a red autumn fruiter. 'Joan J' is currently the heaviest cropping autumn red, but 'Octavia' looks promising. Seedling raspberries may be relatively poor performers but are fun and often have excellent flavour.

Blackberries and their hybrids Grown in the garden, blackberries are productive, but never seem as tasty as the wild ones. Very similar, but more worthwhile growing, are all the various crosses made between black-berries and raspberries. All of these different berries prefer the same rich, well-mulched soil of the woodland's edge, but can often fruit well in poor soils and situations, even in moderate shade or on north walls. All are pruned much the same as raspberries, cutting out the old and tying in the new canes each year. The more vigorous growers need more wires for support, strongly attached to a wall or stout posts. Vigorous and self-fertile, the only common problem is birds and this is particularly true for Tayberries that never even get halfway to ripening unless netted! Thornless versions of these berries are often less flavoured and poorer croppers than the thorny originals. Blackberries benefit from tansy or stinging nettles nearby and they are a good companion and sacrificial crop with grapevines.

Epicurean attentions All these berries rot quickly once picked, so jam or freeze them as soon as possible. Blackberries stewed with apples, strained and sweetened, make a delicious syrup for diluting as a summer drink.

Bob's gourmet choices Few compare with 'Himalayan Giant'. It is highly productive but needs a lot of space – at least three or four paces each way. 'Bedford Giant' fruits earlier and tastes better; the canes are longer than 'Himalayan Giant' but not as thick or prolific, so they are more controllable. 'Oregon Thornless' is decorative and probably the

best-tasting thornless blackberry, but crops rather too late for colder regions. Many thornless and/or short-caned bushy and larger berried varieties have been recently introduced. They include 'Loch Ness', 'Loch Maree', 'Loch Tay', 'Black Butte' and 'Chester', and it will be a while before I can rate them.

Boysenberries are large, well-flavoured blackberries, but make a lot of growth with light crops. Loganberries are crosses between raspberries and blackberries. The only one still worth growing is 'Ly 654', which has a good flavour with a thornless variety.

The Tayberry is like an improved, sweeter Loganberry, but with a much richer flavour. Definitely the best of the whole family, they do better in light shade than full sun and will even do well on a north wall. Japanese wineberries are orange-red and tiny, but the flavour is delicious; children love them and they are best eaten fresh. The canes are bristly, not thorny, and a lovely russet colour.

Blueberries, bilberry, cranberry and lingonberry *Vaccinium corymbosum*, the blueberry, is now cultivated instead of the similar *V. myrtillus*, or Bilberry which has become a scarce UK native. (Closely related is is *V. oxycoccos*, the cranberry, a scrambling evergreen with red berries which is possible to grow as ground cover in the same containers as the shrubbier blueberries.) These need no pruning and rarely suffer much from pests or diseases, but need moist, acid conditions. Although self-fertile, they fruit better if different varieties are grown nearby; they need to be about a pace or two apart. They are all ericaceous, enjoying similar conditions, root bacteria and fungi with rhododendrons and azaleas, so they can be used as ground cover between these. However, don't try to grow them for crops unless you have a genuine acid soil and

almost waterlogged conditions, say, by a pond or stream – alternatively, use large containers (three fill an old bath) and a butt of rainwater.

Epicurean attentions The purple berries of blueberries are delicious in tarts, muffins or made into jelly. Cranberries are invariably used for sauce for turkey.

Bob's gourmet choices 'Earliblue', 'Toro', 'Bluecrop' and 'Brigitta' will crop from midsummer to early autumn. 'Ozarkblue' is tasty but late, while 'Sunshine Blue' and 'Blue Pearl' are most compact. For cranberries, grow the American *V. macrocarpon* 'Pilgrim', 'Early Black' or 'Langlois'. The lingonberry is like a compact evergreen blueberry with cranberry-like fruits and worth growing. The cowberry, *V. vitis-idaea*, has much less merit.

Grapevines These are among the most ornamental and decorative of all plants and easily trained to fit into almost any sunny place. Attractive leaf colours in autumn make the crop almost a bonus. Grapevines are highly productive and tolerant of most soils, except very wet ones, and should not be overfed as this produces growth instead of fruit. They do best against a wall or on wires over a patio. However, they can also be grown in large pots outside, which are brought under cover during hard frosts and, sensibly, while in fruit. Earlier crops can also be achieved by taking pot-grown grapevines into a warm place in late winter; this brings their fruiting forward by months.

Grapes can be formally trained or left to ramble over trees and sheds. Vines are so vigorous that they need hard summer pruning to control them, even if in pots. The method

LEFT *The Japanese wineberry is a must, it is an ornamental and really nice to snack on.* RIGHT *These blueberries straining to get out will be picked off as they ripen, still those further in will survive.*

of pruning under cover is given on page 209 and this best applies to most vines indoors or out. Grapevines have many other specialised pruning methods, such as Guyot and L'Arcure, many of which are more akin to pruning cordon raspberries or blackcurrants, and these are more applicable outdoors in warmer areas than in Britain. Grapes are self-fertile and no problem; even under cover, I've never seen a bad set, although they are supposed to need hand-pollination. Thinning will prevent grapes overcropping, especially in the early years. Thin out the number of bunches to one every couple of feet before the grapes swell, but do not try to thin out grapes in the bunches as it spoils their bloom.

The most troublesome pests are birds, flies and wasps, which are only defeated by netting. Covering the ripening bunches with stockings, paper or net bags works well although, in wet years, may cause the fruit to rot. The best protection is to grow vines in a cage or take them, in pots, under cover. Some varieties are prone to mildew aggravated by dry conditions at the roots and stagnant air. This is relieved by more open pruning, mulching and preventive seaweed sprays, and a sulphur or copper spray, if necessary.

It is vital to obtain a suitable variety of grape. 'Black Hamburgh' is completely unsuitable outside or in most years in the UK, but excellent in a heated greenhouse or conservatory. (Sadly, still one of the most commonly sold, particularly by small nurseries and market stalls, is 'Mueller Thurgau', which is disease prone and for wine, and most newer varieties are frankly disappointing). The time of ripening varies from year to year, but usually from early autumn outdoors and from early summer under cover. Grapes are thought to be inhibited by laurels, radishes and cabbages and aided by blackberries, hyssop and mustard. Outdoors, many pests are controlled by clean cultivation.

Epicurean attentions Without doubt, grapes are best eaten fresh. A longer season can be had by picking the ripest fruits from each bunch which are, thus, judiciously thinned and left hanging until all are used up. When frost is likely, bunches can be cut, when ripe, with a stem. Insert the stem in a bottle of water, put in a cool place and the fruit will keep fresh for many weeks more. Trim back the stem and change the water weekly. Grapes will jam or jelly, but do not freeze well. Naturally, they juice easily and, of course, can be turned into wine.

Bob's gourmet choices 'Boskoop Glory' (B) is the only outdoor grape worth considering. It's a consistent producer of fair-sized, luscious, sweet black grapes that taste good eaten or as juice or wine. It does well in a tub or under cover. 'Siegerrebe' has sweet rose berries which are superbly flavoured. It prefers the warmth of a wall if grown north of southern England, or it can be grown in a tub or under cover. Unusually, it dislikes lime-rich soil but, it's so so tasty, it's worth it. For wine, jam or juice, outdoor reds are consistently better croppers, as they seem to rot less than the whites. 'Triomphe d'Alsace', 'Léon Millot', Seibel, 'Regent' and 'Maréchal Joffre' all reliably produce masses of dark black bunches. 'Phönix', 'Perlette', 'Poloske Muscat' and 'Lakemont' are the better outdoor whites. The Strawberry grape produces well, but the distinct texture and perfume is not to everyone's taste.

Kiwi (*Actinidia deliciosa*) This is one of a family of delightful, edible-fruited climbers. Ideally, they need a warm wall or should be grown under cover to fruit, but they take up a lot of space. They have lovely leaves and buff, rose-like flowers, so allow them to ramble over a shed, tree or pergola. Grown this way, pruning is unnecessary and they have few problems. You must have a male, as well as (several) females, although self-pollinating cultivars are becoming available. *Bob's gourmet choices* 'Hayward', 'Tomuri', or 'Oriental Delight', and 'Blake' are good, as well as the mini-kiwi, *A. arguta* 'Issai'.

Goji berry (*Lycium*) This is a new contender as a fruit, although really more medicinal. It's not brilliant eating out of hand and no better preserved, but is claimed to be very good for you. It is a straggly, vigorous shrub with random thorns. Once established in a warm position, small blooms ripen to rose-hip-like fruits. A better introduction is the honey-berry, *Lonicera*. Most honeysuckles have inedible or poisonous berries, but a couple have palatable ones. These are small, drought-resistant, slow-growing bushes with blueberry-like fruits; two are needed for pollination.

OPPOSITE TOP LEFT *Grapes for wine, such as these 'Madeleine Sylvaner', are successful about every other year.* OPPOSITE TOP RIGHT *Few notice grapevines flowering and they're scented too.* OPPOSITE BOTTOM LEFT AND RIGHT *Thin to leave smaller and more open bunches which will ripen sooner and rot less than those classic Africa shaped ones.* ABOVE *Kiwis are easy enough, if given space or amazing pruning attention.*

ORCHARD FRUITS, TOP OR TREE FRUITS

Apples These are easily stored for many months and can be eaten raw, cooked or turned into juice or cider. The most valuable apples where space is limited are the extra early varieties, late keepers and, of course, those with an exquisite flavour. Most apples can be grown as cordons, at a pace or less apart to squeeze many varieties into a small space, and as espaliers at five paces apart to give high-quality fruit. However, some, known as tip-bearers, such as 'Beauty of Bath' and 'George Cave', are better grown as rarely pruned dwarf bushes.

Apples are not fussy about soil or site, doing well almost anywhere, although very wet sites may encourage scab and canker. Pollinating partners are best provided by

growing several varieties, as many are incompatible. A crab apple will pollinate most others in flower at the same time. Apples suffer minor infestations of many pests and diseases, but as they produce so freely there is nearly always plenty of fruit, especially if the poor ones are removed during successive thinnings. Apply sticky tree bands at the end of summer and keep them touched up all year.

Holes in the fruits are usually caused by one of two pests. Codling moth makes holes in the core of the fruit, pushing out the flower end. They are controlled by corrugated cardboard band traps, pheromone traps, permitted sprays as the blossom sets, and good hygiene. The other hole-maker is apple sawfly which bores narrow tunnels, emerging anywhere. They may then eat into another or even a third. They are best controlled by hygiene, so remove and destroy affected apples during thinning. Also, running poultry underneath an orchard is effective. Most newer varieties are scab-resistant. Old ones get scabby patches on the fruit that are related to blisters and blotches on twigs and leaves. Prune these out to allow more air and light inside, mulch and feed to stimulate growth, and spray monthly with seaweed solution. This will also discourage the canker 'ulcers' often found on poor growers.

Brown rotten patches on apples are caused by bruising or damage, and then infection by spores overwintering on stems and soil, so hinder these with mulching and seaweed sprays. White woolly patches are just a type of aphid and can be killed with soft soap or brushed off. It is believed that nasturtiums growing around the tree eventually persuade woolly aphis to depart. Fireblight appears as brown withered flowers and leaves; prune these out and burn to

prevent it spreading. Apples are strongly affected by replant disease, which is a symptomatic reluctance to grow near, or where, an established apple tree has been. Apples are benefited by alliums, especially chives, and penstemons growing nearby. These are thought to prevent sawfly, as well as woolly aphis. Stinging nettles nearby benefit the trees and, dried as hay mats, help stored fruits keep longer. Remember though, that despite all their apparent woes, most apple trees just go on giving crops year after year after year.

Epicurean attentions 'Discovery' keeps a week or two, but most early apples are only an epicurean pleasure eaten off the tree. The windfalls can be juiced, puréed and frozen. Mid-season and late keepers should be left until they just start to drop, hard frosts are likely or bird damage becomes too severe, and then they should be carefully picked on a dry day. The fruits must be perfect, and the wee stalk (pedicel) must remain attached, for them to store. Use a cupped hand and gently lay them in a tray traditionally padded with dry hay and nettles. As this goes mouldy in the damp, use crumpled or shredded newspaper; if the apples are individually wrapped in paper, they keep longer. Do not store early varieties with lates, or near pears, onions, garlic or potatoes. The ideal rodent-proof store is a dead refrigerator in a shed.

Bob's gourmet choices For the earliest to eat off the tree, choose 'George Cave' and 'Discovery'. For late keepers, you must have 'Ashmead's Kernel', 'D'Arcy Spice', 'Winston' and 'Tydeman's Late Orange' (these last pair need hard thinning to grow to any size). For outstanding, mid-season flavour, have 'James

LEFT AND OPPOSITE *Apples are beautiful in bloom and fruit, and are little work.*

Grieve', 'Orleans Reinette', 'Egremont Russet', 'Pitmaston Pine Apple' and 'Charles Ross'. 'Bramley's Seedling' grows too large regardless, and I reckon 'Reverend W. Wilks' and 'Howgate Wonder' are much better cookers. Unless you can endure the scrappy growth and poor crop to get the quality, flavour and texture, then never grow 'Cox's Orange Pippin'. Very similar and much more successful is 'Sunset' and other Cox derivatives. (True Cox's have loose seeds you can hear when shaken.) Some of the newer varieties also have taste; I'm impressed by 'Jupiter', 'Jonagold', 'Braeburn', 'Katja' and 'Spartan'. Even a 'Golden Delicious' doesn't taste 'old and suspicious' when grown organically at home, although it's a bit prone to scab.

Pears Growing the finest pear is a more demanding task than for most other fruits, but they are beautiful in blossom, especially when trained. Pears need a fairly rich soil, but moisture is the most important. They will not fruit well in quality or quantity if dry at their roots, so always mulch heavily and don't allow grass underneath, as pears suffer badly from the competition. As bushes at four or five paces apart on Quince A rootstock, they are compact and will crop with little attention, but late frosts often damage the blossoms and young fruitlets. Without doubt, most varieties are best grown as espaliers on a wall. 'Jargonelle' and 'Williams' will even crop on a cold wall and also respond well to cordon training on Quince C rootstock. This is most worthwhile, as several cordons ensure pollination and spread the eating season. Most pears need pollinating partners, though some, such as 'Concorde', are self-fertile, but they'll give better crops if cross-pollinated.

ABOVE *Pears left to grow untrammelled crop too heavily and inevitably swell less well.* **LEFT** *A choice pear, 'Doyenné du Comice', deserves hard pruning onto a warm wall.*

'Dr Jules Guyot', 'Conference' and 'Durondeau' are also partly self-fertile.

Pears have fewer pests and diseases to worry about than apples. Leaf blackening in spring is usually from harsh winds. However, if the flowers and leaves wither and go brown, this may be fireblight, which must be cut out and burnt before it spreads. Leaf blistering is caused by invisible mites, traditionally treated with a lime sulphur wash that is no longer available; I find soft soap sprays work. Sometimes, the fruitlets blacken and drop and, if these have maggots inside, it's pear midge. Collect the fruitlets and burn them, and lay heavy mulches. Rake these aside in winter so birds can eat the pest's pupae or run chickens underneath to do the same.

Epicurean attentions Early and mid-season pears are best picked as the first start to fall because they go woolly if left on the tree too long. Pears can be picked more underripe than most fruits and will slowly ripen if kept cool, faster when warm, but keep them humid or they'll shrivel. Late pears need to be left until bird damage is too great and picked with a stalk. They should come off easily, handled more gently than explosives, and carefully watched while ripening, as they go over in a matter of hours after perfection. Late varieties can be kept in the cool and dark for a few months, ripening up rapidly when brought into the warm. Do not wrap pears with paper, as with apples, and never store the two fruits near each other as they cross-taint. Good pear cider is more difficult to make than apple and requires the proper perry pears – be warned. Surplus pears, even those going over, can be washed, chopped and simmered overnight. By morning, you can strain the juice off the pips and skins, then boil it down to a maple-syrup-like consistency.

Bob's gourmet choices Purely culinary pears are seldom needed as dessert varieties can be so utilised. 'Bartlett', also known as 'Williams' Bon Chrétien' (early/mid season), is excellent for preserving and is a good dessert fruit though prone to scab. The best dessert pear is 'Doyenne du Comice' (late season) – sweet and aromatic, dissolving in the mouth. It can reach a large size and weight if trained on a warm wall. Mid-season have 'Clapp's Favourite', 'Dr Jules Guyot', 'Jargonelle' and 'Souvenir du Congrès'. 'Fertility Improved' is hardy and most reliable. For storing 'Glou Morceau' and 'Durondeau' keep into the New Year, 'Humbug' even longer. 'Merton Pride', 'Concorde' and 'Beth' have good flavour and are worth considering. The self-fertile Asian pear or Nashi has several varieties; I grow Kumoi, the fruit is round and gold like a russet apple, perfumed and sweet, and it makes a superb dried fruit like apple rings, but better.

Quinces and medlars These are all decorative compact trees with apple-blossom-like flowers. There are two sorts of quince: cydonias are ancient fruit trees, producing rock-hard 'pears', while *Chaenomeles*, or Japanese quinces, have smaller and even harder fruits on bushier, spiny shrubs. Medlars are pretty trees with contorted branches, large leathery leaves that colour well in autumn, and a fruit like a huge rose-hip or distorted pear. All these odd fruits are self-fertile, suffer virtually no pests or diseases, are tolerant of most soils and sites, though prefer moist ones, and benefit from a wall or shelter in the north of Britain. Plant them three or four paces apart and they will need almost no attention other than harvesting.

Epicurean attentions Both sorts of quince cannot be eaten raw, though they make tasty jellies. They store well and give off an aromatic scent that will fill a kitchen and taint other foods. Included with apple or pear dishes, they impart a spicy aroma and add texture as they keep their shape when cooked. Medlar fruit is only eaten once 'bletted'. They are picked as ripe as possible and stored in a frost-free place. When they go soft and near rotten, the pulp is mixed with cream, liqueurs and honey as a treat, honest – since trying them, I've dug my tree up and burnt it!

Bob's gourmet choices 'Vranja' and 'Portugal' are the best Cydonia quinces, others are very similar. Chaenomeles 'Boule de Feu' is highly productive, with startling red flowers. 'Nottingham' and 'Royal' are reckoned to be the tastiest medlars, 'Dutch' and 'Monstrous' the larger.

Cherries Years of breeding have produced the modern sweet cherry which is a triumph of man's eternal dreaming, as the birds always get them in the end. Morello cherries are more successful, as the birds leave their sour fruits for a moment longer and some

RIGHT *These are won only with cunning and effort in that legendary battle with the birds.*

can be grabbed. Sweet cherries require a rich, well-aerated soil with plentiful moisture at the roots, but without waterlogging. They do not like heavy, acidic or badly drained soil. Cherries can be trained, but this is not easy to do. Sweet cherries should only be grown on the most recent, most dwarfing rootstocks as, otherwise, they make far too much growth to be grown in most fruit cages. They were once grown as fans against large walls, but this requires skilful maintenance pruning. I weave the topmost shoots down and in to make basket-woven tops – it works in a bizarre way. As such, any pruning must be done early in life, and early during the growing season, to avoid silver leaf disease, and only to remove dead and diseased growth.

Morello cherries are much more amenable to soil and site and more confinable, as they respond to hard pruning after fruiting. You will need to remove much of the old wood so that the new can be tied in. Thus, they fit into much less space than sweet cherries (and will even crop on a cold wall), but do take some attention; this is amply repaid if they can be netted. Probably the best way to grow cherries is in large containers kept indoors or in a cage when they are in flower and fruit. Many cherry varieties need compatible pollinators, but some are partly self-fertile. Morello cherries are not only self-fertile, but will pollinate almost any late-flowering sweet cherry.

Rain at any time during flowering causes mould on the flowers, while heavy rain at any time during ripening always splits the fruits. Waterlogging, especially on acid or heavy land, may promote gummosis, which is seen as oozing from the branches. However, this

may also be an attack of bacterial canker. Treatment requires remedial pruning and restoring vigorous growth with feeding, liming and draining.

Cherries can crop despite devastating attacks of black aphid, which does little real damage, even though the shoot tips look pretty bad. The aphid attack soon turns into ladybirds to guard the rest of the garden and it's really the birds who are taking the crop! Where no netting is possible, pull nylon stockings over the branches of fruit, although the birds will still eat through them. Be thankful that cherries escape the wasps by fruiting early in the year.

Epicurean attentions Cherries can be picked and kept for several days if perfect, dry, still on the sprigs and laid on paper in the cool. They can be frozen, but this is fiddly as they need stoning to prevent taint. They do jam well, especially mixed with redcurrant jelly, which makes them set and adds bulk.

Bob's gourmet choices The Morello is dark and sour, so suitable for cooking, jamming or freezing, and for this it is supreme. 'Summer Sun', 'Kordia', 'Cherokee', aka 'Lapins', and 'Sweetheart' are new, mostly self-fertile cherries now replacing older varieties.

Apricots Apricots ripen from early summer and are a gourmet's delight grown at home. The trees are tough, but the flowers come so early that they are nearly always damaged by frosts. That's why, without some protection, good crops occur for me only about one year in five. In the northern UK, apricots will only crop reliably against a warm wall where they prefer to be fan-trained at about five paces apart. In sunnier areas, they succeed as bushes in sheltered spots. The soil should never be waterlogged. For wetter, heavier soils, apricots are best budded onto St Julien A, Mont Clare/Montclair and onto seedling

peach or apricot rootstocks for lighter, drier soils. The major loss of fruit is frosts taking off the self-fertile flowers or fruitlets.

Apricots suffer from ants farming scale insects on them and, occasionally, caterpillars and aphid attacks may bother them. However, more serious is dieback and gummosis; the twigs die back and sticky gum oozes out of cracks in the branches or, fatally, the trunk. The disease is symptomatic of poor growth; fewer weeds, more compost, more mulches, better aerated roots, liming, seaweed sprays and hard pruning are called for. Pruning is not otherwise required for bushes but, for fans, it is done early after the flowers have set and again when the fruits start to swell. Take away half to three-quarters of each young shoot and eliminate any shoots growing inwards towards the wall from the main framework. As they can fruit very heavily in good years, thinning out the fruitlets is as beneficial as is regular watering!

Epicurean attentions Pick apricots only when they start to drop. They do not keep well, but are easily dried or frozen. Apricots make a delicious jam and can be preserved in spirits

LEFT *Believe me, without a net or cage you'll never see these.* RIGHT *Apricots are not only delicious, but much easier to grown than you imagine.*

or syrup and unlike most *Prunus* fruits, apricot kernels are sweet and edible.

Bob's gourmet choice The standard variety is 'Moorpark', while 'Farmingdale' is huge and luscious. 'Tomcot', 'Goldcot' and 'Flavorcot' are new, more reliable varieties, but I rate the old 'Bredase' as by far the tastiest.

Peaches, nectarines and almonds Peaches are one of the choicest fruits to grow at home. Nectarines are slightly more tender peaches without the fuzz, they will not crop in the open in most of the UK, needing the warmth of a wall, but they are much the same as peaches in every other way, as are almonds. These last need the same conditions as peaches, but with less rigorous thinning. All the trees are very beautiful in flower and leaf. They need to be planted five to eight paces apart in a rich, well-aerated piece of soil. They loathe waterlogging, so prefer open soils to heavy, but need heavy mulching to keep them moist. When planted against walls, the fruits often split unless they are watered consistently throughout the season. Peaches should not be planted near almonds as they may cross-pollinate, causing

the nuts to be bitter. All three are benefited by companion plantings of alliums, especially garlic and chives, and stinging nettles nearby, reputedly prevent the fruit moulding.

Peaches grown as bushes are easy, self-fertile and fruitful from early in their life. As they fruit on young shoots, you need to continuously replenish these by pruning them harder and more like blackcurrants than like most other trees. The tops of higher branches are removed to encourage more young growth lower down and to keep the bushes lower and easier to treat. On walls, and especially under cover, peaches are usually fan-trained. Fruiting is then guaranteed because of the frost protection, but flavour may be poorer and pruning must be done regularly. Selected young shoots are allowed to spring from a main frame and then tied in to replace the previous growths once those have fruited. Fortunately, if the pruning of peaches is neglected, healthy bushes respond to being cut back hard by throwing out plentiful young growths, but this vigour lessens as they get older.

More important than pruning is thinning; peaches are prone to overcropping, breaking

branches and exhausting themselves. Thin the fruits hard, removing those touching or anywhere near each other. Do this very early and then again later. Peaches, nectarines and almonds can be grown on Pixy dwarfing rootstocks, which makes them smaller than the usual St Julien A; they can then be grown as small bushes in large pots. This means they can be taken indoors over winter, which ensures freedom from leaf curl, but causes more problems with red spider mite. However, moved outside again when in leaf, they avoid the latter to a great extent and fruit quite well if well-watered.

Peaches suffer great losses from birds and wasps; use paper bags to protect the fruits. Earwigs get inside the fruits and eat the kernel out, but are trapped in rolls of corrugated cardboard tied around the branches. The main problem with all these fruits is peach leaf curl, which puckers the leaves, turning them red and yellow. Severe attacks weaken the tree and, after a couple of years, can even kill it. Spraying with Bordeaux mixture prevents attacks if done twice or so as the buds are opening in late winter. Peach leaf curl can also be avoided if the buds are

kept dry by overwintering indoors or, for wall-trained specimens, a plastic or glass sheet can be hung from the top of the wall. Frosts take off the blossoms and fruitlets most years in the UK, so they must be protected from frosts during bloom and for several weeks after they have set. Dieback and gummosis are symptomatic of poor growth and are best treated by heavy mulching and hard pruning in very late winter.

Epicurean attentions Peaches are best sun-warm off the tree. If picked underripe, they never develop the full flavour or juiciness, but then keep a few days if handled with care and kept cool. However, the slightest bruise and they will rot. Peaches can be dried, jammed or frozen. When almond crops drop, peel and dry them but do not crack them until required. Then they are best blanched to give a clean and tastier nut. Unhulled, they will store in dry salt or sand for years.

Bob's gourmet choices 'Peregrine' has sweet, well-flavoured, yellowish white flesh and it's supposedly freestone. 'Rochester' is similar but with darker yellow flesh. 'Avalon Pride' is allegedly resistant to the dreaded leaf curl. 'Bonanza' is naturally more compact, as are Peento flattened varieties, and so good for tub cultivation. All nectarines are exquisite. 'Pineapple' is tastiest, while 'Lord Napier' is good and widely available. Almond varieties are hard to find; an old Spanish type, Jordan, is still grown but, for roasting nuts, find Texas.

OPPOSITE LEFT AND MIDDLE *Peaches get bigger the further apart, thin at least twice; once immediately and again before half-swelled.* OPPOSITE RIGHT *Nectarines are more luscious and need thinning even harder.* RIGHT *Plums and other stone fruits benefit hugely from early thinning.*

Plums including greengages, bullaces, damson and cherry plums In general, these are all very much alike and are least effort grown as trees at five paces or so apart. Plums like a heavier, moister soil than most other fruits, but do not like cold damp sites. However, some such as 'Victoria' and 'Czar', may do well trained on a cold wall. Liking richer conditions than most fruits, plums can be favourably sited next to chicken huts or compost heaps. Grown as trees, they are best left unpruned and any pruning is always done in mid-summer. Plums wait several years before they start cropping. Speed this up by pulling the branches down, although, if patiently grown as unpruned standards, the fruiting branches will weep and bring the fruit down to picking level. Though some are self-fertile, pollination partners are often required but, even so, cropping is hit and miss as the blossom is so frequently frosted. Irregular cropping makes them overdo it in good years and then they're exhausted for the next couple. That's why thinning

LEFT *Admittedly the flavour of outdoor ground grown fruits can be better, but they come later, seldom as sweetly and often not at all.*

exceptionally heavy crops is necessary and often expediently done by cutting off half of each overburdened truss with shears. There is much maintenance pruning required for training plums on walls, as the rootstocks still do not control them enough, and they prefer a herringbone not a fan shape. Better-quality fruits can probably be had more easily by growing them in pots on the new dwarfing rootstocks such as Pixy or Colt.

Plums suffer from a host of minor pests, although most seem to barely affect the crop. Maggots in the fruit can be almost eliminated with pheromone traps and earwigs by banding the trunk. Mealy aphids often coat the leaves, but it is birds and wasps that destroy most fruit. Birds also damage the buds in winter. I find winding black cotton around them as soon as there is snow or hard frost worthwhile. Plum rust affects the leaves and damages future crops, so avoid having anemones nearby as they are an alternate host. Silver leaf disease is prevented by not pruning except during summer and keeping the tree vigorous, which will also help prevent gummosis.

Epicurean attentions Many varieties of plum will peel and this avoids the well-known side effects of too many plums. I make gourmet jams of the same variety with, without and with double the skins and what a difference this makes to the colour and flavour – try it! All plums make good jam fairly easily; use slightly under-ripe plums for the bite of acidity. They freeze well but need stoning first to prevent taint. Surpluses can be juiced by simmering in water, straining and freezing, or fermenting to wine and, where legal, distilling to that devastating fluid, plum brandy.

LEFT *Damsons are most reliable, rich and fruity.*
RIGHT *Cover it now with a net bag – once ripening the birds and wasps want it.*

Bob's gourmet choices 'Victoria' is ubiquitous; it is dual-purpose (i.e. both culinary and dessert fruits), fully self-fertile, pollinates many others, and worth having for its large, yellow-fleshed, red-flushed fruits in high summer. 'Marjorie's Seedling' is dual-purpose, self-fertile and late cropping with purple fruits. 'Oullins Gage' is dual-purpose, self-fertile and delicious. Believed to be a plum but of gage quality, it is a late flowerer and useful where frosts are a problem. 'Reine-Claude de Bavais' may also have plum ancestry, but makes the most delicious jam. The true greengages have lightly scented flesh and I prefer them for dessert. 'Coe's Golden Drop' is my favourite, but a shy cropper and needs a warm spot or a wall. 'Severn Cross' is a delicious seedling from Coe's but more reliable and self-fertile. The Transparent gages are hybrids with pale translucent flesh and fine flavour. They ripen late and benefit from a wall or sheltered site.

Bullaces are small and generally too acid to eat raw, but make some of the most superb preserves, though varieties are scarce. Damsons are closely related to bullaces, but larger, and resemble blue-black plums distinguished by a delicious spicy flavour once cooked. Their trees are compact and usually self-fertile. The 'Shropshire', or 'Prune Damson', which ripens late has the best flavour but is a light cropper. The cherry plum, or Myrobalan, is often used as a windbreak as it is more shrub-like and can be made into hedges. They are self-fertile and the almost spherical fruits have insipid but juicy flesh, which makes good jam. 'Ruby' and 'Golden Sphere' are new, tastier varieties.

Mulberry If you want to eat these, you'll have to grow them and, although they are slow to come into fruit, I have had them fruit in a year or two from planting. They are traditionally planted as large specimens, but can be fruited earlier and easier in tubs. Mulberries are self-fertile, have few pests and diseases (other than birds) and require no regular pruning.

Epicurean attentions The fruits, which are a bit like black raspberries, are best shaken off the tree onto the grass or a sheet. As well as tasting delicious, fresh mulberries make a good jam and a potent wine.

Bob's gourmet choices There are black, red and white mulberries; all can be eaten, although the black are best. The white are grown for leaves for silkworms.

Figs These big-leaved plants add a tropical look. Do not give them too rich a soil or they make too many leaves and soft growth with little fruit. They need a well-drained, chalky soil and, traditionally, were grown against

ABOVE *Figs crop well here, succulent and prolific, though they're sweeter under cover.*

a wall with their roots restrained by planting them in a sunken brick box. Nowadays, a woven sack of man-made fibre or the drum from an old washing machine will prevent the roots from getting too big, but still allow fine roots, air and water to get through.

Figs crop in the open, but produce better-quality fruits trained on a warm wall at least four paces wide and as high. Where space is limited, figs can be grown in containers. They are pruned during late winter just before growth is about to restart. Sturdy, short-jointed wood is the most fruitful if well ripened; long-jointed green shoots are unproductive and should be removed. To ensure crops, remove every fruit and fruitlet larger than a pinhead in early winter, as these sap the plant's strength and rarely succeed, and also spoil the spring crop as well. Other than birds and wasps, figs suffer few problems except for red spider mite under cover and on walls in hot dry conditions. Figs may benefit from the herb rue growing nearby.

Epicurean attentions Do not eat figs straight away, but keep them a day or so. When they start to soften and darken, they are supreme. Figs can be dried or turned into a syrup.

Bob's gourmet choices 'Brown Turkey' and 'Brunswick' are reliable, similar and ripen from high summer. 'Brunswick' produces the larger fruits, but 'Brown Turkey' is a heavier cropper.

Hazel, cobs and filberts These are easy to grow and are a rich, storable source of fat and protein. The wild hazels have the best flavour which the bigger cobnuts lack. Filberts are those where the husk or beard encloses the nut and are reckoned to be finer flavoured. All make big bushes, which need to be at least three or four paces apart. They will grow anywhere, but crop badly on heavy damp sites, while they do surprisingly well on poor, stony and sandy sites. Hazels are best grown as goblet-shaped bushes on a single trunk. They will still crop if left as thickets, though it is always worth keeping them uncongested and removing suckers to prevent an excessive loss of nuts within the tangle. Apart from thieving wildlife, they seldom suffer many problems. Growing wild they are found in association with bluebells and primroses, with truffles growing on their roots, but my supposedly inoculated trees have never produced any.

Epicurean attentions Like many nuts, hazels taste quite milky and sweet when eaten fresh, so start eating them before they fully ripen. As they ripen and fall off, they can be dehusked and dried, then stored unshelled in dry salt or sand for years. Filberts are stored in their husks, but last nearly as well. Hazelnut macaroons are devilishly good.

Bob's gourmet choices 'Cosford Cob', 'Kentish Cob' and 'Webb's Prize Cob' cobnuts are much bigger than native hazels, but tend to lack the flavour. Red-skinned filberts are tiny but delicious, and I much prefer them.

Sweet or Spanish chestnuts As far north as Britain, these only fruit well after hot summers. As they are rarely self-fertile, several are needed and, for this reason, they are seldom planted in our gardens. They do not like thin chalky soils, preferring a light, well-drained loam or light, dry, sandy soil. To produce nuts, they are best sited on the sunny side of woodlands or windbreaks, ideally of yew or holm oak. Generally, sweet chestnuts are problem-free in Britain, but in America chestnut blight has wiped out their best species. Indeed, if nuts are ripened after a hot summer or two, then the only problems are from the wildlife. Chestnuts are considered healthier when grown near oak trees.

Epicurean attentions Chestnuts are inedible raw, but are traditionally roasted in their shells. They can be used sweet and sour and even made into flour and all sorts of baked goods, and the glorious French *crème de marron* and *marron glacé*. They will store for a year or so if kept cool and dry.

Bob's gourmet choices Better varieties exist, but normally you can only get unnamed seedlings. Look for *Castanea sativa* 'Marron de Lyon', from France. In America, *C. dentata* was their native sweet chestnut, which had smaller better-flavoured nuts, but this was almost wiped out by chestnut blight.

Walnuts These are very slow to grow and to fruit. After fifteen years, my 'Franquette' was just starting to give respectable crops; now it's giving an annual surplus. The nuts are very tasty and nutritious. Walnuts prefer a heavy, moist soil, but detest waterlogging. They are not really self-fertile, so are best planted in groups (it helps to collect catkins on a stick to hand-pollinate the female flowers which come later). Not much grows under walnuts, which are generally bad companions, especially the American

varieties. Therefore, they are best planted at least ten paces apart along drives, rather than grown in the garden where they will become too large. Walnuts need little pruning which must preferably be done early in their life and early in the year. Generally, they are remarkably pest and disease free.

Epicurean attentions Fresh walnuts can be shelled then skinned. Skinning makes them much sweeter and removes all bitterness. The unripe nuts, when soft enough to be punctured with a needle, can be pickled or used to make liqueurs after the manner of sloe gin. The cleaned, unshelled, dried nuts can be stored for a year or so in salt or sand.

Bob's gourmet choices Named varieties of walnut, such as 'Franquette' are scarce but worth searching for. American black walnuts are usually offered as the species here, but there are several named varieties also difficult to find. *Juglans ailanthifolia* var. *cordiformis* is the Japanese heartnut, which may be worth growing. It is quicker to fruit than ordinary walnuts and produces strings of small, easily shelled nuts.

ABOVE *The cobnut is bigger than a hazel and much resembles an acorn when dropped from its sheath.*
RIGHT *Collect nuts as soon as they're ripe or the squirrels will have them.*

7 FEAST ON FRESH HERBS, SALADS & VEGETABLES

Growing for flavour, health, freshness and quality using the easiest and most effective means

Breeders have paid attention to the shrinking of gardens and now most vegetables are available in dwarf or mini forms that are suited to tub culture on a balcony or patio. Huge numbers of once difficult-to-find heirloom varieties have been reintroduced for their flavour or other rather non-commercial properties, though, to be fair, these are often less productive or trickier than modern varieties. And recent breeding has also made some once-difficult crops, such as sweet corn and even watermelons, achievable for the average gardener. Even soya beans are now possible outdoors. We still await truly blight-resistant potatoes with good flavour and any really blight-resistant tomatoes. The overwhelming and spectacular rise of hot chilli peppers is unprecedented, with many people growing these when they've never grown much else, probably because of their ease in pots on windowsills. Now you can find hundreds of varieties whereas, a decade ago, there were very few.

Not only can home-grown produce be one hundred per cent organic, but the varieties are generally better than commercial ones that are cultivated for high yields rather than flavour and vitamin content. Most home-grown crops are annuals, meaning we have to be fastidious over timing and maintain their growth without check. Otherwise, many will bolt and the crops are wasted. Thus, the pragmatic gardener looks to the few perennial crops to minimise the workload. Where space is very limited, culinary herbs are sensible plants to grow. With only a slightly larger area, it is also possible to grow many quick, tasty salad leaves. Only when space and time are generously available should you consider growing the more time-consuming vegetables. Specialise in one plant and you will soon produce first-grade specimens; do 'a bit of everything' and you will rarely show off many triumphs.

Cultural requirements for gourmet crops

Herbs, salads and vegetables need different conditions, depending on their nature.

Herbs Classic herbs, such as rosemary, sage and thyme, are perennials from the Mediterranean and require warm, dry, sheltered spots and not overly rich soil. Herbs that are grown as annuals, such as parsley, dill and borage, need a moister, richer soil and tolerate light shade, while the true vegetables require the best conditions of all: full sun and rich soil.

Although a lack of space may make this difficult, it is a good idea to at least divide off the aromatic perennials because many of them inhibit the germination of seeds, so move them to the edge or to another plot. Indeed, ornamental areas can be made solely from perennial herbs and then need very little maintenance, so grow them in a border next to a warm wall. They also benefit from brick and stone pathways, ornaments and low decorative walls, as all these retain the warmth that such plants love. Most perennial herbs also make useful companion plants, especially to fruit trees and bushes.

Where space is very short, then most perennial herbs will grow in containers, but do not expect them to flourish as they would in the ground. Of course, in pots, they can be stood under cover, in a cold frame or greenhouse, to extend their season. Pot-growing is ideal for mints which are invasive and not easy to control in a bed with other plants.

Do not over-enrich the ground for perennial herbs, as many then produce rank growth and poor flavour. The annual herbs, or rather those grown as annual herbs, do not generally need very rich soil either. A good start is essential and some must be sown in situ. However, most are better sown under cover in pots or multi-celled trays and planted out once the weather is warmer. Growing them to maturity on a seed bed utilises space efficiently once the main crops are planted out, and annual herbs are easy to intercrop amongst vegetables on the main beds. Make sure that your herbs are quickly accessible from the kitchen or include a good path to the herb bed if it is far away. If the main herb bed is not nearby, make a duplicate planting of the more important herbs next to the kitchen door.

Salad beds A salad bed is one plot worked extra intensively for a few years and then best moved on, leaving rich conditions for following crops. Where space is limited, concentrate on salads in their own bed and, if much salading material is required with a larger garden, then a separate salad area is more productive than growing these succulent crops with the main vegetables. Work as much organic material as possible into a salad bed with deep digging. Also, extra dressings of

OPPOSITE *A mixture of plants means few pests proliferate.* ABOVE *What could hope to compete close to a robust stand of potatoes?* LEFT *Salad crops deserve their own area.*

Vegetable gardens Good planning and care is needed for any size of vegetable garden to be productive. Vegetables require the best in soil, sun and situation to crop at all, let alone well. One reason is that many of them are extremely over-bred plants. Many, such as onions and root vegetables like carrots, are naturally biennials and store up nutrients so that they can flower and set seed the following year. However, we eat them before then. Given the best conditions they will grow fat for us, but the slightest check to growth or poor growing conditions leads to bolting (flowering too soon).

The vegetables we grow for fruit or seed, such as peas and beans, are more forgiving but still need good conditions to produce any amount of crop. Hardest of all are the highly unnatural cauliflowers and broccolis. The part we eat is an enormous multiple flower bud which we want to stay immature and succulent, while the plant wants it to blossom and be pollinated. Similarly, a cabbage is an enormous swollen terminal bud and Brussels sprouts are overgrown buds in the leaf axils. Crops such as tomatoes and sweet corn come from hotter climes with longer growing seasons and, although they just ripen in our summers, they must be started off early enough to do so in time. We need to give them protection and warmth, mimicking spring in their place of origin so that they start into growth early enough to catch all the summer's warmth.

seaweed meal will raise the fertility, which is aided by copious watering. This promotes the rapid lush growth that makes for sweet succulent salads. If a permanent site is chosen, then it is worth raising the north end (in the UK) and grading the whole bed down towards the south to create as steep a sun-facing slope as possible. This increases the amount of sunlight falling on the soil and gives faster, earlier starts in spring and longer cropping in autumn.

ABOVE *Once they outgrew the bent wire frames the wood pigeons shredded their outer leaves, but I get the hearts anyway.*

We must give vegetables a rich soil so they can draw on sufficient nutrients, plenty of sunlight, copious water, and enough unchecked growing time to finish the job. A common failing is crowding too many plants together, which makes three of the four vital ingredients rapidly dwindle into short supply. It is far better to grow a few plants well rather than many poorly! This applies to each and every sowing AND to the garden as a whole. Certainly, for the less experienced it is always a good idea to concentrate, initially, on just a few vegetables, adding to the range in following years. So, plan which crops you really want and leave the others for later years.

Comparative value of different crops

Why grow anything you don't like or more than you need? Look around any allotment site and see rows of leathery beetroot, rotting cabbages and withered runner beans. So, before wasting time, effort and money, carefully select what you really want to grow. Time is often limited and is more restrictive than space. A large town garden or allotment can feed a family all year if unlimited time is available, but will provide very little if only a few hours are spent on it. Growing a few crops in quantity takes much less time than growing a little of many.

A good plan is to list vegetables you already BUY each week. Many books offer tables of expected yields, which cannot be taken as more than guidelines, since yields can vary. Some years all of a crop fails and another year you are eating it until it comes out of your ears. Still, some comparison of expected yields helps with initial planning, so you can decide how much ground to give to each crop. In most soils, in an average year, a ten-foot row might produce the relative amounts

ABOVE *This 'Crown Prince' squash may well keep until the next crop matures!*
LEFT *Little plastic collars help water these celery and keep the slugs off.*

shown in the table. This is a rough guide so, when you find that there are just not enough or far too many peas, carrots or whatever produced from your first season, plan to devote more or less ground the following year. The table overleaf also indicates whether a crop is hard, moderate or easy to grow well (although this varies enormously with soil and situation). For example, it is unlikely that any plot will grow both carrots and cauliflowers well, as the former needs a light, sandy soil and the latter a heavy, rich clay. However, I have assessed each according to whether or not it is usually easy or not to produce a crop, bearing in mind their needs and common pests and diseases. I have further indicated whether each crop takes more or less time to reach the same condition that you would purchase it in from a greengrocer. The final columns are an indication of whether that crop costs more or less to grow than to be bought. The biggest expense is the cost of seed, so the total costs vary much more if home-saved seed or expensively promoted 'own brand' seeds are bought instead of standard varieties.

It is difficult to judge which crops are best to grow for saving money. Generally, though, crops such as courgettes, broccoli and French beans, are very expensive to buy compared with the cost of growing them, while most roots and maincrop potatoes are incredibly cheap to purchase, even organic ones. Ultimately, quality, especially freshness, is only obtainable from your own garden. The garden is particularly important for lettuces and saladings, which rapidly lose their crispness, as well as sweet corn, peas and new potatoes. In many ways, these are the best vegetables to concentrate on, while onions, roots and maincrop potatoes could perhaps be left out.

Nutrition from vegetables is affected by their variety, treatment and freshness. Anything grown organically at home of a good variety will always carry more nutritive value than shop-bought produce, as well as fewer residues. However, to get the maximum vitamin value from a small space, concentrate on carrots, spinach and chards for vitamin A; peas, onions and potatoes for vitamin B1; broccoli for vitamin B2; potatoes and peas for vitamin B3; and broccoli, Brussels sprouts and kale for vitamin C.

Where space is at a premium, then the best all-round value comes from growing carrots, and salad vegetables as well as climbing peas and beans. If time is very limited, then courgettes and squashes, beans (especially drying haricots and broad beans) and early potatoes can all be grown with very little work or attention. Onion sets, garlic and shallots are equally easy to grow and take little time, as long as the soil is not very weedy.

LEFT *Sunflowers are greedy. Still, if you want your own seed they are easy.*

COMPARATIVE VALUES OF VEGETABLE CROPS

KEY

CROP

Degree of difficulty to grow well and clean
E = Easy, M = Moderate, H = Hard

TIME

Amount of time needed to grow well and clean
Q = Quick, M = Moderate, L = Lengthy

COST

Cost compared with buying equivalent crop
C = Cheap, S = Same, M = More

VALUE

Ease and cost of growing from saved seed and offsets
C = Cheap, M = Moderate, D = Difficult

CROP	YIELD	GROW	TIME	COST	VALUE	CROP	YIELD	GROW	TIME	COST	VALUE
Beans, broad	8lb/3.6kg	E	Q	C	S	Garlic & shallots	8lb/3.6kg	E	Q	C	S
Beans, French	13lb/6kg	M	M	C	S	Kohlrabi	9lb/4kg	E	M	C	D
Beans, runner	20lb/9kg	E	M	C	S	Leeks	8lb/3.6kg	H	M	C	M
Beetroot	12lb/5.4kg	M	M	C	D	Lettuces	5lb/2.3kg	M	M	C	M
Broccoli	6lb/2.7kg	H	M	C	D	Onions	10lb/4.5kg	M	L	E	M
Brussels sprouts	8lb/3.6kg	H	M	C	D	Parsnips	9lb/4kg	M	M	E	M
Cabbages	10lb/4.5kg	E	M	C	D	Peas	6lb/2.7kg	E	M	S	S
Cauliflowers	8lb/3.6kg	H	M	C	D	Potatoes	20lb/9kg	E	M	S	S
Carrots	11lb/5kg	H	T	S	D	Radishes	6lb/2.7kg	M	Q	C	M
Celery	10lb/4.5kg	H	T	C	M	Spinach	8lb/3.6kg	M	L	C	M
Courgettes	10lb/4.5kg	E	Q	C	D	Sweet corn	5lb/2.3kg	E	M	C	D
Cucumbers, ridge	10lb/4.5kg	M	Q	S	D	Tomatoes	20lb/9kg	M	L	C	M
						Turnips & Swedes	10lb/4.5kg	M	M	S	D

Allocating space, planning and laying out

The vegetable plot needs careful positioning and laying out. Preferably, it should be in full sun with no overhanging trees, and as far away from trees, walls or hedges on its sunny side as practical. Wet boggy sites and low areas should be avoided, as they will cause winter losses and frost damage in spring, but may be ideal for summer salad crops, leeks and celery. The plot should be kept well away from big hedges, especially *Leylandii* and privet, which will steal any goodness. If you wish, these can be isolated by digging a slit trench, cutting the roots, and sealing out by setting them in a plastic sheet.

The plot should not be too far from the kitchen, a water point or the tool/potting shed. The most frequently used path is best hard-surfaced or gravelled to make it pleasanter to use in wet conditions.

Grass paths dividing up a plot are a serious error because they are difficult to keep cut and edged, and also encourage slugs and other pests, so consider replacing such paths with stepping stones.

Square or rectangular plots are best, as other shapes are harder work. The plot must be designed so that the rows or beds run in a direction that allows the sun to shine evenly on them and not cause dense shade behind taller crops. For this reason, a long rectangular plot is best running east to west, while short rows or beds should go north to south. If this means the plot is best aligned askew to the main garden, then surround it with triangular borders to make the whole square and disguise this with screens of fruit or low hedges. However, do not make these too tall or dense, as air must be able to circulate.

BELOW *The frame supported a fleece to keep the caterpillars away, now they've outgrown it, but their heads are secure.*

It is not that important which crop you follow with which, although some combinations can be less satisfactory. For example, potatoes do not happily follow brassicas or legumes if the soil was limed for them. Thus, for many reasons, roughly sticking to the cycle I've mentioned makes sense, but it is not gospel. What you need to take most care with is to ensure that potatoes are not returned to the same spot for as long as possible, that the brassicas are similarly kept away for as long as possible, and that the other vegetables do not return to their previous site from the year before.

Of course, the more elaborate your rotation and the longer the gaps, then the better the results. This is made easier if you grow more different crops in smaller amounts and if break crops, such as flowers, strawberries or artichokes, grow on the plot for a few years. Rotation is greatly facilitated if accurate records of what was grown where and when are kept. Keep a book or a card file and record not only the crop and its position, but also its variety, sowing dates and performance, as these will aid future planning.

Blocks, rows, raised and fixed beds are alternative ways of laying out crops. For those that need support, such as peas, then rows have the advantage. As mentioned before, these should run east to west for long rows or north to south for short. Rows are not essential, though, as you can grow beans and peas in a circle around a pole with strings tied to a wheel on top. Rows waste rather a lot of space with the paths between each of them, which then get compacted and require digging.

For most crops, especially those that are closely planted, such as carrots, block plantings are advantageous. Apart from saving space and reducing digging, it helps with weed control because, once the plants are half grown, their foliage meets and excludes light from the soil, choking out weed seedlings. This also forms a favourable microclimate and prevents moisture loss. Where netting or fleece is used to prevent pests reaching the plants, then rectangular block

Borders and beds around the main vegetable plot will be useful for the perennial crops, such as asparagus or artichokes, and for seed beds and nursery and salad beds which need even more intensive care than the main plot. In the smallest garden, choice is rarely possible and the best use has to be made of what is available. Thick mulches, deep digging, heavy feeding and cunning cropping can be used to squeeze more out of the smallest sunny space.

Rotation Provision for rotation is important (as is explained in Chapter 10). However, it is not necessary to divide the plot into four quarters, as shown in many books, then religiously follow the potatoes, legumes, brassicas and roots cycle. What is critical is that you don't follow year after year with the same crop, or its near relations, on the same ground, but move it around or leave it out entirely for a year or two.

*LEFT Feverfew, pot and French marigolds and evening primrose are encouraged in moderation as companions. **RIGHT** To be effective, fleece and net covers must be in place from the very start.*

planting is obviously convenient. Although row planting is easiest when very large areas are being cultivated, block planting in small beds is much more suitable for most gardens.

Raised beds are becoming popular but most of their advantages accrue from the fact that they are fixed beds. These are simply permanent sub-plots surrounded by narrow paths (packed soil is sufficient). As they are not walked on, they only need digging every seven or eight years and they make block planting easy. However, rows can still be run down the middle if they run north to south. The ideal width is about four feet, as it is comfortable to reach in two feet from either side. Make them no longer than, say, sixteen feet or there is the temptation to walk over rather than around them. Having permanently fixed beds makes record-keeping and, thus, rotation simple, and each bed can also be treated as a separate little plot.

Fixed beds slowly become raised beds naturally as mulches, compost and root residues build up. This raising reduces bending and also the surface area increases as the mulches spill over, allowing extra planting space and increasing aeration and evaporation. This gives an earlier start in the spring, as raised beds warm sooner and, in winter, the crops atop are in slightly warmer conditions because cold air runs off like water. However, raised beds also dry out more quickly in summer and mulches tend to slide or be pulled off by birds. Still, on the whole, their advantages outweigh their problems, especially if their shape is kept to the natural sine curve formed by slumping soil.

This then gives several useful microclimates. The south end is a hot slope suitable for early cropping and tender herbs, while the north end is permanently shaded and suits saladings and leaf crops. The sides are protected from the wind and thus, moist, suiting leeks, roots and saladings. The top is open ground but especially well suited to onions, shallots, brassicas and legumes as row crops and for overwintering vegetables.

LEFT *Good spacing is essential for everything.*

Raising the beds artificially with planks or bricks reduces the area available, removes many of the useful microclimates, and provides hiding places for pests. Paths of packed soil are sufficient but get muddy in the wet. Straw and other mulches harbour pests and are hard to weed. Sharp sand or crushed gravel paths are the best and it doesn't matter if, later, some gets mixed into the soil. Paths add up to one-fifth of your whole area in the vegetable plot and, although plant roots will easily utilise the soil, the surface should not be bare. With more summer droughts and decreasing water availability, prevent

BELOW *Bulk crops such as potatoes need to be grown in blocks for convenience.*

your paths losing water by covering them with either loose mulch or ground-cover fabric or similar. (Recycled nylon carpet lasts for decades and when it gets muddy or weedy you just turn it over.)

Extending the season Using a seed bed makes it easier to spread the harvesting period because when a crop is transplanted, it receives a slight check (and more so the bigger it has grown). Thus, if one sowing of, say, Brussels sprouts or lettuce is divided into three portions and then transplanted to their final positions at ten days apart, then each portion will mature at a slightly different time. Of course, for most vegetables, successive crops can also be ensured by sowing in several batches over weeks or months and by sowing different varieties that mature at different rates. The fastest are usually called earlies and tend to produce less than the slower maincrops. Of course, cloches and growing under cover can greatly extend the season (see Chapter 8).

BELOW *A decent pole has supported heavy crops of tomato plants all summer without failing, an improvement on canes.* **OPPOSITE LEFT** *Runner beans are easier sown late, not early.* **MIDDLE** *Courgettes are best taken small and often.* **RIGHT** *Take tomatoes as soon as they are ready.*

Catch cropping, intercropping and companion planting These are ways to get more out of a small plot, and are made easier if as many plants as possible are raised in seed beds or in pots. However, some crops, such as root vegetables, are best grown in situ and not transplanted. The idea is that many crops, especially the slower-growing ones, do not need all the space available to them all of the time.

- *Catch cropping* is using the quickest-growing crops, such as radishes, baby turnips and saladings, to fill in space before another crop is ready for planting or has grown very big.

- *Intercropping* means growing two crops together. It can also be used when a main crop has finished growing but is waiting to be harvested, such as with cabbages. Another crop can then be planted in between this and, when the main crop is removed, the new crop is already established and rapidly grows to fill the space made available. Care must be taken not to overdo this, as crowding gives poorer results. Crops will compete as badly as weeds unless the spacing and timing are well controlled.

- *Companion crops* are those that combine together well to give added benefits over simple intercropping. Care must be taken not to crowd plants but, as long as sufficient air, light, nutrients and water are available, some combinations of crops do particularly well together. For example, instead of three beds growing peas, potatoes and sweet corn respectively, I find that growing all three crops together on each of the three beds gives a total higher yield. The peas can provide shelter for the other young shoots, the potatoes keep the soil covered and moist, which the sweet corn and peas enjoy, while none shade out the others.

Most importantly, combining and mixing up crops significantly reduces damage from pests and diseases. I have found, for instance, that beetroot plants grown between swedes and parsnips do not get attacked by birds, while brassicas surrounded by French beans suffer far fewer pests. Most useful of all are French marigolds. These should be planted in every plot for their pest-confusing smell. Similarly, some annual herbs are beneficial when grown amongst crops, as their strong scents help hide the plants from the crops' pests. Perennial herbs, such as rosemary, thyme, sage, chives, southernwood, hyssop and lavender, are beneficial when confined to the edges of the plot. There, the scents are effective pest deterrents and their flowers bring in predators and pollinators.

GOOD AND BAD COMPANIONS FOR VEGETABLE CROPS

CROP	DOES WELL WITH	DOES BADLY WITH
Beans, broad & field	brassicas, carrot, celery, cucurbits, potatoes, summer savory, most herbs	onions & garlic
Beans, French	celery, cucurbits, potatoes, strawberries, sweet corn	onions & garlic
Beans, runner	sweet corn, summer savory	beetroot, chards & kohlrabi
Beetroot & chards	most beans, brassicas, onions & garlic, kohlrabi, parsnips, swedes	runner beans
Brassicas, cabbage family	beetroot, chards, celery, dill, nasturtiums, onions & garlic, peas, potatoes	runner beans, strawberries
Carrots	chives, leeks, lettuce, onions & garlic, peas, tomatoes	dill
Celery & celeriac	brassicas, beans, leek, tomatoes	
Cucurbits	beans, nasturtium, peas, sweet corn	potatoes
Leeks	carrots, celery, onions	
Lettuce	carrots, cucurbits, radish, strawberries, chervil	
Onions & garlic	beetroot & chards, lettuce, strawberries, summer savory, tomatoes	beans, peas
Peas	beans, carrots, cucurbits, sweet corn, turnips, potatoes	onions & garlic
Potatoes	beans, brassicas, peas, sweet corn	tomatoes, cucurbits
Sweet corn	beans, cucurbits, peas, potatoes	
Sweet & chilli peppers	basil	kohlrabi, radishes
Sunflowers	cucurbits, nasturtiums	potatoes, runner beans, grass
Tomatoes	asparagus, basil, carrots, brassicas, onions & garlic, parsley	kohlrabi, potatoes
Turnips & swedes	peas, broad beans	

Culinary herbs and saladings

Perennial herbs are the most valuable crops as they are undemanding, yet attractive and useful. They are the easiest of plants to grow organically, as most are rarely bothered by pests and diseases. What's more, they even suppress weeds. Once often used for medicinal purposes, they are still health giving and many are bactericidal. Indeed, most herbs are packed full of vitamins and minerals and make tasty additions to salads and cooking.

Most herbs have good foliage, making them easier to incorporate in ornamental areas than vegetables, and many are also good companion plants with beneficial effects on other plants. Furthermore, in summers with droughts and hosepipe bans, you can pick a succulent salad almost solely from herbs growing in soil that would be too dry for most vegetables (see page 153). Lettuce is certainly not the only salad base; many bland herbs and annual leafy crops are more tasty and succulent, and these are well worth cultivating.

These culinary herbs and saladings have been grouped as perennial and annual, as they benefit from being grown apart. Most perennials are happiest grown in their own sunny bed, as edging companions to fruit, borders and vegetable beds, or as permanent features in ornamental areas. The annuals are better grown as salad vegetables in their own bed or planted out amongst sturdier vegetables. Some gourmet saladings I rate highly are thus dealt with early on with the annual herbs and salads, amongst which I suggest they should be grown, rather than later with the vegetables where they are usually found in the garden. Latin names are given in the following lists only where it may help to get the right plant!

Perennial herbs Most perennial herbs will tolerate, and often prefer, drier, poorer soils than annual herbs. Many come from the Mediterranean region and need some shelter or a cloche to get through our worst winters. It is the combination of damp and cold which kills them, so growing them against a wall is usually sufficient help. Almost all need little maintenance, apart from cutting back dead, overgrown and excessive growth.

The majority are best bought as young plants rather than grown from seed. Also, many are very easily gained from cuttings or by dividing existing plants. Do not divide or move most herbs during autumn or winter. Buy and plant up a new herb bed during spring so that if there has been a hard winter, the nurseryman lost the plants, not you. It is the tender young tips and leaves we use for the most part, so cutting back most herbs each spring removes withered growths and produces a flush of new shoots. Leave pruning until spring so that the old growth protects the new against bad weather. Care needs to be taken not to cut back too far or the plant may die – go no further than where live green shoots emerge from older wood.

MUST-HAVE PERENNIAL HERBS

The following are grown mostly for their leaves:

Bay, *Laurus nobilis*, is a rather tender shrub that suffers from harsh winds while small and is easily lost. However, once established, it becomes a tough, medium-sized tree. It can be grown in tubs and taken under cover in winter, but is then more prone to pests, especially scale. Bay is difficult to propagate and expensive to buy. Use the leaves in savoury dishes, especially with tomatoes and garlic. I find carefully dried leaves taste better than fresh ones. The leaves preserve grains and seeds from weevils, but the burning leaves are allegedly poisonous to us as well as to insects.

Chives can be started from seed or any bits taken from the side of existing clumps. They benefit from being divided every other year, so can be multiplied rapidly. Left to flower, they benefit beneficial insects and are pretty, but self-seed and give less useful leaves. I cut back alternate plants hard. Chives belong to the *Allium* genus and are probably the best to grow to keep fungal diseases down; use them against blackspot on roses and scab on apples in large patches underneath, but be patient as it takes three years for this to have an effect. They discourage aphids on chrysanthemums, sunflowers and tomatoes, and benefit carrots. Also, chive sprays have been used against downy and powdery mildew on cucumbers and gooseberries. Add chives to savoury dishes, especially with cheese, and put loads in salads.

BELOW *Chives make good edgings outdoors and undercover.* **OPPOSITE** *Chives can be started from seed or by division.*

Fennel is a large herbaceous plant with an aniseed flavour. The leaves go well with savoury fish and cheese dishes and are also good in salads. The plant is upright and stately, so can be grown in ornamental areas, the bronze form being particularly attractive. Propagate the green from seed or both by division in spring. Keep fennel away from tomatoes, caraway and dill. It self-seeds viciously unless you deadhead in time! Fennel attracts hoverflies and predatory wasps, and may deter aphids. The foliage feeds larvae of the Swallow-tail butterflies and Mouse moths.

Horseradish, *Armoracia rusticana,* is hard to eradicate once established and any bit of the root will grow vigorously anywhere. Horseradish accumulates calcium, potassium and sulphur. In the USA, a tea made from horseradish has been used against brown rot in apples and against blister beetles and Colorado beetles. Horseradish is traditionally grown with potatoes (here and in China!). However, as it is almost impossible to get rid of, it is best confined to plastic perforated

bags half buried in the potato bed. The grated root can be used in minute amounts on salads or mixed with garlic, chilli, mustard and cider vinegar to make a warming sauce. The foliage feeds larvae of the Green-veined White butterfly and Garden Carpet moth.

Lavender is rarely used in cooking nowadays, but has such a lovely flavour that everyone should try it once with rice pudding – and lavender biscuits are heavenly. There are large and small varieties to suit any garden with a sunny spot.

Lovage, *Levisticum officinale,* is a big herbaceous plant that towers way above head height. It needs moist soil and is propagated by root division or seed. It's believed to aid most other plants by its (not too close) presence. The leaves are used moderately in salads and for giving a rich flavour to savoury dishes, in which it is claimed to be a substitute for salt. It also adds body to vegetable stocks. The stems can be eaten raw, if blanched tender like celery, and the seed used with baked products and in salads.

Lemon verbena, *Lippia citriodora* **or** *Aloysia triphylla,* has an exquisite, lemon-sherbet scent kept by the dried leaves for many years. It's a lovely flavour for salads, fruit salads, sweet dishes and teas. It is not very hardy and is killed above ground by hard frosts, so plant against a warm wall and protect the roots from damp and cold. Easily grown from cuttings, it can be kept in a pot and overwintered under cover, or as a houseplant, but it is then prone to aphids and red spider mite.

Marjoram and oregano both have many varieties, all of which are similar to oregano and essential for Italian food. The leaves can be added to salads, but the flavour goes exceptionally well with savoury dishes. Marjoram has a good flavour when fresh, dried or frozen and can be grown in a pot under cover for winter use. Propagate by seed for the best-flavoured ones grown as annuals and by root division for the tougher perennials. These latter are nearly as tasty and are useful as informal edging or under fruit trees and bushes. There is a particularly attractive golden form that turns buttercream yellow in summer and reverts to green in winter. In flower, these attract many bees and butterflies. The foliage feeds larvae of White Point, Lace Border (also fed by thyme), Mullein Wave, Lewes Wave, Sub-angled Wave, Green Carpet, Black-veined Moth, Shaded Pug and Wormwood Pug, and the flowers feed the Double-striped Pug.

Mints loves rich moist soil and is more than somewhat invasive. To minimise their expansionist tendency, NEVER put them in with other herbs as their roots interpenetrate everything. Grow in pots almost sub-merged in the soil or in beds surrounded by concrete or regularly cut grass. It is one of the few plants to grow under walnuts and they thrive near stinging nettles and aid cabbage and tomatoes before overwhelming them. The odour can be used to repel rodents, clothes'

moths, fleas and flea beetles, while spearmint discourages aphids by discouraging their 'owners', the ants. Mints are famous for sauces and teas, and go well in salads. Best used fresh, they can be potted up for winter under cover. Cool, refreshingly scented forms, such as 'Eau de Cologne' and 'Spearmint', suit ornamental areas, as do golden and silver variegated, and yellow, grey and curly forms, which are mostly less vigorous. Mints make low-maintenance ground cover for large areas and their late flowering is attractive to bees and beneficial insects. The foliage feeds larvae of Orange moths.

Rose petals are wonderful in salads! They can also be used with apple, milk dishes and baked products. See the ornamental section on page 52 for their cultivation. Highly recommended is the thornless 'Zéphirine Drouhin', which smells and tastes divine.

Rosemary is not very hardy, but usually survives if given a warm spot against a wall. It will grow in a pot under cover. Easily propagated from cuttings in spring, it is loved by bees. Delicious with almost all savoury dishes, the leaves and the flowers go well in salads.

Sage is the traditional stuffing herb but also goes well, in moderation, in salads and with savoury dishes. The more compact, multicoloured sages are not very hardy. Easily grown from cuttings or seed, sage needs

OPPOSITE LEFT *Remove most of the flower buds to ensure more fresh leaves.* **OPPOSITE RIGHT** *Go on, put it in some rice pudding.* **BELOW LEFT** *Horseradish is hard to dig next to a tree but can be grown up into a pot of compost.* **BELOW MIDDLE** *Horseradish is better when grown up into a bucket of compost.* **BELOW RIGHT** *The true Lemon verbena, if you don't yet know it then please get some.*

TOP LEFT *Red sage is said to be good for the memory, or was it… * **TOP RIGHT** *Sweet cicely, especially the flowers, are a superb salad ingredient.* **BOTTOM LEFT** *Real French tarragon is nice, the other is horrid.* **BOTTOM RIGHT** *Thymes buzz with bees and are so nice to sniff.*

replacing every few years as it gets straggly and resents pruning. The foliage feeds the larvae of Grey Chi, and Bordered Straw eats the flowers and seeds.

Sweet cicely, *Myrrhis odorata,* has aniseed- or liquorice-tasting leaves, like chervil, and is excellent in salads. The stems, seeds and roots can also be cooked. The plant is very decorative, and sweet, I chew stems and flowers for refreshment on drying days.

Winter savory Summer savory tastes better, but this is shrubbier and survives most winters. Small amounts improve salads, the flavour of beans, and the smell of cooking brassicas. It grows easily from seed, is small and compact, and will crop most of the year, and longer in a pot under cover.

Tarragon Do not confuse the real French with the poor Russian. Taste the leaves: the French is sweet and piquant, the Russian tastes rank and sour. Unfortunately, the hardier Russian comes from seed and root division, and is common. The French needs a warm spot, extra protection from cold damp, and is only propagated by root division – which it needs every third year or it dies out! Tarragon flavours vinegar and is wonderful with eggs and fish.

Thymes are wonderful; they all smell divine and can be used in salads and all savoury dishes. The bees love thyme and it is low-growing, so goes well under fruit trees and bushes if it's sunny enough. Thyme comes in varied scents, colours and forms, and will thrive in poor, dry, sunny situations and lime-rich soils. Try the caraway-flavoured *Thymus herba-barona.* The foliage is the only known food for larvae of the Large Blue butterfly (which, after their last moult, may predate ant larvae), and the Thyme Pug is only known to eat thyme flowers and seeds. The foliage is one of two plants to feed larvae of Lace Border (also fed by *Origanum*) and the Pinion-streaked Snout. And it is one of three plants to feed larvae of Dotted-Border Wave, Light Feathered Rustic, Ashworth's Rustic, Sussex Emerald, Lewes Wave, Annulet and Straw Belle, while V Pug larvae eat thyme flowers.

PERENNIAL HERBS TO GROW IF YOU HAVE THE SPACE

Again, these are utilised mostly for their leaves.

Angelica is a large, tough, but short-lived, self-seeding herbaceous plant that likes shady, rich, moist soil. The stems are preserved candied in sugar syrup. Adding angelica and sweet cicely stems to rhubarb removes the tartness and makes it sweeter. The blooms of wild angelica are visited by 30 species of insect, while the foliage feeds larvae of the Swallow-tail butterfly, and the flowers and/or seeds feed the larvae of Triple-spotted Pug, White-spotted Pug and V Pug.

Bergamot, *Monarda didyma,* is a neat, knee- to waist-high herbaceous plant that thrives on moist soil, and its scarlet or purple flowers make it well suited to ornamental areas. The aromatic leaves and flowers produce a calming drink once sold as Oswego tea. A few petals can add vibrant colour to salads. Divide the clump to propagate the variety; this is worth doing and replanting every third year, anyway.

Citrus Although there is little hope of producing fruit (within a decade), it is worth growing citrus seedlings for the tasty young leaves alone. Finely sliced and in moderation, they give a wonderful tang to salads. These are best sown thickly in a pot and need taking indoors for the cold months.

Dandelion is surprisingly health giving when eaten and does not necessarily cause nocturnal problems. As it is bitter, it is best blanched first by covering the heads with a flowerpot a week or so beforehand. Fry the blanched leaves with bacon! Dandelion blooms attract over 90 different insect species: 7 butterflies and moths, 58 species of bee, 21 species of diptera flies and 7 other, unfortunately including the pesky Mangold Fly, while the foliage sustains the larvae of over two-dozen butterflies and moths.

BELOW *Mint is so invasive yet useful and the flowers are good for insects.*

Good King Henry, Lincolnshire asparagus, *Chenopodium bonus-henricus,* is a vigorous self-seeder and highly nutritious. The leaves and shoots can be eaten like asparagus or spinach, or used in moderation in salads. The foliage feeds larvae of Nutmeg and Orache, and Dark Spinach and Plain Pug larvae eat the flowers and seeds.

Hyssop is a sun-loving perennial and a superb bee plant that makes lovely honey. Supposedly, hyssop benefits grapevines and is helpful against the cabbage butterfly, but radishes do badly near it. The young leaves can be added to salads or to any rich savoury food, but the flavour is strong, bitter and hot, so use with care. Propagate hyssop from cuttings, root division or seed.

Lemon balm, *Melissa officinalis,* resembles a mint as it has the same tendency to spread, though not by root but by seed. Compact and dense-growing, it excludes weeds wherever it is planted and will flourish almost anywhere you choose to put it. It has a refreshing, clean, lemon scent. Although lemon balm can be used in salads, soups and teas, it doesn't taste as good as it smells. In flower, it is beloved by bees. Lemon balm is easily propagated by root division.

Rue is poisonous and an irritant, especially in hot weather. It was once used sparingly to flavour food, especially cheese, but I cannot recommend this. However, rue is a beautiful plant, easily grown from cuttings or seed.

Sorrel, *Rumex acetosa,* is easy to grow, spinach-like and can be used like spinach or in soups and salads if you like sour flavours. It likes moist, lightly shaded soil and tends to spread; grow it from seed or root divisions and replant every few years. The foliage feeds larvae of Brown-Spot Pinion, Sweet-Gale, Knot Grass, Small Copper and Plain Clay.

Watercress is easy if you have clean, running water, though it is possible to get crops with only a trickle available down a water trough. It can be grown in mud, but then makes much poorer stuff. It's best in a clean gravel with sparkling, aerated, lime-rich water. The watercress sold in shops can often be rooted; it bolts and reseeds, but is best when regularly replaced by cuttings.

LEFT *Most herbs are well suited to growing in pots.*

Annual herbs and salads

Most annual herbs are best started off sown in situ in mid-spring. They resent transplanting, although are easier to manage if started in small pots or cells like vegetables. Pot them up, if necessary, then harden them off and plant out after the last frost. If sowing direct, mark out and station-sow as for vegetables, but for most annual herbs, there is no necessity to sow or thin to one plant per site. Sow most annuals fairly shallowly; after sowing, cover with clean potting compost, press in a cane to mark the site, and then firm down well. A label aids later identification. With most, the flavour is ruined by the onset of flowering, so successional small sowings are a good idea. The younger shoots and leaves are the more tender, and most herbs become more succulent with adequate moisture. They all grow lusher in a richer soil, though this may spoil their flavour – some exceptions will be noted.

ANNUAL HERBS BEST SOWN FREQUENTLY THROUGHOUT THE YEAR

These are used mostly for their leaves and best sown in batches, often throughout the year.

Chervil will grow in shade, needs moisture and loathes transplanting, like parsley. It's easier to grow, though, with a milder, subtle flavour. It may keep aphids off lettuces. Sow thickly in situ from late winter till autumn. Chervil will self-seed if left to flower, but if the plants are cut down beforehand, they often produce new crops of fresh foliage. Very highly recommended, chervil enhances other flavours best when raw or only slightly cooked. The wild plant blooms were recorded as being visited by 73 species of insect, and the flowers feed larvae of the Double-striped Pug.

Dill has a fresh, clean flavour. The leaves and seeds are added to pickles, sauces, cheese, salads and fish dishes. Sow dill in pots or in situ. If left to grow waist-high, it flowers and attracts hoverflies. Dill allegedly attracts bees. It's not liked by carrots, but aids cabbages and may help lettuce, onions, sweet corn and cucumber as it repels aphids and spider mites. It appears to hybridise with fennel! The blooms are visited by 46 species of insect.

Land cress resembles watercress, but grows almost anywhere, even in window boxes if kept moist, and gives a peppery flavour to salads. Surface-sow in situ and keep cutting back.

Purslane, *Portulaca oleracea,* is an infuriating plant as it is hard to grow from seed, but self-seeds happily. Useful as a salad crop, it needs to be grown quickly and kept cut back hard for flushes of the young succulent shoots. Get fresh seed and sow it on the surface of a layer of sterile compost on top of the soil where it is to grow. If you succeed, let it flower and seed, then it will appear everywhere. It's the richest plant source of omega oils.

Radishes can be sown in situ anywhere, a few seeds at a time, every week from spring to autumn. They're very quick, but definitely not nice unless eaten young and tender, as they get too hot. If ordinary radishes are allowed to go to flower, they are good for beneficial insects and then produce pods that are tasty and nutritious while still small. The variety 'Munchen Bier' was developed for that purpose. The Black Spanish and Japanese radishes are sown after mid-summer and are more like turnips than radishes, so treat them as such.

Rocket, *Eruca* subsp. *sativa*, has spicy peppery leaves and the flowers add interest to salads. It tastes best when grown quickly in moist conditions. Cut back for new flushes. Sow often and thickly. Rocket is prone to flea beetle but, otherwise, has no problems. Sow instead of radishes because it is the best salading.

ANNUAL HERBS AND SALADINGS (SOWN ONCE OR TWICE A YEAR)

Basil is one of the tastiest herbs, going well with tomatoes, with which it also grows happily, and these make a trio with asparagus. It has been sprayed as an emulsion against asparagus beetle and used as a trap plant for aphids. There are purple-leaved, tiny-leaved and lemon-flavoured versions, as well as the usual sweet basil. Use basil leaves in salads, with cheese and with garlic in every tomato dish. Freeze and dry any surplus for winter, as this is, sadly, a very tender plant. Start basil off in pots in the warm and grow alongside tomatoes or peppers. Watch out for aphids and cut the plants back before flowering.

ABOVE AND OVERLEAF *Dill and coriander are easy seed crops and can be grown for their leaf and seed.*

Claytonia, winter purslane or miner's lettuce, is a potential weed as it seeds and comes up everywhere. However, it grows well, even in mid-winter, under cover on any soil. It's tasty in salads; all the leaves, stalks and flowers are edible. Surface-sow anywhere and thin if you wish. Let it self-seed, as you will want perpetual supplies, and give it shady, moist, rich conditions for lush growth. You'll like it, chickens love it and children will eat it.

Corn salad, lamb's lettuce, is a useful winter salad crop, best grown under cover to keep the weather and dirt off the leaves. It can be sown direct or in pots from spring until mid-autumn, spaced a finger or so apart. Left to flower, it resembles small forget-me-nots and self-seeds. Pick leaves rather than the whole plant.

LEFT *Basil is not easy outdoors, it prefers warmth under cover.* CENTRE *Sow a series of batches of mixed salad leaves, as these are sweeter when young.* RIGHT *Miner's lettuce, Claytonia, is a must have – try it.*

Iceplant, *Mesembryanthemum crystallinum,* makes excellent ground cover for barren, hot, dry sites. The leaves can be used in salads or cooked like spinach. Sow in pots and plant out in early summer. It has a peculiar texture and strange taste.

Lettuces and endives are amongst the easiest crops to grow well, yet are often badly grown. Never sow a lot of seed at once but, preferably, in batches in a seed bed and planted out later. However, the best way is to use multi-celled packs. Sow a few cells each of several varieties every few weeks through most of the year. Thin to one plant per cell and plant out as catch and intercrops, putting them in as you pull other plants out. They do best amongst cucumbers, carrots, radishes and strawberries, but may not prosper near broccoli. Lettuce can be partly protected from aphids by growing chervil nearby. Their root aphid overwinters as eggs on poplar trees, later infesting the leaf stalks and forming galls that split in mid-summer when the aphids move on to lettuce. Anthocorid bugs destroy these galls and reduce the pest numbers.

If it is hot, sow lettuce in the shade, as they will not germinate if very warm. Lettuce has been shown to take up natural antibiotics from the soil. Birds need keeping off with black cotton and use slug controls. Water thoroughly to avoid slow growth, which makes the leaves bitter. Salad bowl and cutting varieties are not uprooted but eaten on a cut-and-come-again basis. Cos lettuces are tall and need tying up for blanching to avoid bitterness. During winter, grow lettuces under cover to protect them from the weather and hungry creatures.

Endives are grown like lettuce, but must be blanched or they are too bitter. They can also be cropped on a cut-and-come-again basis. Sow from early summer or, better still,

a foot apart from early summer to autumn. Late crops need a cloche or cold frame to protect their growth. They benefit from a moist, rich soil and slugs may cause problems.

Parsley is very nutritious and is used in countless dishes, as well as a garnish and salading. It is biennial, so flowers in the second year. Let it go to seed, as self-sown plants are always best. Sow soaked seed on the soil surface and hardly cover the seed. Sow once in spring, and again in autumn, for two years and then use self-sown seedlings. Thin plants for seed to one per foot. It will revel in rich moist conditions and will stand moderate shade. Parsley freezes and dries well, and plants can be dug up, potted and moved under cover or cloched for fresh winter leaves. The bigger, continental, flat-leaved variety has more flavour than our common curly-leaved form. The foliage feeds larvae of the Mouse moth.

Shungiku is a decorative chrysanthemum that's edible and rich in vitamin C. It is also a good companion plant, keeping pests away. Used like pak choi and as chop-suey greens, it has a strong flavour and gets bitter once flowering. However, the flower petals are good in salads. Very tough and easy to grow, sow direct from late winter to autumn or sow in pots under cover.

Summer savory is traditionally grown and used with broad beans. The tips are tasty in salads and it adds a lovely flavour to savoury dishes. Do not allow it to flower or the flavour goes. Sow direct or shallowly in pots; it can be dug up and potted for winter use under cover, but dries perfectly well anyway.

ABOVE *Herbs start to lose flavour as they come into flower, so pick early.*

start them in cells like lettuce. Lettuces, especially the wild form, sustain several of the more pestilential larvae. Roots feed the Small (Garden) Swift Moth, roots and leaves feed the Great Yellow Underwing Moth, foliage the Grey Chi and Shark, and flowers and seeds are eaten by Broad-barred White and Small Ranunculus.

Mustard and cress are the easiest of all saladings and quicker than rocket. Just sow densely in short rows on the flat, any day of the year. Spray water gently on, then cover each batch of seed with a clean mat. Once the seed has germinated well, remove the mat and cut with scissors when two inches high; they don't regrow.

Pak choi, leaf mustards and Chinese greens, are fast-growing, pest- and disease-resistant additions to dishes: raw in salads and cooked in stir-fries. These are highly productive and can be cropped as cut-and-come-again. Sow in pots or direct, then thin to just less than

VEGETABLES SUITABLE FOR SALAD BEDS

Celery is difficult so, unless you have a rich, constantly moist soil, grow celeriac instead. Celery must never dry out, is prone to bolting, and suffers from slug damage. It needs careful blanching; self-blanching types are hardly such and tougher textured. Swiss chard gives a superior stem for braising and is easier to grow, so substitute this for celery and add other flavourings. However, celery does well with beans, tomatoes and leeks, and benefits brassicas by deterring cabbage white butterflies. If left to flower, celery and leeks will attract many beneficial insects, especially predatory wasps.

Ideally, sow celery thinly on the surface in tiny pots or cells in early spring in a propagator. It is difficult to sow individually, so thin early and pot up into bigger pots before planting out about a foot apart in trenches, under plastic bottles or cloches in early summer. They must never be allowed to dry out. Once the plants are three-quarters grown, remove poor leaves and surround each plant with newspaper collars and earth them up to blanch them – take precautions against slugs and do not believe claims of self-blanching types. If you only want celery flavour from the leaves, then sow it direct and thick like parsley and let it self-seed.

Alternatively, grow celeriac instead. Started the same as celery, it requires the same moist rich soil but is more forgiving, easier to grow and no blanching is needed. The peeled root is used grated raw, braised or in other ways where celery flavour is required. Strip off the lower leaves as the root starts to swell, and store once mature in a cool, frost-free place. Discourage celery rust with a tea made of nettles and *Equisetum*. The foliage of the wild form feeds larvae of the Swallow-tail butterfly.

Chicory produces heads like a bitter lettuce and is grown the same way; they may be solid, or round and looser. The popular dark red Radicchio (Rossa de Verona) adds colour and a subtle bitterness to salads. This is sown direct, or started in cells like lettuce, and planted out in early summer. However, some varieties of chicory, such as 'Brussels Witloof', can also be left unharvested until late autumn, when the roots are lifted with the foliage cut off and stored in a cool place. Then, when wanted, they are packed in sand in a box and kept in a warm dark place where they start to produce solid shoots called chicons. These, finely sliced, are a superb addition to winter salads. If not lifted, chicory may overwinter and produce early leaves for cutting before bolting. The root can be roasted and ground to make a coffee substitute. The foliage feeds larvae of Feathered Footman and Feathered Brindle, and flowers and seeds, the Marbled Clover.

Chinese cabbage must be sown in situ, a foot or so apart in rich moist soil, or it will quickly bolt, as do most varieties sown before mid-summer. In dry conditions, Chinese cabbages suffer from flea beetle before they bolt and are eaten by slugs in wet conditions. New varieties may just do sown before mid-summer, but most only do well sown from soon after until mid-autumn – later sowings need cloching.

Florence fennel is similar to celery with an aniseed flavour, and is considerably easier. It is best sown early or mid-summer, in situ or in cells, then planted out when very small, a foot or so apart. Do not let the plants ever dry out or they bolt, as will many early sowings. The leaf can be used as fennel and, if the swollen bulb is cut off above the root, it resprouts.

Garlic is the most pungent of the onion family and an effective accumulator of sulphur, which may explain its ancient reputation as a fungicide. Garlic emulsion has also been used against aphids, carrot root fly, onion fly, codling moths and snails, and peach leaf curl. As a companion plant, it is especially good for roses and fruit trees. Keep garlic away from beans and peas, although it may follow them in rotation.

Plant cloves in autumn for the biggest yields (but not too shallow or too deep). The holes should be between an inch or two deep, and at least a foot apart. Fill in afterwards with gritty, sandy compost and firm well. Garlic can be planted until late spring, but the earlier the better. Dig the crop up before the leaves totally wither and blow

BELOW *Let onions fall down naturally, don't help as this may let in neck rot.*

and tough. 'Purple Vienna' is easily available, but far better is 'Superschmelz' which, given space, can get very big and still remain crisp and tender.

Spinach For those who want the real thing, sow in situ from early spring until late summer, although you can start spinach in cells or pots if planted out while still very small. It is worth feeding the soil beforehand with ground seaweed or sieved compost, as this crop needs moist rich conditions or it bolts. Protect the plants from birds with black cotton, use slug traps and never allow them or the plants to dry out. Growing spinach through a plastic mulch keeps the soil off the leaves, as well as aiding growth. Round seeded spinaches are the best for summer and, for winter and early spring, use prickly seeded spinaches. Sow them similarly, but during late summer. Cloches will keep the weather from messing up the leaves, but may encourage mildew. New Zealand spinach is another non-spinach grown in the same way, but is far better in hot dry conditions and more reluctant to bolt. It needs twice the space, at up to two foot apart, and is convenient if started in pots.

away. Dry them in a warm, airy place. If you fail to dig any garlic bulbs, they will show their position when they sprout. Then they can be dug up, split and replanted for the next crop. Rocambole garlic is similar, smaller bulbed and more disease-resistant, producing an edible cluster of bulbils in place of seeds.

ABOVE *Well I did it the once – but then I couldn't break the string up for use, so now it's gone over…* RIGHT *Kohlrabi need a makeover, they've got potential.*

Kohlrabi A tough, disease-resistant crop, this is like a turnip but easier and not as hot. Do not grow with brassicas, tomatoes, strawberries, peppers or runner beans, but mix with onions, beets and ridge cucumber. Kohlrabi looks odd but is easy, highly nutritious and immune to most pests and diseases. It can be cooked, but is best used raw, grated or as crudité sticks. It will grow in relatively poor conditions and, unlike turnips, can be transplanted from a seed bed, cells or pots. Sow in succession from mid-spring to mid-summer. Eat kohlrabi before it gets large

ANNUAL HERBS USED MOSTLY FOR THEIR FLOWERS

Borage is one of the best bee plants, a good accumulator of minerals for compost and grows well with strawberries. The flowers add colour to beverages and salads. Sow in situ, thin to a foot or so apart, and then allow to self-seed. Kept renovated with occasional trimming, the plants can be in flower most of late spring and summer. Not only is it a useful green manure, but it also makes a rich liquid feed and the foliage feeds larvae of Queen of Spain Fritillary, Crimson-speckled and Bright Wave moths.

Nasturtiums are edible in all parts. The flowers make colourful additions to salads, while the young leaves add piquancy. Pickle the seeds and pods as a better substitute for capers. Sow after the last frost in a moist place, or in pots, and grow at a foot apart. Do not overfeed or there will be few flowers.

Pot marigolds, *Calendula,* have edible flower petals (do not try French or African marigolds). Use the petals freely in salads and with seafood; they are surprisingly good in stews. Sow in pots or direct any time, at a foot each way, and let them self-seed. The flowers and seeds feed larvae of the Bordered Straw, and the foliage feeds the Cabbage moth.

Sunflowers are usually grown for their seeds, but the petals are bittersweet and the young heads can be eaten while in bud, like globe artichokes. For good heads, sow in early spring and give each plant at least a foot each way.

TOP LEFT *Pot marigold petals are okay fresh in salads, but try them flavouring a beef and vegetable stew – mmmm.* TOP RIGHT *Try Nasturtium flowers with shrimps and mayonnaise, another mmmm.* BOTTOM LEFT *Borage flowers go pink as they age.* BOTTOM RIGHT *More edible bits than you'd guess.*

ANNUAL HERBS GROWN FOR THEIR SEEDS

All these give bigger crops per plant if given enough space, say a foot each way. However, the total yield is safer if they are crowded a bit, so sow a hand width or so apart each way.

Anise, *Pimpinella anisum*, is a pungent, annual herb often used in ointments against insects, their bites and stings. A host plant to predatory wasps, it deters aphids. The flavour goes well with sweet and savoury foods; the leaves are used fresh and the seed dried. Sow in warm soil after the last frost.

Caraway is sometimes difficult to establish and takes one and a half years to crop, so it is best sown in situ in early summer, or autumn if fresh seed is available. The feathery leaves are sometimes used in salads and savoury dishes, the tiny pungent seed likewise – the latter is good on baked products, too.

Blossoms have been recorded as being visited by 55 species of insect and the foliage sustains larvae of the Swallow-tail butterfly.

Coriander seeds were once used a great deal. Often added to bread or baked dishes, they give a warm spicy flavour that improves almost every dish or salad. Nowadays, the leaves are also, if not more, popular. Coriander repels aphids and has been used as a spray against spider mites. Sow thickly in situ in late spring for the leaf; thin to a hand's width apart for the seed.

Cumin seeds provide a curry flavour and need to be dried well to keep (they can also be used like black pepper). Station-sow in early summer, at a finger or so apart, and support the plants with sticks to stop the seed-heads falling over and getting dirty. Black cumin is seed of *Nigella sativa*. The closely related *N. damascena* seeds, love-in-a-mist, are also edible in moderation. Both have a spicy, aromatic flavour that is pleasant, especially with spicy, sweet, sticky buns. Sow in spring in situ.

Poppies, *Papaver somniferum*, have been grown for their seed and use on baked products for as long as they have been grown for opium. They are a weed and self-sow wildly. Give them full sun and after flowering pick the ripe heads before they shed. Growing for opium is, of course, illegal but I believe you can still grow poppies for seed in the UK. The number required for home baking are only a few dozen heads. Although loved by bees for pollen, they have no nectar. The foliage of the native red poppy feeds larvae of the Bright Wave moth.

LEFT *Ornamental opium poppy seed can be used on baked products, as it contains none of the drug.*
OPPOSITE *Pop over a paper bag held in place with a clothes peg to catch the seed when it ripens.*

Vegetables

This section deals with the individual needs and uses of each vegetable to help you produce crops for normal household consumption organically with the least effort. I have given sowing periods, but these are only guidelines as they vary according to area and season. The depths given for sowing are maximums, planting distances are for vegetables grown in blocks to optimum size but, again, these may be varied tremendously depending on whether you want small, young or larger growing specimens. Seed packets carry sufficient instructions for larger and smaller varieties and distances for row planting.

Despite the loss of most old varieties, there are still many to choose from. Although I recommend those I have found good for flavour, new ones come along constantly and it is worth trying different varieties to see what suits your soil, situation and taste.

I have also expressed an opinion on whether it is worthwhile growing crops, depending on its culinary value, reliability, effort required and space taken. The perennial vegetables are given first, as they offer the best value all round. The legumes are rated the next most valuable group, as they also create soil fertility. They are followed by alliums, roots, brassicas, cucurbits and others – with potatoes last, as they are a lot of work compared with the cost of a sack of organic ones.

PERENNIAL VEGETABLES

Asparagus is a luxury crop and expensive to buy, but the home-grown is so much sweeter. One of the lily family, asparagus takes time to build up large enough resources to throw good thick spears; three years, usually, before it becomes productive. Yields, however, are best in full sun in a permanent bed on its own with lots of space. Asparagus rarely suffers from pests and diseases, though the beetle can be troublesome, or rather the small slug-like larvae which are easily controlled with soft soap.

Grow asparagus under fruit trees and grapes to save space. It grows well with basil and tomatoes – the latter hides it from the asparagus beetle, while a root secretion from asparagus kills *Trichodorus*, a nematode that attacks tomato roots. Parsley does well with asparagus, but onions and possibly other alliums are disliked. Sow in situ or otherwise get one-year-old crowns to plant as early as possible in spring. Plant the fleshy roots on a mound in a trench at a good stride apart each way. Do not take a spear until three years from planting and never after the start of summer. Likewise, never remove the ferny foliage until it's dried up. Darken the soil with soot and do not mulch if you want the earliest spears; you can force plants with cloches.

Epicurean attentions Green asparagus has more flavour than white blanched spears, but may be bitter if not fresh. Steaming is best for home-picked asparagus; boil shop-bought asparagus with salted water to remove any bitterness.

Bob's gourmet choices New all-male hybrids are offered that do not waste energy producing seed. Otherwise, there is little to choose between varieties; I prefer female plants as they give thicker, more succulent spears. 'Gijnlim F1' is polyploidal (which means it has an extra set of chromosomes) and produces very thick spears.

Seakale is rarely grown, despite being mostly unaffected by pests and diseases and providing a tasty crop in early spring. Ideally, get planting 'thongs' of a good, long-selected local variety. Sadly, only 'Lily White' is usually available, so alternatively sow in a seed bed and grow the best plants on for a year. Transplant them to their permanent position, a stride apart, in late winter and grow them on till autumn. Put bottomless buckets over the crowns during dry weather and fill a foot deep with a mixture of peat or leaf mould and sand. When the shoots appear in spring, remove the bucket and filling, and cut the blanched shoots and head off at ground level. Left to sprout and grow, the root and crown will crop for many years.

Epicurean attentions Steam the cleaned shoots for three quarters of an hour and serve with a Hollandaise sauce or butter for a luxury treat. If the bitter flavour is too much, then boil instead of steam and change the water twice.

Rhubarb is the first 'fruit' to crop. It will grow in between other fruits, in ornamental areas or as ground cover, at a good stride apart. Rhubarb is not too fussy about shade, site or position and rarely suffers from pests or diseases. To force for earlier crops, cover the crowns with a bottomless bucket, barrel or stack of tyres lined with a little loose straw. Give the crowns compost every year or two to keep up their productivity. It is worth buying certified virus-free plants initially, as these produce more freely. You can also grow some varieties from seed.

Epicurean attentions Pull the stems with a twist, rather than cutting them. Stop at midsummer, as the sourness becomes too much. Rhubarb can be eaten in desserts, frozen or made into jam and wine.

Bob's gourmet choices 'Timperley Early' is best for forcing and 'Victoria' is very good. 'Glaskin's Perpetual' can be pulled for longer before getting too acid, and all old varieties, like 'Holstein Bloodred' and 'Early Champagne', are worth finding.

OPPOSITE ABOVE *Asparagus fern (with pot marigold flowers) builds up the crowns strength to crop again next year.* OPPOSITE BELOW *After cutting stops, asparagus shoots become fern-like to feed the crown and roots.* RIGHT *Globe artichokes from seed are variable, can be thorny but are usually tasty.*

Globe artichokes and cardoons Artichokes are large attractive plants; their blue flowers are beautiful and attract bees. For best results, give them their own bed of rich soil and rotate every third year or so. Rarely affected by pests and diseases, they may be lost in hard wet winters, unless protected with straw or a cloche. Ideally, procure offsets of good stock of artichokes in early spring, as they do not come true from seed. Sow in pots in spring and later transplant at a good stride or two apart. Select from this stock after a couple of years, building up the plants to tell their worth.

Cardoons look similar, but are grown annually. Bind up and wrap the leaves in late summer to blanch the hearts for winter. Cardoons are always grown fresh from seed and the skill is to keep them growing without check, in rich moist soil, to make a succulent heart for blanching.

Epicurean attentions If aphids or earwigs get in artichoke heads, soak them in salt water before cooking and the pests float off. The hearts can be frozen for winter use and are scrumptious on pizza and in patés.

Bob's gourmet choices 'Green Globe' and 'Vert de Laon' are excellent. Purple artichokes can taste better than the green, but have small thorns on the bud scales; try 'Purple Globe' and 'Violetto di Chioggia'.

Jerusalem artichokes are a good, nutritious standby crop for when the potatoes fail. These tall plants are useful as quick, easy windbreaks and, being related to sunflowers, get on well with sweet corn. Their dense growth suppresses ground elder, and even *Equisetum*. Plant the tubers one to two fingers deep, a foot apart, in early spring. They are difficult to eradicate, so are best confined to wild corners. They only keep well left in the ground and are immune to pests and diseases. Straw over their bed in late autumn, so you can dig them unfrozen in deepest winter.

Epicurean attentions Try them peeled, sliced and deep-fried, or as a soup with anchovies and shallots.

Bob's gourmet choices 'Fuseau' has golden, chocolate-vanilla-scented flowers and longish tubers. 'Dwarf Sunray' is shorter, flowers more freely, and has thin-skinned tubers.

Mushroom kits are available, which are very expensive per mushroom produced, and unreliable unless you follow the instructions religiously. Starting with fresh strawy horse manure and mushroom spawn is a lot of work for risky results. The critical thing is to get the ambient conditions perfect. Without a cellar or similar, success is rare, as they prefer a fairly constant temperature. I believe my lack of decent yields is due to the low humidity where I live; in wetter climes more success is likely. Mushrooms are probably least irksome as a perennial; pare back rich, lush turf by a warm, damp hedge base, mix the spawn in with the soil, then re-cover with turf. If lucky, you harvest, if not... Surpluses are easily dried or frozen.

Epicurean attentions The stalks of mushrooms are tough, so save these up, dried or frozen, for making stock or soup. Gently fry mushrooms in butter with salt, freshly ground black pepper and lemon juice.

Bob's gourmet choices Shiitake mushrooms are so expensive to buy that their kits almost look good value! The fresh mushrooms are fantastic, almost garlicky and delicious.

LEGUMES

Legumes enrich the soil by fixing nitrogen in nodules of bacteria on their roots. In some soils, the first few crops may be poor, as these bacteria are not present. Inoculate your soil with the bacteria, available from commercial seedsmen for use with alfalfa, or use a little compost or soil from a nearby friend (without brassica clubroot) who grows peas and beans well, to add to the water for your first seed drill. When clearing these crops, cut off the stems at ground level to leave the root systems to enrich the soil. They all enjoy lime in the soil, so apply this during their rotation. Mulching with a thin sterile layer after sowing suppresses weeds among them without risking their own emergence.

Broad beans are nutritious and easy to grow. Extra-early crops of long-pod varieties may be had from early winter sowings in mild years. Broad beans can be planted with potatoes, both in the autumn for the earliest crops if winters are mild, or in spring when the young beans protect the early potato shoots from wind and frost. Grown with gooseberries, they discourage sawfly caterpillars. Follow broad beans with sweet corn because they leave a rich moist soil, while the stumps give wind protection to the maize's young shoots. I sow them at about three or four to the foot and finger deep. Pinch out the tips after flowering as this prevents black aphid attacks, or use soft soap later. Growing summer savory nearby helps discourage the pest. Black ants protect the aphids from predators, so destroy their nests.

Epicurean attentions Broad beans go well with summer savory and, if de-skinned, make a base for a most delicious paté. They freeze well and can be dried for use in soups.

Bob's gourmet choices 'Aquadulce Claudia' is the hardiest, while 'Express' is quick and productive but not as tasty as the tendered 'Windsor' sorts. For small gardens, the dwarf 'The Sutton' is handy but, for us gourmets, it has to be 'Red Epicure'.

French and haricot beans are known as waxpod, snap, string, green or just dwarf beans (though there are also running French beans that climb). They are prone to late frosts, cold winds, and slug and bird damage, so benefit from plastic bottle cloches and mulches of grass clippings after sowing. The latter encourages slugs but keeps the soil in better condition. They do well with celery, when planted in rich moist soil, and produce earlier crops with strawberries, which also benefit. Sow under cloches from late spring till late summer, an inch or so deep, at a foot each way. For gourmet haricots of the most floury texture, grow suitable drying sorts and give the plants a warm dry site so that they ripen well. Cloches may help towards the end of the season. There are climbing varieties that grow like runner beans and need supports, but have the finer texture and flavour of dwarf French beans (which, incidentally, are the best for growing out of season under cover).

Epicurean attentions Pick the green bean varieties regularly to keep them producing. The pods are finest when you cannot see the bean seed shape from outside and the flesh snaps crisply. Store the dried beans in the pods in a dry, rodent-proof place, and start soaking them the night before they're wanted for cooking. They freeze well, and the seeds can be dried for winter use.

Bob's gourmet choices 'Masai', 'Radar' and 'Aramis' are my favourites. For drying haricots, 'Brown Dutch' and 'Horsehead' are reliable. 'Blue Lake' and 'Largo' are good climbers. The popular borlotti are Italian climbing French beans, needing a warm site to do well.

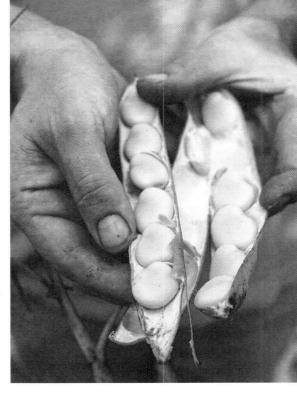

OPPOSITE ABOVE *Globe artichokes and cardoons are almost identical initially.* OPPOSITE LEFT AND RIGHT *Are these food or fatal? If you planted bought spawn just there and it looks just right, then it is alright.* ABOVE *Broad beans are both generous and early crops.* BELOW *You've not eaten fresh peas raw? A must!*

Runner beans are highly productive climbers, but have a coarser texture and flavour than French beans. They need to be well mulched and watered to thrive, and should be kept picked. Support them on poles, wires or strings. Netting is better and wire netting best. All of these can be suspended from posts, walls or fences. Runner beans can be a problem late in the season when they may shade out other crops. This may benefit some, especially celery and saladings, but only when enough water is available. Brassicas, especially Brussels sprouts, which are sheltered while small, grow on once the beans die back, flourishing on the nitrogen left by them. Try sowing the shorter varieties to grow up and over sweet corn. Runner beans are perennial and can be protected or overwintered as dormant 'tubers' for an earlier crop. Sow the seed in late spring in situ, two or three inches deep, and the same apart in rows. Varieties with coloured flowers and purple beans look good in ornamental areas. *Epicurean attentions* These are usually best eaten smaller. Surpluses can be frozen, salted or pickled and the dried seeds used in stews.

Bob's gourmet choices Grow 'Desirée', 'Kelvedon Marvel', 'Scarlet Emperor' and the nearly stringless 'Butler'. Dried 'Czar' seeds are as good as butter beans. 'Red Rum' is prolific.

Peas are more work than most vegetables but are delicious and, as legumes, enrich the soil for other crops. One of the few crops better grown in rows, I have modified the way they are usually sown and supported to save as much work as possible. First, grow short varieties; although they produce less, they do not need as much or as strong support and do not shade out other crops as much. Do not use pea-sticks, which are time-consuming to put up and take down. Instead, use galvanised chicken netting on strong canes or metal stakes. It's quick and easy to erect and, in autumn, the dried haulm can be stripped off, the roll wound up and any remaining haulm burnt off, destroying spores and pests. If you have enough, bend the netting bottom back and over the row to make a guard against birds.

I sow peas an inch or two apart, and an inch or two deep, in one well-watered and drained slit trench, made with the edge of a spade. After sowing firmly infill with soil and firm down. I use a thin sterile mulch over the row to keep weeds down. My peas come through grass clippings but, in wetter areas, sharp sand is safer. It is expensive to buy pea seed, but self-saved seed comes true so use this. You don't even have to shell out the seed, as I've laid the pods end to end in the slit, watered well, and had complete success. In dry conditions, peas are quicker to germinate if soaked for an hour or so before sowing. Adding a dash of seaweed solution helps disguise their smell from mice.

As peas need support, grow them down the middle of a bed and grow potatoes, brassicas, carrots or sweet corn on either side.

For succession, sow peas from late winter till late summer (some can be sown in late autumn for overwintering). Although these early crops rarely do well unprotected, they avoid most problems. Pea guards keep birds from eating the seeds and young leaves, but not mice, so use traps for these. Do not worry about mildew because, if the plants are moist enough, they won't suffer. One good watering when the flowers are just finishing will improve yields substantially. To avoid seeing maggots in your peas, see the tip in Epicurean attentions about cooking them in their pods. *Epicurean attentions* Pick peas early, not late! Pod them immediately, blanch and freeze, or cook and eat soon after, with joyous haste and lots of butter and mint jelly. I cook the peas in the pods and serve them whole, so that you can eat them like asparagus. Surplus peas can be dried on the vines and used in winter soups and stews (remember to soak overnight first). *Bob's gourmet choices* The round, seeded varieties are the hardiest, but not as sweet. 'Meteor' is probably most reliable, but 'Douce Province' is sweeter. 'Feltham First' and 'Jaguar' are good for overwintering. The wrinkle-seeded varieties are sweeter, so for later sowings grow 'Cavalier', 'Kelvedon Wonder', 'Onward' and 'Hurst Greenshaft'. Petit pois are small, sweet, wrinkle-seeded peas that take a lot of podding, so use the eating tip above. Grow 'Calibra' and 'Waverex'. Mangetout peas have edible pods, so podding is not necessary when young and tender, but they rapidly get too tough to eat. Sugar-snap peas are similar, but much improved with thicker sweeter edible pods. Asparagus peas are more like a vetch and are not peas. The best that can be said of them is that they grow in poor conditions and have pretty flowers.

LEFT *Runner and running French beans are very economical in terms of time and space.*

ALLIUMS

Easy to grow and store, growing alliums is a must. They accumulate sulphur and impart some disease resistance to plants nearby and their flowers are good for attracting beneficial insects.

Shallots are the easiest vegetables; simply put healthy cloves in very shallow depressions, at about a foot apart, and fix in place with a handful of sand. Do this from midwinter on, and even during the prior autumn in mild areas. They will need replanting if birds and worms pull them out of their holes but, otherwise, rarely suffer any problems. When the leaves have withered, lift the crop and store in a dry airy place, selecting the best clumps for next year's 'seed'. New varieties, such as 'Golden Creation', can be grown from true seed.
Epicurean attentions Pickled shallots are much better than onions.
Bob's gourmet choices 'Golden Gourmet' and 'Longor'.

Leeks are very hardy, take up little space, and rarely suffer from any problems in a rich moist soil. They may not do well, though, in hot dry conditions. Grow leeks with onions, celery and carrots, where they will decrease attacks of carrot root fly. They hide brassicas from pigeons. Leave unused leeks to flower as they are loved by beneficial insects. Sow them shallowly indoors in mid-winter and in a seed bed in mid-spring. Transplant in late spring to about a foot apart. When transplanting, make deep holes, insert the leeks and align them so their leaves hang out of the way; then water in well with dilute seaweed solution. If leek moth is a problem in your area (eating out the centre), cover the crop with fleece from when young. Or, cut back hard in mid-summer when an attack is first spotted, as leeks usually recover well.

Epicurean attentions Surround leeks with paper collars and be careful not to let grit get in the middle. Trim and wash carefully for the same reason.
Bob's gourmet choices For autumn leeks, sow 'The Lyon' or 'Argenta'. For winter use, 'Musselburgh' is hard to beat and 'Neptune' has attractive blue foliage.

Onions suffer a few pests and diseases but, most years, still produce good results in favourable weather. Grow them in several different ways to split the risks and extend their season of availability. Easiest of all is to buy onion sets; these are not cheap, but usually avoid many of the problems. Plant onion sets from late winter to mid-spring, but the earlier the better if the ground is ready. Plant in very shallow holes, a hand's breadth or so apart. Keep putting them back as the birds and worms pull them out, or fix them with a handful of sand. Onions are convenient for intercropping where space is available, especially between brassicas, but keep them away from beans.

LEFT *Garlic is the simplest most remunerative crop.*
RIGHT *Leeks do better in heavy clay with plentiful rain.*

Onions can also be sown direct, but are best sown under cover in mid- to late winter in pots or cells. Do not worry about getting more than one plant per cell, as two or three grown together will produce smaller, harder onions that keep longer than big ones. Plant the seedlings out in mid-spring and use closer planting, down to one every three inches, for small long keepers and much more space for big ones and clumps. In late summer, you can direct sow Japanese onions for overwintering. These crop before mid-summer when onions are expensive to buy, but do not try to store them as they go off easily.

If onion fly is a problem in your area, grow sets, which rarely suffer or grow under netting or horticultural fleece. Spring sowings can be mixed with carrots as an intercrop, which helps hide them from the fly. If the leaves get a grey mould, dust them with wood ashes to check the attack. You must never break or damage the leaves or

bulb when cultivating, so weed around onions by hand. Once the bulbs start to ripen, allow weeds to grow as they will take up nutrients and help the ripening process. Never bend the leaves down to help ripening, as this lets in disease. Lift the onions from well underneath with a fork or sever the roots with a sharp knife, dry off under cover in an airy place, and store on open trays rather than tie them up in bunches.

For small pickling onions, sow thickly so they crowd each other. Sow spring onions the year before in autumn or winter for spring use, and then again every few weeks for succession.

Epicurean attentions Peel onions under water, slice them into rings and segments, as these cook differently.

Bob's gourmet choices 'Sturon' and 'Stuttgarter' are excellent. 'Giant Zittau' is good for pickling, 'Bedfordshire Champion' is a good keeper and 'Southport Red Globe' makes a lovely change. 'Senshyu Semi Globe' and 'Imai Early Yellow' are the best Japanese onions. 'Paris Silverskin' is the ultimate pickling variety, especially good in piccalilli.

LEFT *Start onion sets in cells first, then you only need plant them once.* BELOW *Onions need it dry and airy to store well, cold seldom hurts them.*

ROOTS

These are often highly nutritious, as their deep roots tap levels of soil further down than most plants. They are soil breakers and improvers, as they leave fine roots and foliage enriched with minerals, particularly the beet and chards. They do not need a dug soil because the fine taproot will go straight down into the hardest soil if it is moist, and the seed has a firm covering of soil to push against. They are mostly biennials, building up their reserves to flower the next year – thus, bolting into flower early can be a problem. Remove bolters to prevent them encouraging others. I use a two-prong fork, made from the middle of a four-prong digging fork, to lift out roots with minimal disturbance.

Carrots must be grown under an old net curtain or horticultural fleece to prevent carrot root fly damage. They are plagued by this; numerous herbs and strong-smelling remedies have been used as deterrents with some success, mostly from intercropping onions, chives and leeks. Most carrot root flies can be stopped by a simple barrier of anything thigh-high around small beds. However, the best preventatives are crop rotation and a physical barrier to stop the fly laying its eggs by the seedling carrots.

Carrots need a stone-free, light soil. Heavy clay soils need lightening with organic material and sharp sand, well mixed in. Do not overfeed or use fresh manure, as these will cause poor flavour and forked roots. Heavy soil may be improved the year before sowing with a green manuring of flax. I find carrots follow onions well on a light soil. Do not disturb the soil deeper than an inch and the seedling carrots will grow straight down. Sow successionally and shallowly from early spring through until mid-summer. Station-sowing, at three or less per foot apart, is best

if you want large carrots for storing but, for handfuls of baby carrots, I prefer broadcast sowing. Rake the soil, then water heavily and let it percolate away. Mix the seed with sand, and sow this side to side and back and fro. Cover the seed with a half inch of used sterile potting compost or sharp sand, pat down and cover with some fleece, well pegged down. Unwanted carrots left to flower attract hover-flies and beneficial wasps. I keep most of mine in the ground over winter, just covered with straw and a plastic sheet. Geese love them!

Epicurean attentions Carrots keep best with dirt left on them and washed when needed. Carrots stored near apples may acquire a bitter taint.

Bob's gourmet choices 'Amsterdam Forcing' is the best quick carrot; surpluses freeze well and it's excellent grown in a cold frame. 'Early Nantes' and 'Chantenay' are nearly as good and can be sown from late winter under cover, and right through to late summer for little ones for winter. 'Sugarsnax' and 'St Valery' are good summer carrots with a sweet crunchiness rivalling (shop-bought) apples and a better flavour. 'Autumn King' is superb, if a bit coarse, for winter storage. 'Kingston' is an improved storer. 'Yellowstone' is a very good yellow, but generally avoid white and red varieties as they are poor doers. For shallow soil or containers in the greenhouse, 'Rondo' is useful as it grows short and round like a radish. For maximum vitamin A, 'Juwarot' is superb, having double the average amount.

Parsnips, Hamburg parsley, salsify and scorzonera are similar roots that are not difficult to grow, but take a long time. Hamburg parsley produces a parsnip-like root that is grown and used in the same way, but tastes of parsley; don't use the leaves like parsley. Salsify and scorzonera are like long, thin parsnips with a much better flavour.

ABOVE *Carrots given good spacing swell well (i.e. sow thinly!).*

These all rarely suffer from pests or diseases, other than the usual soil pests and carrot root fly, from which they are protected with cloches or fleece. If left to flower, they are good for beneficial insects and are best intercropped with peas or lettuce. They keep well in the ground, though it is wise to dig some up to store in a shed when hard frosts are likely. Sow in early spring, three seeds per station, at about a foot apart, and protect with a wee cloche as germination is slow. The seed does not keep, so use fresh every year. Thin to one seedling once they emerge and forget about them until harvest.

Epicurean attentions Parsnips taste better after the frost has got to them. Parboil them and make into French fries. Salsify and scorzonera do not store well, so dig up immediately before use, parboil without

peeling, slip off the skins, and fry the roots in butter. Young scorzonera shoots can be eaten in salads.

Bob's gourmet choices 'Tender and True', 'The Student' and 'Gladiator' are good choices, 'Avonresister' is most canker-resistant and 'Excalibur' is very sweet.

Turnips and swedes can be started in cells if planted out while still small. However, they do much better sown direct, half an inch deep and up to a foot apart, from early spring right through to late summer. Other than flea beetle, they rarely suffer from pests and diseases, but can become tough and hot grown in dry conditions. They grow well in the shade of peas or intercropped with French beans. Eat turnip leaves like spinach. Swedes are like turnips, but sown in late spring, either direct or in cells and transplanted while small. Swedes do very well interplanted with broad beans. They are ideal for autumn and winter use, as they stand and store better than turnips.

Bob's gourmet choices 'Golden Ball' is the best all-round turnip and will store reasonably well in a cool place. 'Snowball' is quick to grow and more succulent, but 'Purple Top Milan' has the flavour for turnips. 'Acme Purple Top' and 'Marian' are both reliable Swedes. 'Twede' does well in poor soils, and 'Best of All' is the hardiest.

Beetroots and chards Red, yellow and sugar beet are very closely related to leaf beet, perpetual spinach and Swiss chard. Originating from maritime regions, they need trace elements more than most crops. Thriving on seaweed products, they do poorly in impoverished, chemically fertilised soil. Good mineral accumulators, one quarter of the mineral content of their leaves is magnesium, which is extremely valuable when added to compost. Grow with French beans, onions and brassicas, especially kohlrabi. Birds eat the seedlings and young leaves, so use wire netting guards, black cotton or plastic bottle cloches.

Sow in pots or cells under cover in early spring, plant out and sow in the open from late spring to mid-summer. Beets do well sown one seed capsule to a pot, cell or station, then transplanted and left unthinned at a foot or so apart to give clumps of smaller beet for pickling. Sown direct and thinned, they can be grown larger for winter storage. Chards, leaf beets and perpetual spinach are effectively beetroots grown for their leaf and stem instead of their roots. They are treated similarly, but must be thinned to about two foot apart. They will carry on producing until the hard winter frosts and often sprout again in spring.

Epicurean attentions Swiss chard stems braised in a cheese sauce are delicious. The green leaf can also be used like spinach; keep pulling the stems and it comes again.

Bob's gourmet choices Especially recommended are the 'Egyptian Turnip Rooted' beet, the yellow 'Burpee's Golden' and, for pickling and slicing, 'Forono' or 'Cylindra', which have barrel-shaped roots. For winter storage, grow 'Crimson King', and where bolting is a problem try 'Boltardy'. Ruby chard is brightly coloured, but 'Fordhook Giant' or 'Lucullus' taste better.

OPPOSITE *Same soil, same space, four different varieties.* **ABOVE AND BELOW** *Beetroot seldom suffer much, other than bird damage.* **LEFT** *Swedes do best for me with broad beans.*

BRASSICAS

The cabbage family is highly bred and very specialised, needing rich soil and plenty of lime. Brassicas are all prone to clubroot disease so, if you do not have it in your soil, NEVER bring in any brassica plants from elsewhere. Do without as, once present, this disease is almost incurable. If you must buy in brassica plants, choose only those grown in sterile compost. Wallflowers and stocks can carry the disease and it may be introduced with muck, so compost it thoroughly before use. Clubroot can be decreased in virulence by liming the plot very heavily. And you can give your crops a head start by growing them in pots filled with sterile compost, so that the infected soil does not touch the young roots.

Although best sown direct, brassicas can

be started in small pots and planted out as soon as possible. The better crops are sown in a seed bed, thinned to three inches apart, lifted and planted back again when they are about three inches high. They are then transplanted to their final site when they have a couple of pairs of real leaves. All brassicas suffer badly from bird damage, so use black cotton or wee cloches while they are small. Brassicas benefit from growing herbs nearby, such as chamomile, dill, peppermint, rosemary and sage. These help confuse their pests.

In general, brassicas grow well with peas, celery, potatoes, onions and dwarf beans, but not near rue, runner beans, lettuce or strawberries. Cabbage root fly attacks them when they are transplanted, so use pieces of cardboard, old carpet underlay or roofing felt cut up into about a foot square, and make a slit to push around the stems. These lie flat on the ground and prevent the fly laying its eggs in the soil by the stem. The dreaded caterpillars can be hand picked or sprayed with *Bacillus thuringiensis*, or the adults can be kept off with nets. Whitefly, which are different to the ones in greenhouses, are not much of a problem but can be controlled with soft soap, as can aphid attacks. Flea beetle makes little pinholes in the seedling leaves, so keep the area wet to discourage them.

When planting out brassicas, mix a handful of sieved garden compost, seaweed and calcified seaweed in with the soil you return to the planting hole, unless you have very rich soil. Brassicas are good for our health and are the most reliable overwintering crops available in the spring. They all need sowing in spring and transplanting a couple of feet apart or so by early summer. Read the seed packets carefully.

LEFT *Cabbage can be had fresh, or stored every month of the year.*

Cabbages are terminal buds and to get them to swell without opening is a marvel of controlling nature. Constant unchecked growth in rich moist conditions is required. Cabbages can be produced for use every day of the year, and some can be close planted for small heads. In early spring, apply a liquid feed to get slow overwintered greens moving again, but don't overdo it as this spoils the flavour.

Epicurean attentions Don't cut a whole cabbage in one go. Instead, cut a section out and cover the rest of the head with foil, as it keeps fresher in the garden than in the fridge. All cabbages may produce a bonus crop of little ones if the root is left in when the head is cut and a cross cut is made in the top of the stem.

Bob's gourmet choices For early summer cabbages, start 'Greyhound', 'Golden Acre' or the compact 'Hispi' in pots under glass from late winter and plant out in spring. Then sow the sweet 'Caramba' and the red 'Marmer', 'Minicole' or 'Stonehead' from early spring in a seed bed, and plant out in late spring. For early autumn cabbages, sow 'Grand Prize', 'Winningstadt' and 'Red Drumhead' from late spring and plant out in early summer. For late autumn and into winter, sow 'Holland Late Winter', 'Christmas Drumhead', 'January King', 'Celtic' and 'Savoy King' from late spring and plant out in summer. When hard frosts threaten, pull the winter cabbages up, roots and all, and hang them upside down in a cool, frost-free shed or cover them in straw and a plastic bag. For spring cabbages, sow 'Myatt's Offenham', 'Wintergreen' and 'Spring Hero' in late summer, plant out in early autumn and protect against harsh weather. Fortunately, there are now clubroot-resistant cabbages, such as 'Kilaton', which is a significant breakthrough.

Broccolis Sprouting broccolis are useful spring varieties that form many small heads instead of one big one, while Calabrese is an autumn broccoli. All are highly bred and require rich conditions and heavy soil to form their swollen immature flowerbuds. They all do best sown directly in situ but can be started off in small pots and planted out well before their root system fills the compost. They need to be at least two foot apart each way and three suits the sprouters.

Epicurean attentions Bend the surrounding leaves over the curd to prevent the sun turning it yellow.

Bob's gourmet choices Grow early purple, late purple and white sprouting broccolis for succession in early spring. All varieties are good, 'Claret' excellent. The Calabrese varieties are currently changing annually: 'Belstar', 'Green Sprouting' and 'Fiesta' cover early, mid- and late, 'Aquiles' will grow early, late or over winter. 'Romanesco' is different, delicious with a superb texture and flavour, but quite difficult to grow well! Try sowing direct in situ, in mid- to late spring.

Cauliflowers are only really cauliflowers during the warm months. The winter-hardy ones are, botanically, broccoli, which are tougher than true cauliflowers. They are the most highly bred and the most difficult of the family to grow well. The part we eat is an enormous, multiple-flowered head suspended in the bud stage. Any check or damage will lead to 'button' heads. There are red and green cauliflowers, and dwarf ones that take less space. They all require rich moist soil, so do not expect good results on light soils. As they are so highly bred, sowing dates are critical – read the packet! Sow at least two foot apart each way and three for big heads. Cauliflowers can be had most of the year with successional sowings of

TOP *Calabrese/summer and autumn broccoli need rich, moist soil.* BOTTOM *Romanesco broccoli, made from asparagus-like fractal spears, is gorgeous, but not easy to grow.*

different varieties, but it is more difficult to get all of these to do well than for cabbages.

Epicurean attentions Subject to the same problems as the other brassicas, they need most attention, as the shape and texture of their heads makes pest problems more detrimental than for, say, cabbage where the outer leaves can be discarded. When the curd starts to swell, bend side leaves over to keep the light from yellowing it.

Bob's gourmet choices As with broccoli, there is much breeding and varieties are changing frequently, though 'All the Year Round' and 'Armado April' are still popular. The first is renowned for not-quite-year-round successional cropping and the latter for overwintering to crop in spring. 'Pavilion', 'Maystar' and 'Snowball' are current good performers. On light or poor soils, and in small plots, grow mini-caulis that produce small heads; sow suitable varieties such as 'Avalanche', 'Nemo' or 'Igloo' in situ at a hand's breadth apart. Fortunately, there are now clubroot-resistant cauliflowers, such as 'Clapton', which is a significant breakthrough.

Kale is the hardiest of all brassicas and will give you tasty greens in spring when all else fails. It is very nutritious, fairly resistant to clubroot and cabbage root fly, and rarely eaten by birds. Sow in late spring and plant in early summer.

Epicurean attentions Try the smallest leaves, chopped fine with the first chives and parsley, in mayonnaise on buttered toast. Deep-fried kale leaves are what you may get when ordering crispy seaweed, which is at least a nice change from boiled!

Bob's gourmet choices Kales have become more popular, especially dark lamb's tongue-shaped 'Nero di Toscana', 'Dark Tuscany' or 'Black Tuscany'. The traditional 'Dwarf Green Curled' and 'Pentland Brig' are commonly available, but the tasty old 'Asparagus Kale' has been lost commercially. The 'Jersey' or 'Walking-stick' kale is interesting, long-lived, really a fodder crop, so neither good eating nor, eventually, very good walking sticks either.

Brussels sprouts One of the hardier brassicas, Brussels sprouts have the same family tendencies, differing mainly in a tolerance for runner beans and a liking for really firm soil. They need to be two to three feet apart, and in loose soil are best in threes, as a tripod tied together at the top, ready for the windiest weather.

Epicurean attentions If you want firm tight sprouts, plant extra deep and extra firm. If you want the sprouts to swell more quickly, nip out the terminal shoot – it's a tasty dish on its own.

Bob's gourmet choices Brussels sprouts can be available from autumn until spring if several varieties are grown. Sow successional varieties from early spring till early summer, transplant by mid-summer in well-firmed soil and plant extra deep. Grow 'Bedford Fillbasket', 'Nautic' or 'Cascade', 'Seven Hills' (mid-), 'Doric' and 'Trafalgar' (late). Try 'Noisette', which produces tiny nutty sprouts, and 'Rubine', which are small and red. The tops can be eaten as spring greens.

LEFT *Not eating enough greens? Try fast frying finely shredded kale for garnishing savoury dishes.*
BELOW *Nipping the top out a month before Christmas makes sprouts swell more.*

CUCURBITS

Courgettes, marrows, squashes and pumpkins are all closely related. It is not worth saving their seed because they cross-pollinate too freely. They all need similar conditions, especially rich soil and warmth at the start.

Courgettes (zucchini) give large numbers of small fruits from each plant. If you stop picking, they produce few more and those left grow into marrows. They need a very rich soil and flourish growing on the compost heap. Grow courgettes amongst sweet corn, peas and beans, but avoid having potatoes nearby. Sow in pots in the warm, in late spring, and plant out three feet apart once the last frost has gone. Also sow direct under a cloche or plastic bottle in late spring. Watch out for slug damage but, otherwise, they have few pest or disease problems. If courgettes distort and become warty, suspect virus disease and destroy the whole plant promptly.

Marrows are treated exactly the same, except most varieties produce long stems which can be trained up fences or along wires. Grow them under and over well-established sweet corn or up sunflower stems. Squashes and pumpkins need the same treatment, but more space at four feet apart. Most of them keep better than marrows but are you going to use them? *Epicurean attentions* Picked with a short stalk when fully ripe, marrows and squashes can be stored hung from a garage or shed roof in old stockings or tights. Pick courgettes small, as they taste better and far more are produced. *Bob's gourmet choices* 'All Green Bush' and 'Defender' are well-established courgettes with many new contenders. Yellow varieties seem to perform less well than green, but add colour to dishes. Avoid spherical and round courgettes, as they go over too quickly when not picked. 'Long Green Trailing' is still

the best marrow and 'Green Bush' is a compact variety, more like a courgette plant. Vegetable spaghetti is just a marrow with stringy insides – only worth growing if you like it! Butternut squash is very good for summer, autumn, and into winter. 'Crown Prince' is the longest storing squash for winter. 'Turk's Turban' and 'Uchiki Kuri' are well flavoured and good in soups and stews, baked or roasted. 'Jaspee de Vendee', an old French sort, is very sweet for preserves. Avoid custard or patty pan varieties with scalloped edges where space is tight, as they waste a lot on shell. Pumpkin plants proper grow really big, take even more space, and have little culinary value unless you want pumpkin pie for months on end. Grow courgettes instead.

Ridge cucumbers, gherkins and Japanese cucumbers have a fine texture and flavour if grown well, but often have little prickles on their skin. They can benefit from a cold frame or cloches, and can be grown in a cold greenhouse or tunnel. In hot summers, ridge cucumbers do well planted under sweet corn or sunflowers. They also grow well with dill, peas, beans, beet and carrots, but dislike

LEFT Courgette flowers can be used too – stuffed and cooked. RIGHT Few crops can crop so heavily as courgettes.

potatoes and most strong herbs, especially sage.

Sow the seed on its edge, half an inch deep, in individual pots in warmth in late spring. Keep warm and pot up until ready to plant out in early summer. Space at least two feet apart and provide some protection. Or, sow in situ under cloches in early summer. Most trail like marrows, so can be grown up fences or over trellis once they are vigorous enough to fill the cloche or cold frame. It does not matter if they are pollinated, as it does not make them as bitter as with pollinated indoor cucumbers. Gherkin varieties for pickling are more reliable. The Japanese cucumbers are the easiest to grow. *Epicurean attentions* Gherkins are best picked small so check them daily. Dill goes exceptionally well with all cucumbers. *Bob's gourmet choices* 'Bush Champion' still reigns, 'Marketmore' is reliable, 'Paris Long White' the least wind-inducing. There are a host of others, newly bred, that are better still. I don't like the round 'Crystal Apple', though some do. 'Vert petit de Paris' is still *the* gherkin.

POTATOES

Potatoes are easy to grow, but need care to give worthwhile yields. They like soil well enriched with organic material and can be a lot of work. To reduce the work-load and to help with dry conditions, I have modified the usual growing method.

As they are prone to diseases spread on the 'seed' potato tubers, buy new certified stock every year. However, it is cheaper to grow self-saved tubers for a couple of years and buy new stock before yields drop or after a year with disease. Only save tubers from healthy plants and never from those that yield badly. Egg-sized tubers are usual, bigger ones are better; green bits do not matter. Organic gardeners are advised to grow early varieties, which give lower yields but crop quickly. These can then be harvested before potato blight becomes a problem, usually after mid-summer during a warm wet period. Second earlies also miss most blight attacks, but the more productive maincrops need to grow on into late autumn to give full yields.

Blight is recognised by blackening foliage that smells bad and all the plants are rapidly affected. Do not confuse it with natural withering as the crop matures. You can prevent blight by spraying with the permissible fungicide Bordeaux mixture, but this is not recommended. If blight appears, cut off the haulms before it runs down them and wait a fortnight before harvesting the tubers. Remember blight is rarely a problem if you grow mostly earlies and second earlies, and these will store almost as well as maincrops anyway. I grow maincrops as well and have yet to suffer blight badly most years. In soil that has long grown potatoes, parasitic eelworm nematodes increase in numbers until crops of all but immune varieties fade away. However, planting *Solanum sisymbriifolium* clears the infestation by awakening the pests and then starving them.

As soon as you can each year, purchase your 'seed' and chit it. This means laying the tubers in a tray and keeping them in a frost-free, slightly warm place with lots of light so they start to grow short green shoots. They must be rose-end-up (i.e. the eyes) not the haulm end (wee bit of root often attached). Earlies need chitting more than maincrops. As soon as weeds start to grow vigorously on your plot, it is time to plant the seed. Plant earlies five or six inches deep and only a foot or more apart; maincrops a little deeper and at least a couple of feet apart. To produce many small new potatoes, leave on all the shoots but remove all the shoots but one or two if you want fewer, bigger tubers. (These wee shoots can be potted up in the warm and grown on to produce extra plants.)

Conventionally, the 'seed' is planted in a trench with ridges for earthing up, but I prefer to dig large individual holes. I use a small post-hole borer, put the 'seed' in the bottom, and infill with soil mixed with sieved garden compost (do not completely fill the hole). Once the shoots appear, add soil around them when a frosty night is predicted, and continue to drag soil up around the shoots until you reach mole-hill size. From then on, earth up with a mulch of straw, leaves or grass clippings. The latter are excellent but put them on in several thin layers when the weather is dry to stop them going slimy. Protect the foliage against frost when it is too big to earth up; newspaper sheets will do.

Once flowers appear (they don't always), search among the clippings and soft soil for tubers big enough to eat, but leave the

ABOVE *Grown in bags of compost gives very clean, early crops.* **LEFT** *It is unearthing buried treasure.* **OPPOSITE** *'Arran Victory' (for mash) set aside for 'seed' and compost grown King Edwards (for roasting, obligatory for Christmas dinner).*

smallest to grow on. This saves digging up a whole row for the first meal and increases overall yields. If birds continuously drag the mulch aside, then the tubers develop green poisonous bits from the light. To avoid this, take sheets of newspaper, tear slits to the middle, push these around the foliage, and replace the mulch on top. If scabby patches appear on the tubers, they only spoil the appearance. Avoid them by mixing grass clippings with the planting soil and compost. Incorporating well-wilted comfrey leaves also works and adds potassium as well.

To increase yields significantly, water potatoes heavily on flowering. Remove any poisonous seed-heads that come after the flowers. To get the longest-storing potatoes, cut the haulm off and leave the tubers for a fortnight before digging as this gives them tougher skins. However, the most important factor is to dig them up in dry conditions. Be careful not to bruise them and take out small damaged tubers first. Leave the best to dry in the sun for an hour, but no more, then keep in paper bags in a cool, frost-free place. I also force potatoes under cover for early new potatoes, see page 205.

Epicurean attentions Do not let them freeze or they go sweet and pick up taints easily. Adding potatoes can 'remove' excess salt from a dish. Try steaming potatoes for better flavour, leaving on the skins and peeling after cooking.

Bob's gourmet choices There are hundreds of varieties to choose from, which are becoming more widely available again. I grow 'Sutton's Foremost', 'Epicure', 'Sharpe's Express', 'Rocket' and 'Dunluce' for my earlies. For maincrops, I grow the wonderful, but low-yielding 'King Edward', and for salads, the divine waxy 'Pink Fir Apple', 'Linzer Delikatess' and 'Charlotte'. 'Cosmos', 'Picasso' and 'Valor' are best for baking and chipping. Try as many as you can!

SWEET CORN

Sweet corn is almost uniquely Anglo-American and relatively unknown to Continental Europeans. Traditionally grown in a hillock covering a dead fish, the modern alternative is incorporating fishmeal, seaweed meal or compost, as this crop needs a rich moist soil. So, sweet corn should follow legumes or be sown with them. It grows well with peas or beans. The light shade makes the space underneath sweet corn ideal for growing ridge cucumbers, squashes, courgettes, marrows and even melons in warmer climates. Sweet corn can also be interplanted with brassicas or sunflowers – I find potatoes are a good intercrop, keeping the soil moist and providing the young shoots with more shelter.

Sweet corn has few pest or disease problems, but is hard to grow in cold wet conditions. Thus, it is often started off under cover in deep pots to give it time to crop. I sow some indoors in pots in mid-spring and sow a second and third lot a week apart direct during late spring. Each sowing or planting hole is dug deep and wide, and partly refilled with soil and sieved compost with extra ground seaweed. The seedlings are planted out deep, but refilled in two stages, and then later earthed up further above ground as they mature. This encourages rooting from the base of the stem and helps keep them upright. Similarly, when sowing, each site is made and improved and the seed sown at the bottom but only covered with an inch or two of soil at first. Whether transplanted or direct sown, the hole and seedling are covered with a plastic-bottle cloche until the plant is a foot or so high to protect it from cold winds.

Sweet corn is best grown in blocks and about two feet apart each way to ensure wind pollination. If you grow some varieties

near certain others flowering at the same time, they may cross, potentially giving mixed or rather non-uniform results. The 'super sweet storage gene' or 'stay-sweet longer' gene may be disabled, which won't matter if you eat your cobs fresh, anyway. You can also grow an extra early crop under cover with one plant to a bucket. The female plants will not be wind-pollinated if they are grown under cover, so save the male pollen in a paper envelope as often the female silks mature a bit later. A good watering once the cobs start to swell is worthwhile.

Epicurean attentions Cook within half an hour of picking or it is not as sweet. I run in with the cobs to plunge them in already boiling water. Sweet corn is bulky but freezes well after blanching, so strip it from the cob for use in soups.

Bob's gourmet choices Grow several varieties and compare, as the range is wide. The non-F1 'Kelvedon Glory' and 'Golden Bantam' are still excellent, and you can save their seed. 'Northern Extra Sweet' proves very reliable, 'Butterscotch' and 'Lark' tasty and 'Conqueror' slow but it has big cobs. Mini-cob varieties produce those treats that are sometimes served as a food substitute. Popcorn varieties are worth trying if you think it will be a hot summer!

OPPOSITE ABOVE *First crops in buckets undercover!* OPPOSITE BELOW *When the male tassel emerges, start to water even more liberally.* ABOVE *Female silks 'helped' by fondling alternately with male tassels on top of plants.* BELOW *Some varieties, particularly popping corns, have attractive pink silks.*

8 SHELTER FROM THE WEATHER

Grow more crops and flowers for more months of the year

The real cost of greenhouses and plastic tunnels has come down, making them more affordable, although the cost of heating has gone skywards. Still, by adding cheap, bubble-plastic insulation, we can all grow tender crops and flowers more cheaply. Also, the breeders have given us more cold-tolerant and disease-resistant varieties, for example, the modern mini-cucumber is easy to grow; a sowing in mid-winter in the warm will crop before spring and give huge numbers of fruit. Outdoors, we can use low, plastic tunnel cloches to enable earlier, near-tender crops, and grow salads all year round. Much of being a successful gardener is about fitting plants to the microclimate and the most radical way of affecting this is to grow plants under cover, which allows for varying degrees of control, depending on what you are using. For example, a cloche or two extend the season; a cold frame allows a wider range of plants and more successful propagation; and a greenhouse, conservatory or polytunnel (especially if frost-free) opens up whole new areas of gardening. If you can supply heat, then you will be able to grow pineapples or, with more height, bananas!

GARDENING UNDER COVER

Cloches create significant weather and pest protection, allowing you to extend the growing season by several weeks at both ends. Their clever use makes growing grapes and melons successful, even in the north of England. Traditional cloches are now widely replaced with low plastic tunnels, but these are not as warm at night as the old glass ones. The simplest cloches are no more than clear plastic sheets stretched over low frames and held down with weights or pegs. The better ones use the more rigid, longer-lasting polycarbonate or similar. In any case, some ventilation is always required on hot days and extra cover at night, if full use is to be made of them. And used continuously, cloches can cause dryness underneath if rainfall is patchy and rain is rarely heavy enough to soak sideways into the middle. Cloches are most useful for getting earlier crops of favourite vegetables and are best set in place a week or two early to pre-warm the soil. They are then used for protecting young tender plants, such as tomatoes or courgettes, and after can be full of melons all summer. In autumn, use them to protect crops from the weather or for winter saladings.

Large plastic water bottles make excellent cloches for growing plants to quite a large size, and even the smaller ones work well – cut the bottom off and discard the cap. (For many crops, cylindrical, clear plastic tubes (i.e. with no bottoms or tops) are sufficient protection from the worst weather and pests – and do not over-heat in hot weather.) It's simple to make big cloches or cold frames from clear plastic bottles, held together with waterproof clear tape. Create a hollow box with bottles stuck together upright as the walls, but don't cut the bottoms off or discard the tops. Add clean water to each to weigh them down. Then the bottles also act as heat reservoirs. On cold nights, some could even be refilled with warm water from the house to give extra protection. Later in the season, making a small hole near the bottom of each with a screw in it will allow trickle irrigation when the cap is loosened. Clear plastic bottles full of water can be stacked like bricks to build a sheltering cloche wall around a treasured plant while it establishes or through winter. And similarly placing such bottles amongst the plants in coldframes and the greenhouse helps keep them cooler by day and warmer by night.

Cold frames are big cloches, usually sited in a warm sunny spot. The better ones are well insulated, but be careful not to cook the plants by leaving the lid closed on a sunny day. A cold frame can be covered at

OPPOSITE ABOVE *Newspaper retaining wall for bed, plate glass traps the sun's heat and cloches keep the melons warm.* OPPOSITE BELOW *Walk-in cover is a luxury – you can grow as much as you need and lilies are for cutting.* BELOW *French marigolds making a grand display in autumn.*

night with a blanket and kept frost-free for longer through the year by popping in bottles of hot water, allowing you to start off and grow on tender plants before planting them out in late spring/early summer. In summer, a cold frame can produce good crops of cucumbers, peppers or even a decent melon or two. A cold frame is useful for propagating plants from seeds and cuttings and for overwintering nearly tender plants. With a soil-warming cable, a compost heap or hotbed under-neath, you can achieve great things – even good melon crops – but then you are better off putting the whole set-up under walk-in cover.

Greenhouses and plastic-covered tunnels One of the most useful garden accessories is walk-in cover, which provides better shelter and warmth because the extra volume produces a more stable environment. A greenhouse or a plastic-covered tunnel (a polytunnel) can give a really early start and protection from pests and weather. You

can use them for winter salads or flowers, plants a little too tender for outside, and forcing or protecting fruit trees.

A greenhouse is lighter and warmer than a polytunnel and the frame can usually be used as a support for staging, potting benches or plant supports. This makes a greenhouse more suitable for plants growing in pots and for perennials. Metal-framed greenhouses are more ugly than the wooden-framed ones, but will last much longer. A polytunnel is uglier still. Although cheaper, it can be colder, very humid and is harder to ventilate. The plastic cover needs replacing every few years, which makes it poor value ecologically. However, you can move it around if space allows, making a rotation possible. As they can be moved, they are most useful for growing annual or short-lived plants directely in the soil and for forcing fruit trees and bushes in tubs.

Site both polytunnels and greenhouses with their longest axis east to west to maximise sunlight and do not site in heavy shade. Water nearby is essential. Electric light and power allows for evening work, while heated propagation further increases the value of the area. Make sure everything is securely built and that you have adequate ground fixings against strong winds. Although extra plastic insulation will keep greenhouses and polytunnels warmer, it reduces the more valuable light too much. I go for a triple layer plastic cover in winter and add extra light because this is cheaper than the heat saved. Ventilation, preferably automatic, must also be adequate for hot weather.

Conservatories are nice for early spring sowing in pots and potting up seedlings. But most plants prefer more humid conditions than we or our furniture can tolerate, so opt for cacti and succulents or plants that like dry atmospheres if they are staying there. Other types of plants will appreciate spraying with water regularly to keep them happy. Ideally, grow conservatory specimens in pots, then they can go out in summer – or in winter, as many deciduous plants, such as peaches and grapes, need the dormancy induced by a cold period outside.

Heating The value of any cover is much greater if it can be kept frost-free. On the smallest scale are tiny seedtray-sized electric propagators, which are very convenient for germinating and rooting, but so small the plants cannot grow uncongested for long. Thus, we want to keep a larger area warm. This may range from simply adding insulation to a cold frame at night and popping in a couple of cans of hot water, to a full scale automatic system with hot air blowers.

The more heat, the earlier you can start cropping and the more different plants you can grow, but it is expensive. A paraffin stove is cheapest, but causes damp and fumes. (However, I use one in the

spring, for extra heat for a week or four, when planting up my polytunnel with tomatoes, and so on.) With electricity available, then a fan heater is most useful and can come with a thermostat. This is the cheapest way to heat, as the capital cost is so low and most heat is needed at night which is off-peak, cheaper electricity. Gas can be as cheap to run, but is more costly to install and any leaks or fumes may damage the plants. Oil is very similar to gas. Solid fuel heating is cheap to run but a lot of physical effort, unless very modern equipment is installed. With a conservatory or when the greenhouse is nearby, it may be simplest to extend the domestic heating to warm it. Soil-warming cables are very cheap to run. They heat the soil underneath plants and keep the roots warm, which is often more important than warm top growth. They can be used to make propagators, to heat cold frames or to warm an area of floor inside a greenhouse for more tender plants. This can even be in an indoor cold frame. Passive heating is ideal and, with better insulated glazing and a big back wall, the the sun has been used almost unaided to keep homes warm, so why not a greenhouse?

A better cold frame or a bigger propagator Falling between the cold frame and the freezer, I find the best solution is a dead deep freezer. Although best stood inside a greenhouse, it can work against a sunny wall or sunk in the ground. Fit it with a ventilated glass or plastic cover for daytime and it becomes a superb cold frame. At night, shut the lid

to keep in the warmth. You will need a false floor to bring the plants near to the light. If you cover this with sand, you can run a soil-warming cable in it to keep the freezer warmer still for using like a giant propagator. Without electrical heat, you can supply extra warmth by putting in bricks that have been warmed on a radiator or, alternatively, bottles full of hot water.

Hotbeds are not often made nowadays, perhaps because many gardeners regard them as ineffective. However, when I first saw how hot a big compost heap gets, I started to put a thick

layer of soil on top before covering with a cold frame. Without doubt, this is an effective way to grow high-quality cucumbers and melons. Hotbed mixtures are just compost heaps; traditionally, strawy dung is used, but I find grass clippings work fine. I use stacks of big tyres to hold the mixture of three-quarters grass clippings, an eighth soil and an eighth straw. These can be interchanged as the heat drops and the mixture slumps. The topmost tyre holds the compost and the plant, which is usually sown in situ under an extra cloche.

Ventilation You cannot over-ventilate if there is sufficient heat. The greater the through-put of air, then the healthier the plants, as they consume the carbon dioxide and fresh dry air usually reduces mildews and moulds. However, never suddenly chill the plants by opening up too soon or, worse, too late when they are half cooked. To prevent overheating under cover, automatic vents are indispensable. Automatic fans are another good investment. A small electric fan can even be solar-powered – just to move air when conditions are hot! It is hard to ventilate sufficiently in cold springs because the vents have to be kept shut. Since there is then little change of air, fortify the air under cover with bottles of fermenting wine or beer that give off carbon dioxide.

OPPOSITE *Hmm … time for the machete I think.* ABOVE *Just a compost heap is a hotbed and is good for melons and marrows.* LEFT *Propagator – a dead fridge on its back, half full of sand with a soil warming cable and some glass (Porsche side windows).*

Water control Under cover, air moisture is very important. Too much encourages moulds and botrytis; too little, mildew and red spider mite. In general, during the growing season, it is best to err on the side of too moist, so spray the walls, plants and floor with a fine jet in the morning so that it can dry before nightfall. It will save time if you arrange an overhead sprinkling system for plants under cover. Sprinklers are inexpensive and will soon repay their cost but, for only a little more, you can have seep hoses and trickle feeders which use water more efficiently by applying it directly to the roots. In a greenhouse with a larger investment, a microchip-operated system will accurately maintain soil and air moisture levels, as well as the heating and ventilation. Less expensive systems can be run with timers or simple moisture sensors. In a polytunnel, the air conditions tend to be too moist and so more heat or ventilation is required.

ABOVE LEFT A hose is essential undercover – not so much for watering, as for hosing down and misting. **ABOVE RIGHT** *Sarracenias catch flies, lots of them, easily.*

Light Under cover in very hot weather, plants may cook, which is why you need good ventilation or glass shading or blinds. The problem is worse when cold dull weather is suddenly replaced by non-stop sun. The plants effectively get sunburnt, just like us. Generally, though, the problem is usually one of insufficient light, often made worse by over-hanging trees or buildings. Pruning may allow in more light and dark areas can be lightened with white paint. All glass and plastic should be kept scrupulously clean to prevent further light loss. Electric light can supplement weak winter sunlight and may be used for early sowings and valuable plants. Ordinary incandescent bulbs are counter-productive as they give the wrong spectrum. Special fluorescent tubes and discharge lamps, though expensive, are made for the purpose. I believe it is better to add extra layers of insulation to retain heat and add extra artificial light to compensate the young plants at the start of the year. The light to give brighter conditions is much cheaper than the extra heat required without those extra layers of plastic insulation.

Pest and disease control under cover While a cloche isolates a plant to an extent, it is still in the soil and only temporarily covered. Growing under walk-in cover is more artificial and requires more intervention, as the natural systems cannot control pests and diseases unaided. Using chemical fumigants is not organically sound, although a greenhouse or tunnel can be cleansed thoroughly with a steam jet. The natural alternative is to build up semi-natural systems (see page 235) and encourage beneficial predators for pest control. Do this by supplying water in saucers and film canisters, nests made of straw-filled pots, sections of hollow-stemmed plants, and rolled-up cardboard tied in dry nooks and crannies. Include ground-cover plants under staging and place rock piles in shady corners for beetles, spiders, frogs and toads. I hang strings just to give my spiders good frames for their webs. Companion plants bring in and feed more predators and pollinators, such as ladybirds, hoverflies and lacewings. I grow French marigolds in the greenhouse or tunnel, especially by the door, as these keep whitefly out, but attract bees and hoverflies. Sweet tobacco and wild tobacco (*Nicotiana sylvestris*) are also beneficial as their sticky stems trap insects like thrips. Introduce bought-in predators to control specific pests. Remember, you must refrain from using even organic pesticides and yellow sticky pest traps or the predators may suffer.

Soil care under cover In the greenhouse or polytunnel, grow plants to fruition directly in the soil rather than in containers, as it saves on watering and compost. A greater root run gives plants the most stable conditions and the best chance of finding nutrients for themselves. Even with a rotation and moving the plants around each year, and adding copious amounts of garden compost and lime, the yields may start to drop after five years or so as the soil becomes worked out (although I have never known this to happen). The answer is to dig out the topsoil and replace it with compost and fresh soil from a clean part

BELOW *Mixing plants up helps controlling problems, or at least stops them spreading.*

of the garden. This is hard work, but is less work than carrying, filling up and watering loads of containers every year. For the paths, I use old carpet and cardboard to cover bare soil, as this prevents weeds and moisture loss and stops the splashing of soil onto crops, while rolling back the strips allows me to pick off slugs and other pests. In my tunnel, I've made a practical solid path from old flat radiators – their white enamel surface also throws back light.

Hardening off tender plants the ideal way I start off all my tender plants in a heated dead freezer propagator. Then I move the hardiest out first into a cold frame in the greenhouse, one section of which is heated. As they get bigger, they move to the unheated section and then to the greenhouse proper. Some of them are hardened off and go outside. As each type of plant moves through the sequence, it leaves space for others so that I can raise dozens of plants with little total space or much electricity. The general order is indoor tomatoes and cucumbers first, followed by peppers and aubergines. As the first of these move on, outdoor tomatoes, sweet corn and indoor melons

ABOVE LEFT *Wall flowers give early flowers for cutting and cheer.* **ABOVE RIGHT** *Most chives are live-headed but a few are left to flower.* **LEFT** *Early, really early, crops of new potatoes and sweet corn can be had.*

are sown, and then the other cucurbits. Sweet corn, ridge cucumbers and courgettes move from the warmth, then the squashes. This leaves space for indoor cucumbers, melons, watermelons, and okra, the last of which stay all through summer as they need the extra heat.

WINTER SALADS AND FLOWERS

Winter salads are wonderful when there are fewer other fresh foods available. Most perennial herbs, such as rosemary, don't need or like protection, but some are usable much longer if potted up and taken under glass. These include thyme, winter savory, tarragon, chives and sage. Any cover, even a humble cloche, can provide more green saladings any day of the year. It is wind and weather protection that helps most and often bright sunny days in winter. Even under cover, these annuals need sowing while the soil is warm in autumn. Thereafter, they make slow growth but can be cut carefully on a regular basis to provide lots of tasty and healthy fodder. Of most value, in my estimation, are: rocket, claytonia, parsley, chervil, corn salad, lettuce, spring onions, cress and mustard, and, of course, radishes.

Winter flowers are luxuries you can afford once you have a light, frost-free place. There are so many, but my favourites are greenhouse cyclamen, which are easy from seed and great value, and citrus, which are wonderful and almost always in flower. Gardenias have an opulent heavy scent and bloom. Almost any bulbs can be forced, and primulas and pansies can be cheerily had with only a cloche. For an impressive display, sow *Schizanthus* in mid- to late summer in cells, pot up under cover, and in the winter you will have many 'orchids'.

Bonus crops under cover

Longer seasons are the productive gardener's reason for wanting more covered space. Growing under glass or plastic simply adds weeks to either end of the growing season. The first advantage comes from having somewhere to raise many plants that will finally mature outside. Without such early protection, they would not be ripening before the autumn frosts. You can also grow plants that require a much longer and hotter growing season by keeping them indoors throughout, so many things you just wouldn't dream of can be grown in colder climates and others become easy.

New potatoes are, to my mind, one of the most delicious and valuable crops. When many people are only planting theirs on Good Friday, as is traditional in the UK, I am eating mine. Most of my effort and heated growing space is taken up with new potatoes forced in pots. I sow the 'seed' of 'Rocket', and other very early varieties, as

soon as the days lengthen after mid-winter's day. I grow these first in pots and move them up to black bags of compost. More batches are started every week or so until early spring when further batches can be started under cloches and in my unheated tunnel. Late crops are also easily had by starting earlies off in big pots after mid-summer. These are brought under cover before the frosts and kept dry once the foliage dies.

Sweet potatoes are an easy crop to grow if you start them off in late winter in a propagator and grow them on in a plastic tunnel. I find the tubers are hard to get to sprout. Any are then best detached and grown on, rather than left on the tuber and, from then on, propagation is best by overwintering young layered plants. They crop at the end of a long season and do best in mounds or in very large pots so that their compost or soil is warm. I prefer the large, orange-fleshed varieties, often from North Carolina, to the thinner, yellow- or white-fleshed varieties, although the latter are easier croppers. Do not let the vines touch the ground or they will rot. It is better to tie them to canes and gain more light as well.

Tomatoes can be grown outside in sheltered gardens, but are much more reliable grown under cover. Start them off in individual cells or pots in a propagator in late winter for indoor crops and early spring for outdoor ones. Pot up twice and keep them warm until hardened off and planted out, a couple of feet apart, in spring under cover or early summer outdoors. Most varieties, indoors or out, are normally

ABOVE RIGHT *Sweet potatoes crop after summer, with bigger crops the later they grow.* BELOW RIGHT *Extra early and extra late means fresh tomatoes from May until January.* LEFT *New potatoes before Easter, and strawberries too.*

grown as single cordons tied to canes with all the sideshoots rubbed off. I grow some plants as double and triple cordons, though, as these give bigger early crops. Early removed sideshoots can be potted up, as they easily root to make more plants. I grow a couple of plants in small pots to crop extra early. These are disbudded and deheaded once one truss has set. They then ripen sooner than when the plant is allowed to grow on.

ABOVE *Truly ripened on the vine.*

Indeterminate types, or non-deshooted plants, produce many sprawling stems and are more often grown outdoors. To keep the stems and the fruit of these off the soil, I place old wire baskets over or around the young plants, which then grow up through and onto them. These can also be covered with plastic sheeting to act as cloches while the plants establish. Out of doors, tomatoes always benefit from cloching or at least wind protection from nets on stakes. These can be used later to cover the plants to keep the birds from eating the fruits.

Feeding is not really necessary in rich loamy soil, but is needed in poor soils, pots or containers. For early crops, be careful not to overfeed as this produces growth instead of fruit. I find fruit from slightly underfed plants tastes best, though starved ones just do badly. Remember, it is tomatoes you are after, not lush, tropical-looking plants. Comfrey liquid, in moderation, is ideal for feeding tomatoes; but seaweed sprays are more beneficial.

Watering is best done well, but not too often for plants in the ground. Never allow them to get checked as this causes blossom end rot, a brown blotch on the flower end of the fruit. In pots or containers, water frequently and keep the medium constantly moist once growth starts vigorously.

Pollination is free outside, but you can hand-pollinate under cover with a cotton-wool bud. However, I plant *Alyssum* and marigolds instead to pull in the poll-inators.

Tomatoes rarely suffer badly from pests and diseases, especially if grown with French marigolds and basil. Under cover, whitefly may appear but can be dealt with by *Encarsia formosa* predators or soft soap. Grow the tomatoes directly in the ground in the greenhouse or tunnel, rather than in pots; the extra watering and feeding for pots can never replace a free root run. The soil may become tired if tomatoes are grown in it year after year, so dig it out and refill the top foot with enriched fresh topsoil every few years. Most other problems are caused by poor nutrition, low temperatures or water stress. Tomatoes ripen best on the plant, but these stop others setting, so leave a ripe one (or a banana) in the greenhouse to help them ripen. At the end of the season, pull up the plants and hang them upside down in a warm airy place to ripen the remaining fruits. **Epicurean attentions** Tomatoes freeze easily without blanching for use in soups and stews. The skins slip off if they are scalded in hot water for a few seconds.

Bob's gourmet choices Grow several varieties for different uses and flavours. Under cover or out of doors, 'Gardener's Delight' is the best, 'Sungold' a close second. I find 'Matina', 'Shirley' and 'Alicante' to be the most reliable early tomatoes under cover, while 'Geo' 'Stupice' and 'Ferline' are reliable for later.

The miffy, but fabulous, 'Pink Brandywine' and 'Marmande' beefsteaks produce large tomatoes. To get really big ones, limit them to three or four per plant at a time. 'San Marzano' and plum-type tomatoes taste poor raw, but wonderful cooked. 'Golden Sunrise' is yellow and adds colour to salads, but also makes a good jam with lemon juice. Do not even consider 'Moneymaker'. Outside, tomatoes that escape blight longest are 'Ferline', 'Legend' and 'Histon Cropper'.

Peppers, sweet and chilli may even just succeed out of doors in southern Britain in very sheltered warm gardens. Sow them in pots, preferably in a propagator, in early spring, repot monthly and plant under cover in early summer at a foot or two apart. Tie them in to canes to support the crop. Peppers often crop better under cover in large pots. Aphids may cause damage early on and watch for slug damage to ripening fruit. Do not let roots in pots get too hot in the sun; shield with another pot or foil.

ABOVE *Little hot peppers are usually hotter than bigger varieties.* BELOW *Green peppers turn red, orange or yellow as they ripen.*

Epicurean attentions Most varieties go red when ripe. The chilli varieties are often hotter, the smaller the fruits. Peppers dry and store remarkably easily. Put a whole, unbroken, just-turning-ripe habanero pepper in rice for flavour with a distinct, but not too lasting, burn!
Bob's gourmet choices Sweet and hot both come in a staggering range. In general, for flavour, avoid the decorative, weird-coloured or super-hot. 'Jumbo', 'Jumbo Sweet', 'Marconi Rosso' and 'Bellboy' are reliable, big and tasty sweet varieties. 'Hungarian Hot Wax' is highly recommended. Habanero varieties are hot and tasty.

Aubergines or eggplants are related to tomatoes, potatoes and peppers. They are often grown with the latter as they like the same warm conditions, but they should be kept away from the first two. These are definitely greenhouse crops and need continuous, warm, moist, rich conditions. Sow in pots in warmth in early spring and repot monthly. Plant under cover in early summer at two feet or so apart. Tie in to canes to support the crop. Aubergines are prone to red spider mite and aphid attacks.
Bob's gourmet choices Try 'Long Purple', 'Black Beauty' and 'Black Enorma'. In general, avoid original white egg or mini-aubergines.

Okra is not difficult to grow if light warm space is available; treat them as aubergines, but do not feed them. You need several plants to get enough to use, so they are not awfully practical. Pick the pods while small to add their peculiar slimy texture to stews.

Frame or indoor cucumbers are closely related to melons and squashes. They need continuous high temperatures and very high humidity, with a really rich soil, although some will crop in warm sunny frames in

good seasons. Sow indoor cucumbers in pots in a heated propagator, during late winter or spring, and pot up regularly until planted in their final position. Take care not to let the neck where the stem leaves the soil get damaged or wet, as it will easily rot – to avoid this, grow them on a little mound of sterile compost. They trail like marrows, so can be grown up strong strings or wires. They are prone to red spider mite and mildew, so need regular syringing; adding seaweed solution or nettle tea may prevent downy mildew. Cucumbers of older indoor varieties have male flowers (those that have no tiny cucumber behind them), which should be removed before opening. This is so the female flowers on the plant are not pollinated, otherwise bitter fruit results. All-female varieties are rarely completely so – be vigilant. The seed is expensive but, given warmth and rich conditions, cucumbers (especially the new, smaller ones) give quick results and are productive early in the year.
Epicurean attentions Pick cucumbers early in the morning, for maximum crispness.
Bob's gourmet choices Varieties are now so much improved, you can't believe how easy they are. 'Carmen', 'Tiffany', 'Cumlaude' and 'Flamingo' are fantastic, full-size cucumbers. The mini-fruiters, 'Zeina', 'Cucino' and 'Silor', are superb for snacks, packed lunches and kids!

ramble under sweet corn or sunflowers, for example. On the ground, place the young fruit on a piece of wood or tile to stop it rotting. Under cover, melons are usually trained up strong strings and the ripening fruits supported in bags or nets.

Epicurean attentions Pick melons when they give off a scent and the stalk will start to pull out. Chill for a day or so, then let them gently warm before serving.

Bob's gourmet choices 'Galoubet' and 'Sweetheart' are well worth trying in an unheated greenhouse or frame in a warm garden, but only expect good results in hot years. 'Charentais' and 'Ogen' are better, but need warmth. For exquisite melons, try 'Jenny Lind', 'Emerald Gem', 'Blenheim Orange' and 'Galia'.

Watermelons are even more difficult than melons in a cold climate, but I just manage them in my heated cold frame and poly-tunnel. They are started in much the same way as indoor cucumbers and need similar conditions, but prefer a more open gritty compost, more sun, and lots of water. They seem to be the ultimate red spider mite attractant! Try 'Blacktail Mountain', 'Red Star' and 'Malali'.

Melons need warm, moist, rich conditions. Treat them the same as cucumbers, but provide even more heat to keep them growing well. Don't let the neck where the stem leaves the soil get damaged or wet, as it will easily rot. Instead, grow your plants on a little mound of sterile compost. Forget conventional advice on getting four equal-sized fruits – simply nip out the tip of the vine and take off all of the fruits bar one and then you'll have a melon worth having. They are even more prone to red spider mite than cucumbers. I sow out-door melons direct in a cold frame on top of a freshly made compost heap in late spring. In warmer regions than Britain, plant out melons where they can

Sweet corn, though not usually grown undercover, can give very early crops before mid-summer, either in the border or bucket-sized tubs. Save male pollen from top tassel flowers to dust the later female silks that come from the cob ends. Sow in pots in late winter and move up regularly, water and feed generously.

Tender and early perennial fruits

Almost any fruit can be grown under cover to extend the season or just to keep off the birds. Cherries are worth growing in pots and only need moving under cover when in flower or with ripening fruit. Peaches thrive likewise. Being kept indoors all winter prevents peach leaf curl while, in spring, the flowers are protected from the frosts. Then they can go out once it's warm to return just for the few weeks when the fruit is ripening. Some fruits merit special attention, as follows:

Strawberries are probably the most rewarding crop to have under cover. Although you can plant in borders under cover, they soon get miffy. Far better is to pot up runners in summer, grow these on in big pots outdoors, and bring them in from late winter onwards for very early forced crops. Alpine strawberries force easily, as do most summer fruiters. The autumn fruiters can ripen fruits better and for longer if grown in pots and taken in well before the first frost. For those who strive against the greatest

disadvantages, the newer, day-length, neutral varieties may make it marginally easier to produce fresh strawberries in mid-winter.

Grapes are one of the best fruits to grow in a greenhouse or conservatory, where they are less subject to rot, frosts and bird damage. Although they can be planted inside, planting them in a border just outside the greenhouse gives them a bigger root run. Bring the vine inside through a hole, make sure the hole can be enlarged as the stem grows, and insulate the outside stem. You *may* find it better to grow vines in large containers because this confines their roots, so reducing the pruning required and allowing for many varieties to be grown in the space taken by just one vine, but they will need more water. Heat is used under cover to start growth sooner. Then grapes can be had for mid-summer or earlier, and some of the more luscious but long-season old varieties can be grown, such as 'Madresfield Court' and the difficult 'Muscat of Alexandria'.

ABOVE *Grown indoors, strawberries are admittedly slightly less tasty, but very early and very welcome.*
LEFT *Grown outdoors they taste better, but come later.*

Less heat is used if you take the vines outdoors after they have fruited to ripen and harden the wood outdoors in late autumn. Prune them once the frosts have come and leave them out until late winter or early spring, when bringing them under barely heated cover will start them into growth. Once under cover, be careful not to let them get a chill or draught as the sudden change can precipitate mildew attacks.

Prune hard. Grapes fruit best on last year's wood, so, in the UK a framework is usually formed along horizontal wires. This is because sap always rises, so if any of the canes are significantly lower than the rest of the vine they will get little sap and not fruit. It is better to fill a high wall with two vines, one for the lower tiers and one for the higher than to try and cover it with only one plant. A year after planting, cut back really hard to three buds to get only one or two strong re-growths; these should grow up to the level of the wires. In late autumn, cut these back well below the wires; their re-growth in the third year then can be trained up to and along the wires and eventually trimmed back to make the frame.

Once the frame is made, which will take at least a couple of years, the pruning becomes more complicated. Select and cut back the younger growths to form fruiting spurs in good places on the framework. This is best done in a couple of stages. All shoots are trimmed in summer to three or four leaves beyond the flower trusses – except any growths wanted to replace or extend the framework. If no flower truss appears by the sixth leaf, stop it anyway and mark those canes for later removal – do not use these for next year's spurs if alternatives are available! Any later re-growths are also cut back to prevent congestion and to redirect energy to the ripening fruit. Then, in winter, remove every surplus bit of wood, leaving well-placed spurs tipped with one small piece of young wood with a bud or two. All else is removed, except where needed to extend or replace the framework. Occasionally, a strong young shoot from lower down can be used to replace ugly, worn-out spurs or a whole limb of the frame.

In pots, grapes are pruned even harder to a stump with only a couple of shoots with a couple of buds on each. Ideally, four or five equal and fruiting shoots emerge to be tied together at shoulder height and later trimmed not far above. These are then cut back to a bud or two apiece in winter. Be brave, as you can rarely over-prune grapes if you leave some firm, well-ripened, medium-sized *young* wood. Especially under cover, thin the fruit bunches down to a reasonable number if you want size and quality and to keep the vine from exhaustion. The vine will set plenty, so remove three out of four in a good year!

Make sure grapes, especially those grown in pots, never run out of water because if they slow down and restart growth, the grapes will split. Vines suffer from many common pests and diseases and the usual remedies apply to these (see page 241).

Epicurean attentions 'Golden Chasselas' ripens the first grapes in mid-summer and still carries slightly wrinkled but edible fruits in the New Year. Spraying my ripe grape bunches with neat, high-proof white rum cleans them of mealy bugs and other pests.

Bob's gourmet choices Under cover, 'Muscat Hamburg' (black) is supreme and 'Black Hamburg' (black) is good where warmth is available. 'Golden Chasselas' ('Chasselas D'Or') (white) and 'Buckland Sweetwater' (white) are both remarkably sweet and reliable. 'Siegerrebe' is exquisite, but it dislikes lime-rich soils.

Citrus trees wait a decade before fruiting when grown from pips, but grafted plants can be obtained, which will fruit while small. Citrus need frost-free conditions and an open, gritty, rich, almost ericaceous, potting compost in large containers (preferably made from terracotta or wood slat, as the roots need good aeration). Drill multiple breathing holes in plastic pots.

Citrus like nitrogenous feeds. I add fresh, human, recycled liquid fertiliser to their water once a week during the growing season. Water copiously and then allow to drain (don't let the plants ever dry out). Citrus are very easy to look after, but suffer from aphids, red spider mite and scale insects, so need regular and careful inspection. A hard prune in late winter keeps them compact and provides propagation material. Do not keep them under cover all year round – place them outdoors in summer. Not cheap to buy, they can be multiplied by cuttings which fruit more readily than seedlings.

Epicurean attentions Marmalade is easy to make, so I freeze all home-grown orange and lemon skins to add to a jelly made with yellow tomatoes and white currants. The flowers have a divine scent, making it worth having the plants for that reason alone.

Bob's gourmet choices Lemons seem easiest and can produce fruit almost all year round; 'Meyer' is the most reliable. Oranges require more warmth and bigger pots, tangerines and kumquats are similar and worth having, while grapefuits are the hardiest of all, but not highly productive.

OPPOSITE FROM ABOVE *Glazing units and heat retaining flooring bring this vine on weeks ahead of the rest.* BELOW LEFT *By growing in a tub under cover, you get about five bunches very early.*
BELOW RIGHT *'Muscat Hamburgh', my favourite variety.* RIGHT *Grapefruits are the hardier amongst the common citrus.*

Tropical delights you may not think possible

Out of curiosity many of us have started off seeds from an unusual fruit we've eaten such as mangoes and lychees. However, some of these exotic plants will easily fruit with just a little more attention. For instance, the Swiss cheese plant, given a big pot and light, produces large, arum-like flowers that ripen into delicious, banana-sized cerimans or fruits. If you want an impressive houseplant that also crops, try eddo or taro. The 'tubers' of these colocasias are eaten, especially in West Indian cookery. Watch out for the irritant skin on the tubers, though. With only a plastic tent inside a plastic tunnel, a soil-warming cable and a household fan heater, I have fruited all of the following exotics with surprising ease here in Norfolk. The fruits with their seeds are readily available from most supermarkets.

Cape gooseberries are surprisingly easy. The seed is best ripened in the fruit until the pulp wrinkles up. The plant is perennial, but flowers

and fruits better in the second year when it produces abundantly all summer and autumn. Hard-prune in late winter or early spring. It uses a lot of water! Take a cutting in early autumn, keep it warm and pot up in spring. Then, never prune, but entwine every shoot up a cane as soon as each is long enough to form a spherical ball of immense productivity.

ABOVE *Cherry/Strawberry guava – a real superfruit and winter cropping.* **LEFT** *You can eat fresh Cape gooseberries all winter.*

Peanuts are for kids of all ages. You start them off in cells in the warm, grow them in the ground (not in pots) and get compact, soft-leaved, clover-like plants with yellow flowers. When you dig them up at the end of the season, you have peanuts, simple as that.

Passionfruits are equally easy, although they don't survive long, cold, damp winters very well, even under cover. They are so quick to grow and fruit that you can often have fruits the first winter after an early-spring sowing. Sow seeds of supermarket fruit early in warmth, pot on, and train up canes. Do not keep hot, just frost-free.

Guavas surprised me. The hard object from the supermarket, hardly fit for jam, produced an attractive compact shrub. This fruited the second year with the most lusciously perfumed and succulent fruit I could imagine, so try these! The mountain, cherry or strawberry guava, *Psidium cattleyanum*, is the most wonderful fruit and I do not know why we don't all have one. It's a neat, bushy, small-leaved evergreen that's nearly hardy and enjoys a similar treatment to citrus. It produces purple fruits over a long season that are very, very tasty and rich in vitamins and anthocyanins. In fact, with a couple of bushes treated differently, I have fresh fruits from early autumn to spring. A must!

Lemon grass is essential to much Eastern cuisine and is expensive to buy. Look for fresh stock in the supermarket that hasn't been cut too close to the stem, leaving a tiny bit of the root crown. These root easily if potted up over some heat or even in a glass of water in summer. Once growing, this makes magnificent mounds of lemon-scented grass, which can cut the fingers if mishandled. Detach and trim plump new sideshoots to use for flavouring.

Ginger is also expensive to buy, yet almost any part of the fresh root with a bud will grow if detached, potted and given some warmth. I grow ginger on in the warm in big buckets, which, by winter, produce pounds of root each.

Pineapples are harder. They need it hot, must never get chilled, and require two or three

years to crop. In time, they will flower and fruit if given bottom heat and a bucket-sized pot of rich, well-drained compost. Choose a good, healthy, crowned pineapple, cut off the crown immediately above the fruit, and let it dry for several days. Then peel away the lower decaying leaves and you will usually see the first roots there. Pot up, arrange a little bottom heat and a hot sunny position, keep the centre dry in winter, and then be patient as the reward will be worth it!

Bananas are actually easy but, as they grow very tall, we can only grow the dwarf *Musa acuminata* 'Dwarf Cavendish', which still needs about ten feet or three metres to open its leaves. To guarantee tasty fruits, grow from an offset, not seed. The 'bulb' can be brought into the UK from the Canary Islands, where it is widely grown. Sometimes, unnamed banana plants are sold in supermarkets and garden centres, but avoid buying ornamental bananas such as *M. basjoo*. The *true* 'Dwarf Cavendish' has light purple shading in the middle of younger leaves. However, pot it up, plant it in the ground under cover, and keep it warm, and in a year or two it will fruit – honest! After fruiting, cut down the 'tree' and allow the biggest replacement shoot to stay, removing all the others. A plastic dustbin is a tad too small for a pot; an old bath or water tank is better.

ABOVE RIGHT *In my tunnel within a tunnel, front to back: lemon grass, melon, ginger,* Impatiens, *chilli, mango,* Aloe, Monstera, *guava,* Cape gooseberry *and* Nicotiana. BELOW RIGHT *Young pineapple plants – a slow but very rewarding crop.*

9 HARVESTING, STORING & SHARING OUR BOUNTY

Easy and effective ways to spread the enjoyment of our bountiful produce over even more months of the year

The once-common techniques of processing and storing crops are skills that many of us need to relearn. However, the tools to help us are much improved. Simple dryers and juice extractors are now widely available, excellent fruit and root stores can be made from redundant fridges and freezers, and even bottling and deep-freezing have become easier with the cost of the equipment falling in real terms.

As more and more people become aware of the value of home-grown produce, they are taking up the challenge – in particular, there seems to be an explosion in the number of varieties of chutneys being produced at home. The backyard chicken has returned, with many more now being kept for their delicious eggs, and often with an interest in keeping heritage breeds. Even the backyard pig is returning and sales of sausage-making machinery and home smokers have

become substantial. Much credit for this reawakening interest in good food may be laid at the door of TV cookery programmes, although they concentrate more on meals than methods of preservation. Still, I'm sure that will come in time, too.

SUCCESSFUL HARVESTING
Harvesting is the most glorious job of the year – digging potatoes is like searching for buried gold, while cupboards filled with jam jars and the deep freezer become our treasure chests. The season of plenty is soon over, however, so harvest and store diligently. Remember: store only the best, eat fresh the rest, and compost what's left. In temperate climates, we also only have a short growing season of about half the year. In the UK, for example, we need to harvest most of our crops before the first autumn frosts. So, successful harvesting and storing are as important as growing the crops well in the first place. Refer back to the last chapter about how to extend the season at either end by growing under cover.

While the harvesting time for most vegetables is not that critical, most fruits are only enjoyable when perfectly ripened. Melons are

improved by chilling first, but most fruits are tastiest eaten straight off the plant. Of course, long-keeping apples need careful picking for storage if they are to last many months. The best date for picking fruit will vary with the cultivar, the soil, the site and the season. This can only be determined by experience, as these factors all vary considerably. If you want to store them, fruits need to be at just the right stage and most store best when picked just under-ripe. They may keep for longer picked younger, but this will be at the expense of flavour and sweetness. On any tree, the sunny side ripens first. Fruit will also ripen earlier where extra warmth is supplied – next to a wall, window or chimney, or just close to the soil, are good places for early fruits. Likewise, when the rest of the fruit has gone, you may find some fruits hidden in the shade. So, wait for the fruits on the sunny side to ripen – the rest of the crop is probably then perfect for picking to store or process.

Vegetables usually have a long season for picking, while many are easier to store than fruits because they are less prone to rots. Indeed, some, such as parsnips and most roots and brassicas and leeks, are best left in the ground if protected against hard frosts. Some, such as squashes and the onion tribe, just need careful drying and keeping in an airy, frost-free place. Other vegetables store very well, but always plan your week's cooking, harvesting and storage to save on too much running to and fro. For example, petit pois peas ripen and go over rapidly, but, if you plan ahead, then you can harvest them to use fresh on the day and process the rest in one efficient swoop.

Harvesting herbs is best done at the last minute for fresh use; if you are going to store them, pick them at their peak, often just before flowering. Crunchy salad crops are a special case and should be picked at dawn with cool dew on them for maximum crispness.

OPPOSITE *A motley crew, but their eggs are divine.* ABOVE LEFT *Unearth storing potatoes carefully so they're undamaged.* MIDDLE *Note these 'brickies' gloves, designed for grip they also clean up spuds nicely.* RIGHT *Set to dry in the sun for an hour or two to toughen their skins.* BOTTOM *Nothing beats really fresh asparagus.*

have dried off, but before they are warm. Similarly, it is helpful to chill and dry off many crops initially by leaving the store open on chilly dry nights and closing it during the day for a week or two after filling. Most fruits are best removed some time before use so any staleness can leave them. Care should be taken not to store early and late varieties together or any that may cross-taint. Vegetables need to be kept separate from fruits! Obviously, do not situate your store in the same place as strong-smelling substances such as paint. Likewise, stored straw, although a convenient litter, will taint if it gets damp (shredded newspaper or stinging nettles are safer).

Always inspect stored crops regularly, as they can go off very quickly, and don't store everything for ages merely for the sake of it. Instead, select and store well that which you will use.

SIMPLE WAYS OF STORING

Although we occasionally store some crops, such as pears, for a period to improve their condition, we usually store most crops just to extend the season. All crops for storage must be perfect; any blemish or bruise is where moulds start. There is absolutely no point storing anything that has any real damage. Use immediately or process the crop into juice, jelly, chutney or purée, and so on. Choose varieties suitable for storing; many early croppers are notoriously bad keepers! Waxing fruits is undoubtedly good for extending their life, but could help shorten yours. Some will keep as well wrapped in paper or oiled (vegetable) paper. Another early method of deterring mould was dipping fruits in a sodium bicarbonate solution and then leaving them to dry before storing.

Common, long-keeping fruits and vegetables, such as apples and potatoes, can be stored at home for months, even up to a year. The major problems, apart from moulds, are shrivelling through water loss and the depredations of rodents and other big pests. The house or garage are too warm, cold or dry for storage purposes. I personally find dead deep freezers and refrigerators make excellent stores, being dark, at a constant temperature and frost-free. Provide some ventilation by cutting small holes in the rubber door or lid seal. Condensation usually indicates insufficient ventilation, but remember that too many draughts will dry out the fruits. The unit can stand somewhere dry outdoors, as it needs no power. Kept in a shed, it is out of sight and better protected against the cold, although it may even get too warm. Extra frost protection is ensured in extreme conditions by putting a sealed bottle of warm water inside the unit each night and morning.

When putting crops in store, leave them to chill at night in trays or bags and then load them into the store in the morning when they

OPPOSITE *'New' bicoloured carrot.* **ABOVE LEFT** *Leftover potato sets, kept in case a gap appears.* **ABOVE RIGHT** *Shredded paper pads nicely and absorbs any leakers.* **BOTTOM** *Pears need to be inspected daily, so don't wrap them up.*

SIMPLE WAYS OF PROCESSING

Because many crops go off too quickly, they are best processed if you want to preserve them for longer. The most valuable crops to process are herbs and fruits, as vegetables take more effort. An important point to consider is that, even if rotten, fruit bottled or jammed gone mouldy is rarely as harmful as preserved vegetables gone off, which can be extremely hazardous. So, if you skimp on instructions and detail, then you'd best stick to processing fruits!

Juicing is the very best way of storing fruit, other than turning it into wine, but that's another book! Not all crops can be easily juiced, though. The harder fruits and vegetables are easier with electric machinery, but many can be squeezed to express the juice, or heated and/or frozen to break down the texture, then strained. Sugar or salt may be added to taste and may also improve the colour, flavour and keeping qualities. Juices may be drunk as they are, as squashes diluted with water, added to cocktails, and used in cooking. Fruit juices take less space in a freezer than their original crop. I freeze mine in wax cartons and plastic bottles, cleaned first and with a wee space for expansion. (Vegetable juices should only be consumed fresh, for safety.)

Grapes are the easiest to press and the most rewarding, and you can still ferment the pips and skins afterwards. Such wine tastes no worse than most of my regular tipples, though that is little praise. They are best crushed first to break the skins. Most of the currants and berries can be squeezed in the same way. Apples must be crushed first

and then squeezed. They will go through the same equipment, but more slowly than the more juicy fruits. Pulpy firm fruits, such as blackcurrants, pears and plums, are best simmered with water until soft and then the juice is strained off. Repeating the process and adding sugar to the combined juices is also the basis for jellies. Raspberries, strawberries and fruits with such

ABOVE *Apple juice, fresh pressed and chilled, is a nectar of the gods, too much makes you fart like the devil though.* LEFT *Although not all ripe yet, this bunch will turn into a very palatable juice.*

delicate flavours are best frozen, then defrosted and strained, when a pure juice unchanged by heating is obtained.

Suitable equipment for processing large amounts is widely available if the quantities are too large for kitchen tools. Many different presses and crushers are sold or hired for home and small-scale winemakers. Home-made juices last longer in the refrigerator and keep for months or years if deep-frozen.

Jellying and jamming both preserve fruit in a sugary gel. They differ in that jelly is made from only the juice, without the seeds and skins, while jam contains whole fruits or pieces of fruit. A conserve is just an expensive jam, usually implying more fruit and less sugar or filler. (Freezer jams are conserves made with so little sugar that they go mouldy quickly unless kept frozen and then used from the refrigerator.)

Almost any fruit can be jammed or jellied – and there are many only palatable if treated in this way. The fruit is cooked to the point of breaking up the cells, so that the juices run. The juice is then turned into a gel with sugar, which also acts as a preservative. Most fruits need to have up to their own weight of sugar added to them to make a setting gel.

Jellies are made from the strained juice and set clear and bright. Many people prefer them because of the absence of seeds, skins, etc., although others prefer the texture of jams because of these things. So, fruit for jam requires more careful picking and preparation because the odd sprig or hard fruit is not strained off. My solution for, say, blackcurrants, is carefully to pick the very finest berries first and then more roughly pick the bulk of the fruit to jelly. The bulk is simmered down to a juice, strained, and then *before* it is set with the sugar, the finest berries are added and quickly cooked. White sugar, not brown, is traditionally used for jamming and jellying, unless a strong (caramel) flavour is required. Honey is not really successful, as the flavour is strong and it goes off when heated as much as when making jam. Similarly, concentrated juices can add too much flavour. The amount of fruit can be increased and the sugar decreased the better your technique, and the quicker you can eat a jar!

Ideally, simmer down the fruit with the minimal amount of water, strain (if it is for jelly), add the sugar, bring to a boil, skim off any scum, and then pot in sterile conditions. Hot jars and clean lids put on *immediately* improve results. Store once cold in a dark cool place. Some fruits are difficult to set, particularly cherries, aronias and strawberries in a wet year. Adding chopped apples to the jelly fruits or their purée to the jams will supply the pectin needed to make any fruit set. Extra acidity for a pleasing tartness is often achieved using lemon juice. However, whitecurrant juice is a good substitute and redcurrant even better. Adding white- or redcurrant juice is also an aid to setting difficult jams. Their flavour is so tart yet mild that their jellies make good carriers for more strongly flavoured fruits in shorter supply, especially for raspberries and cherries.

Important tip! It is quicker and easier to make four five-pound batches of jam than one twenty-pound. And the result is always better – large batches have a low heating and evaporating surface compared to their volume and take much longer to process, so the fruit degrades more. Remember: quickly simmer down to a pulp, add the right

ABOVE RIGHT *Small batches cook quicker and better than large ones, note sugar pre-warming.* BELOW RIGHT *Small jars, hot from oven, fill then seal promptly.*

amount of sugar, bring back to the boil, skim, pot and seal. No standing around watching some great cauldron bubble all day!

Chutneys, sauces and pickles are really just jam-making with vegetables! But, because these are so prone to going off, we add vinegar and salt to the sugar (or even use these to replace it entirely). Many vegetables are combined with fruits in chutneys. Tomato sauce is ripe tomato jam with vinegar and spices, while many other sauces are based on this with more or less chilli/tamarind/pepper added. The vegetables may be salted first, but are often almost raw in pickles, such as piccalilli. What healthier food?

Drying loses some flavour, but concentrates the food into a much smaller volume than preserving, so use dried herbs sparingly. Many foods can be dried if sliced thinly and exposed to warm dry air. Sealed in dark containers and kept cool and dry, they will keep for long periods to be eaten dried or reconstituted when required. However, in the humid air of the UK, and much of maritime Europe and North America, drying is not quick enough and nor is it helped by low temperatures in these regions. Making solar-powered dryers – wire trays under glass with good ventilation – allows for fruit to be dried to a larger extent, but in regions with the highest humidity the food may still go mouldy before it dries. I slice the food thinly and hang the pieces, separated by at least half their own size, on long strings over

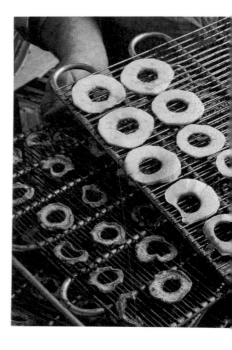

my cooking range. This provides the dry warmth and ventilation needed to desiccate most within a day or two or even just overnight for the easier ones such as apples.

Oven-drying with artificial heat is risky as it can cook the food, destroying the value, texture and keeping properties. It is possible, though, if the temperature is kept down and the door kept partly open. Oven-drying is convenient for finishing off partly dried samples after you have done other baking; the decaying heat desiccates well with little risk of caramelising or burning.

Herbs for drying are best gathered once the dew has dried off them. Then, hang them in small bunches, upside down, in a very airy place. Bright light bleaches out the colour, so some shading may be necessary. Once completely dry, crush them to go in jars or seal in paper bags in a tin.

Freezing captures flavours lost by drying. It is good for herbs, which can be frozen and need almost no time to defrost, and can be conveniently frozen as portion-controlled ice cubes in water or oil. Most fruits freeze easily with little preparation, unlike vegetables which need blanching first. This involves chopping up the vegetables and immersing them in boiling water for a minute or more, then chilling them again before freezing.

Obviously, only the very best produce is worth freezing. Most fruits turn to soggy lumps in a pool of juice when defrosted, which is not as appetising as the well-textured fresh product. However, they are still packed full of sweetness, flavour and vitamins, so are well worth having for culinary uses, especially in tarts, pies, sauces and compôtes.

ABOVE *Drying reduces the volume significantly.* **LEFT** *Not the best place to hang herbs, but handy for drying seed heads.* **OPPOSITE ABOVE** *A lid traps the hottest molecules from escaping and taking aroma away with them.* **OPPOSITE BELOW** *A tub of beans ready for adding to every soup and casserole.*

For most fruits and blanched vegetables, merely putting them in sealed freezer bags or boxes is sufficient. However, they can freeze in a block, making later piecemeal usage difficult. Freeze them loose on open wire drying trays or greased baking trays, and then pack them afterwards. Cut or damaged fruits need to be drained first before freezing them. Or if you have a sweet tooth, they can be dredged in sugar, which absorbs the juice. Stone fruits are best de-stoned before freezing or the stone can give an almond taint. The tough skin of fruits such as tomatoes or plums is easiest removed after freezing and before use. Do this by carefully squeezing the frozen fruit under very hot water and the skin should slip off easily.

COOKING EFFICIENTLY, ECOLOGICALLY AND ORGANICALLY

Having achieved freshness, flavour and quality with all your home-grown produce, don't spoil your wonderful ingredients by using a rancid oil, a stale spice or an adulterated one. Grind your own from

fresh ingredients and always buy 'organic' if you can. And, of course, there are many ecological alternatives to everyday household products that are preferable to anyone with a greener outlook.

Multiple waste buckets make sense – have one for compost, one for hens, one for recycling and, lastly, one for the dustbin. The latter should not get full too often as, obviously, there won't be many tinned, bottled or pre-packaged products in a grow-your-own household!

A pressure cooker or steamer are more efficient for cooking than boiling and, with planning, several meals can be cooked together for simple reheating later. With a freezer, this becomes easier and you can make your own range of home-made ready-meals for those rushed days.

If you wish to cook as organically as possible, I advise you to stop using aluminium or non-stick surfaces, especially with acid or salty liquids; copper and brass are dangerous for most cooking purposes! Stainless-steel, enamel or, failing that, cast iron is preferable.

Flavourful guidelines Bay leaves add aroma to every savoury dish and basil can be almost as widely used, especially with tomatoes and any combination with garlic. A parsley or cheese sauce will go with almost any savoury dish or enliven a plate of steamed vegetables. Mint and horseradish sauces are delicious eaten with most vegetables.

A bunch of herbs for soups and other dishes should contain a sprig each of parsley, thyme and bay, although I always add rosemary as well. A *bouquet garni* is the same thing but is tied up in a bit of cloth with some peppercorns.

Fine herbs (*herbes fines*) for French-style egg dishes and sauces are just finely chopped chervil, chives, parsley and French tarragon.

Mixed herbs are anything you like, but usually parsley, thyme, marjoram and summer savory.

Angelica and sweet cicely can be used to make rhubarb and fruit dishes sweeter, while bay or lavender can be added to milk dessert dishes. There are countless different combinations, so try to experiment.

Most vegetables and fruits can be peeled. Although the fibre in the skin is good, the skin of tomato and potatoes can be an irritant to some people. The area under the skin contains the most valuable nutrients, so it is often best to cook them first and then slip the skins off after. Water that has been used to steam or boil food is full of goodness and should be used as a stock or at least added to the compost heap.

A better salad Bored with the blandness of many salads, I experimented by adding fresh herbs to enliven them. I also reasoned that more varied foods, especially using more herbs, would provide healthier nutrition. Once I started, I soon found the herbs started to outgrow the lettuce and cucumber portion. With some summers too hot and dry for growing lettuces, I discovered that, by blending many herbs, I could make delicious salads without any lettuce or most other conventional saladings at all. The more herbs I blended, the more pleasant the overall taste, as long as the very bitter and strong herbs were used with utmost moderation. Although some more conservative friends have looked askance at strange mixes, they have nearly always gone on to enjoy them.

The basic principle is to use as many different edible herbs as possible without letting any one flavour dominate. Take small quantities of each herb and chop them finely. By varying the proportions, the mix can be adjusted to suit most tastes. Of course, for some people, the flavour will be too strong so, background salading vegetables can be added to dilute the herbs and increase valuable nutrients and texture.

For much of the year, it is possible to continually crop small amounts of very many different herbs. However, the choice is not as wide in late winter and early spring. It is at this time that the hardier herbs and vegetables can be valuable. They provide the most part of salads, reducing the need for expensive, bought-in, out-of-season produce.

ABOVE *An old chip basket for washing carrots before they come indoors.*

Flowerdew's super salad Add, mix and adjust to taste as available, finely chopped portions of the following:

Small amounts of rosemary, thyme, sage, marjoram, sweet cicely, summer savory, shungiku, coriander and fennel.
Larger amounts of parsley, chervil, dill, French tarragon and basil.
Lots and lots and lots of chives and rocket.
Varying quantities to taste of mint, nasturtium leaves and flowers, purslane, iceplant, good King Henry, grated horseradish, land cress, citrus leaves, radicchio and alpine strawberries.

Mix all the above up thoroughly to be diluted with background saladings of: shredded carrot, grated red and green cabbage, shredded kohlrabi, chopped red and green pepper, cucumber and gherkin bits, tender curly kale leaves, corn salad, Claytonia and even lettuce, chicory, endive, almost any edible green, and baby peas. Then, add pot marigold, day lily (Hemerocallis), Pelargonium and shungiku petals, borage and rosemary flowers, some violets, pansies, bergamot and loads of rose petals. When ready to serve, top with sliced 'Gardener's Delight' tomatoes and sprinkle over hull-less pumpkin, poppy, celery and sunflower seeds. I rarely use salad dressings on this. Instead, I prefer to keep it dry and serve it in combination with a well-moistened dish such as taramasalata, houmous, egg mayonnaise, and so on. (I have also often eaten, but cannot recommend including, very small amounts of clary sage, salad burnet, lovage, hyssop, winter savory, lemon verbena, lemon balm and lavender.)

Bob's toast topping This is a very nutritious meal for those in a hurry. Simultaneously soft-boil an egg(s), make some toast and chop up finely a handful of any tasty herbs, but especially chives and chervil. Put the chopped herbs in a small bowl and add (to taste) grated cheese, mayonnaise or salad cream or similar, some tomato ketchup and a dash of hot chilli or Worcester sauce. As soon as the egg is cooked, shell and chop it into the bowl, mix quickly and spoon onto the buttered toast. This goes well with my super salad and the Kohlslaw to make a mega-healthy meal.

Kohlslaw Like coleslaw, but this is made from grated kohlrabi instead of cabbage. Carrot, apple and onion are also added, mixed with mayonnaise (or similar) a little garlic and paprika. I often add grated celeriac, red and green peppers and small amounts of dill and other herbs. This is a moist dish to complement the salad and to go with baked potatoes or the toast topping.

HOUSEHOLD PRODUCTS: POT POURRI AND STREWING HERBS

The medicinal uses for herbs require a book of their own, so I will not venture to deal with them here. It is worth noting a few of their more handy uses around the home, though. Handfuls of fresh or dried herbs, wrapped in a cloth and held under the hot tap, create a wonderful and relaxing bath to finish off a hard day in the garden. Pot pourris are air fresheners made from dried herbs. Special recipes are quoted needing exotic ingredients, but any dried herb in a bowl will give off its own aroma. My favourite is based on lemon verbena leaves with some rose petals, 'Eau de Cologne' mint leaves, and *Thymus herba-barona*. Try whatever you have available.

Dried herbs tied in bags keep pests out of drawers and cupboards; lavender is the best base for this. Strewing herbs offer a better, if dusty, means of scenting a room than pot pourri and make ideal floor coverings in potting sheds. Perhaps unsuitable for the home, I prefer mints and cotton lavender for working areas, hyssop by the wellie rack, and lavender in the summerhouse and car footwells. In the fruit store, I use southernwood to give a clean scent and drive away pests. Use the barbecue to scent the air and drive away gnats and flies by adding small bundles of fresh or soaked dried herbs to the coals.

TOP LEFT *Rather oddly, I like aged bay leaves, most prefer fresher.* TOP RIGHT *By drying individually it's quicker, with less flavour lost.* BOTTOM *Seed heads laid on paper to finish ripening and drying fully.*

Sharing our garden with backyard friends

Along with the satisfaction of growing your own food and flowers, the greatest joy of successful organic gardening is spying a rare butterfly, a grass snake or a dragonfly by your pool. All the natural fertility you make in your soil, the many forms of life it supports, and the sustaining habitat you provide attract and multiply many and varied forms of wildlife. These are disappearing from the wild and our aim is to bring them to strength again within our bounds. Even though we may lose some crops to them, they give us pleasure, control many pests and improve our fertility. Surely we can afford to share a little of our surplus with them?

Not only may we have wild friends, but we can also keep pets and livestock. Livestock are a cunning way to convert medium-grade household and garden wastes into high-grade food and composting material. By giving animals food that we don't eat, we can recycle the food value back as eggs, meat or milk. This is also a way of converting the surpluses of summer into a more storable form. Don't be put off by the added responsibility of looking after animals – having chickens is easier than owning a cat or dog – and their eggs are far better!

Chickens It is an exceptionally good idea to run chickens underneath fruit trees, as they improve the fertility, control the grass and reduce pest problems to a minimum. Bantams lay as many, but slightly smaller eggs, and are more prone to escapism than the bigger breeds. Marans or Rhode Island Reds are good breeds for most households.

A couple of hens can be kept in a mobile ark and run on a small lawn which is moved each day. It is gratifying how much grass they then neatly eat. For several birds a hut is needed. Site a permanent hut next to the compost heap or by plum and peach trees, as these will benefit from the increased droppings. Ideally, though, the hut should be mobile, so that the hens can get access to different areas. The more they run around on new sites, the better the egg quality and production will be. And you don't need a cockerel if you just want eggs.

The birds will need nice fat perches in their hut, nest boxes, water, grit and oyster shell. They can be given back eggshell, but only if it is baked and crushed first. Household scraps, plus garden wastes and grain, will make a couple of hens happy and they will give you eggs from early spring to late autumn for about five years. In winter, you just do without eggs, unless you give them extra light and hot mashes. Their parasites can be kept down if you give them a dust bath to roll in. Chickens love their greens and if you let them amongst brassicas they choose cauliflower and broccoli leaves first, but also really like lettuce, beetroot and chard leaves. In some areas, foxes may be a problem. A solid hen house with a simple pop-hatch that can be opened in the morning and closed at dusk will keep them safe. Automatic ones are also available. Keep them in until late morning so that they lay in there and you can find the eggs!

LEFT *Geese are useful converters of grass to egg.* **OPPOSITE** *Although there will be times you curse them, backyard hens can be hugely productive of top quality eggs and meat.*

predators and because they can't escape. Of course, once they are introduced, almost all pesticide use has to stop. Introduce them early in the season, but not before the pest has appeared or they will starve. If pest populations get large before the predators arrive, thin out the numbers with traps, trap plants and safe sprays first. Follow the manufacturer's instructions on the packets.

The minute predatory wasp, *Encarsia formosa*, is very effective at controlling whitefly, while *Phytoseiulus persimilis* is a mite that eats red spider mites. Slugs and snails, vine weevils, chafer grubs and leather jackets may all be controlled by watering on solutions of appropriate parasitic nematode eelworms. *Aphidoletes aphidmyza* is a parasitic midge for controlling aphids. Mealy bug predator, *Cryptolaemus montrouzieri*, is a ladybird; its white, shaggy larvae rapidly control mealy bugs. Cabbage white, and other similar caterpillars, can be killed with the disease *Bacillus thuringiensis*; this is sprayed onto the crop and, as the caterpillars eat, they pick up the spores and soon die. This disease occurs naturally and is no danger to us or the

environment. *Trichoderma viride* is a predatory fungus used to prevent other fungi attacking pruning wounds. It's applied before, or instead of, a sealing compound. It can also be used to cure silver leaf disease in plums and Dutch elm disease if these have not progressed too far. Pellets are inserted into holes drilled in the trunk and the predatory fungus permeates the tree. *Trichoderma* apparently prevents posts rotting and has been used in watering systems to prevent wilt in seedlings. Unfortunately, it is not available to amateurs in the UK.

10 Organic Pesticides

Organic gardeners prefer not to use poisonous substances unless they are needed to save a valuable crop. They are there as a last resort, but we should not disrupt ecosystems that have slowly built up. Take especial care not to harm bees, and only use poisons after the bees have retired. Newer pesticides based on natural products, such as plant oils, garlic and chilli extracts, and even milk, are proving efficacious and becoming available under trade names as they are cleared for legal use in the UK. Follow the instructions on the packaging as to their uses, application rates and precautions. Keep them in a safe, secure place.

Pesticides used to control insects Soft soap is just that. Traditionally used to kill aphids, red spider mite, whitefly and other pests, it has been reformulated to be more effective. Extremely safe to use and made from natural products, it is the preferable insecticide, but cannot deal with larger insect pests such as caterpillars or wasps.

Pyrethrum is available to UK gardeners in a liquid form, but is not suitable for organic purists because it is supplied with a synthetic synergist. The powdered form is sold for

killing ants, but is not yet cleared for other insect pests such as small caterpillars. Pyrethrum also kills beneficial insects and fish but is very safe for mammals.

Derris (rotenone) liquid or powder is extracted from various tropical plants and kills most insects and caterpillars, friends and foes indiscriminately. However, it is particularly effective against mites, but also lethal to fish, pigs and tortoises. It breaks down in sunlight and is slower to act than pyrethrum. Derris is being withdrawn because of doubts about its safety and is not now recommended.

Quassia solution is made from a tree bark and kills aphids, but few beneficial insects. Quassia is no longer available as a preparation except combined with other more unacceptable ingredients.

Pesticides used against diseases Bordeaux mixture is a fungicidal suspension of copper sulphate and slaked lime. It is a chemical, but allowed under organic standards as it is not considered very harmful to us or soil life. It is effective against potato blight, peach leaf curl, raspberry cane spot and many other fungal diseases. It is a preventative, not a cure, and must be applied thoroughly and in good time.

Sulphur is the pure element, and allowed under organic standards as a control for powdery mildews on fruit, flowers and vegetables and for preventing rots in overwintering bulbs and tubers. Take care with fruit trees and bushes as a few varieties are allergic to sulphur, so read the label carefully.

Sodium bicarbonate solution was once used as a fungicide against gooseberry mildew, but is not allowed under UK pesticide legislation. However, the similar potassium bicarbonate is available and works against a range of powdery and downy mildews and black spot of roses.

The usual diseases and their treatment

Mildews are broadly of two types: powdery and downy. The powdery forms generally do less damage than the downy, grey mildews. They both attack plants under stress, 'eating' them from the outside. The commonest causes are plants too dry at the roots and stagnant air. Good growing conditions, plus careful pruning and training to let in air and light, will do much to alleviate mildews. Having many alliums growing nearby may offer some protection, but needs time to work. Removing diseased material speeds up the effect. *Equisetum* tea, seaweed, garlic and nettle sprays, mustard seed flour and milk are all claimed to make plants tougher and more resistant. Bordeaux, sulphur and potassium bicarbonate are also effective controls.

Rusts, in many ways, are very similar to mildews. Like mildews, they tend to appear on different plants at the same time. This is because the conditions are suitable and not because the rust has moved from one to the other as, in general, they do not. However, some rusts do have alternate hosts whereby they spend part of the year on one plant and then move to another for winter. For example, wild *Berberis* harbours wheat rust. Hygiene and the permissible fungicides cited for mildews are usually effective if used in time.

Botrytis or grey mould is usually associated with high humidity. Improved air flow and drier conditions can help. Some fungicides may help as can, surprisingly, spraying on fresh urine.

Wilts and rots are soil-dwelling organisms that attack unhealthy plants which soon succumb. Rather than futilely sterilising the soil, add live garden compost and the goodies will soon eat the baddies! *Trichoderma* also proves useful, but is not available to amateurs in the UK.

Bacterial or virus diseases Hygiene, healthy plants and the control of vectors (disease-transmitting organisms) spreading the diseases are the most effective controls. For example, removing the mite-swollen big buds from blackcurrants helps prevent reversion attacks. Hygiene and sterilising tools with alcohol is important.

ABOVE RIGHT *Although disfigured, these leaves are still mostly functional.* **BELOW RIGHT** *Another 'disease', but in fact it is wasp damage.* **LEFT** *It's easy at first to imagine disease but in fact it's typical aphid damage.*

The usual pests and their treatments

Ants Black ants bite but do not sting, red ants sting. Ants are attracted to the honeydew excreted by aphids. Black ants milk and move aphids to better feeding grounds and overwinter aphids and eggs in their nests. They effectively keep almost all predators away from their flocks! They may also do the same for other pests, such as scale insects, whiteflies and mealy bugs. Ants may, however, predate some other pests. They uproot seedlings, and even large plants, with their burrowing. However, the pulverised soil aids other plants, especially as it contains immediate and potential plant food as finely divided organic material. The main problem is their arrival in the house or store. Strewing the mint family, especially spearmint or pennyroyal, will repel them. Growing mints or tansy near their entrance point will also help. Non-drying sticky bands are a very effective preventative measure. Nasty option: put out some sugar, watch where they take it home, then pour boiling water down their hole. Nematodes are now available that do not kill the ants, but irritate them so much that they move away!

Aphids are generally considered a plague, but often do little real harm. They do not suck sap, but allow it to be pumped through them, taking what they want and letting the sticky sweet sap residue fall on leaves where it turns mouldy. This spreads virus diseases but, otherwise, aphids are usually just taking surplus nutrients without affecting growth overall. The curling of leaves, especially leaf tips, actually has the same result as summer pruning. For many plants, redcurrants and sweet cherries in particular, withering the tips causes young buds lower down to convert to fruit buds instead of staying vegetative. There are many different aphids and some are specific to a few plants. Chives discourage aphids on many plants, and nasturtiums, although attacked themselves, will keep broccoli clear. Ladybirds and hoverflies are the best control, so use attractant plants like *Limnanthes douglasii*, buckwheat and *Convolvulus tricolor*. If these fail, then soft soap works well. Under cover, there are diseases, parasites and predators available to control aphids.

Flea beetles make many tiny holes in the young leaves of plants, such as turnips, radishes and Chinese cabbage. They dislike moist conditions, so frequent watering is most effective. Interplanting lettuce or spinach deters them and they are discouraged by mint, wormwood and elderberry leaves, as well as pieces of tomato plant. Sticky flypaper waved close overhead thins them out rapidly, as they jump up when disturbed.

Slugs and snails can be stopped with barriers of salt, lime, wood ashes, creosote, pine needles, crushed eggshell or sawdust. They are also reluctant to climb over smooth rings cut from plastic bottles. Trap them in slug pubs: saucers or yogurt pots half full of fermenting beer, in which slugs obligingly drown themselves. ('Friendly' ground beetles also drown, unless you give them some twigs to climb out on.) Slugs and snails also unwittingly congregate under tiles, melon or orange shells, and upturned saucers from where they can be collected. There is a parasitic nematode available that you water on to the soil to kill them. Do not destroy the

ABOVE AND BELOW *Ladybirds do control pests, but not always soon enough. Still, holed leaves allow more light to fall on previously shaded ones below so are less detrimental than you imagine.*

predatory slug, *Testacella*, which is large, yellowish and has a small, but noticeable, vestigial shell on the tail end. It eats other slugs, and worms, but was quickly killed by a diet of poisoned ones so is now almost unknown.

Red spider mites are a serious threat to plants under cover, on walls and even in the open. They cover shoots with a fine webbing that repels sprays and turns leaves yellow and desiccated with thousands of tiny pinpricks. Spraying water and keeping the air humid discourages them. Attract them with sweet tobacco plants which are then composted, spray with soft soap and introduce a biological control. The predator *Phytoseiulus persimilis* is tiny, but still bigger than the pests, and works very well if introduced early enough.

pest, which becomes a mass of eggs. This soon proliferates, and they cunningly hide on the backs of leaves and branches. Hand-pick minor infestations, spray with soft soap and buy in predators. Mealy bugs are very similar but mobile. Treat them with bought-in predators such as the beetle, *Cryptolaemus montrouzieri*. The bugs are attracted to potato shoots so can be trapped there and then sprayed with soft soap. Other predators are available.

Whitefly are mostly a problem under cover. Though unrelated to those outdoors on brassicas, the same physical methods and poisons work for both. Thin out flying adults with a vacuum cleaner, use trap plants, and spray with soft soap. Indoors, introduce the commercially available biological control, *Encarsia formosa*. The white scales on the fly turn black once attacked by the wasp. As these fly when disturbed, infestations of aphids or other less mobile pests can still be controlled by dipping the plant tips, where the pests concentrate, in soft soap solution. Remove yellow sticky traps from greenhouses once these wasps are introduced. Other predators are available.

New Zealand flatworms are a new pest in the UK, mostly confined to the non-lime-rich wetter west and north. They destroy true worms and damage fertility. Attract them with worms as bait in buried jam jars, piles of flat tiles and under bricks, and so on. Do not handle them as they exude irritant slime; old scissors come to mind…

Scale insects and mealy bugs are most troublesome on plants under cover and on walls. The little flat helmets hide an aphid-like

ABOVE LEFT *Slug pub, setting wee sticks so beetles can climb out.* **ABOVE RIGHT** *Nectar gives adult predators the energy to catch more pests.*
LEFT *Not pest, or disease, but splitting after sudden prolonged heavy rain.* **BELOW** *Big eyes, moves fast, not common – then it must be useful.* **OPPOSITE LEFT** *Ladybird larvae pupate, then emerge as adults.*
OPPOSITE MIDDLE *Ants can be lured into filling pots with their 'eggs' for us to steal away.*
OPPOSITE RIGHT *Even if not sealed, such barriers exclude a multitude of opportunistic pests.*

Wasps are very beneficial early in the season because they hunt other insects in great numbers. However, trap them when they turn their attention to fruit. A bottle half full of water and jam, capped with foil and with only a small hole, allows the wasps to crawl in but not fly out. Do not use these near flowers or with honey, as bees may be lured in too. Dust wasps with flour, follow them home, and then destroy the nest by puffing poisons in the entrance when they fly home at dusk. Repeat a week later. If unsure, call in a professional.

Vine weevils The adult weevil is dark grey, beetle-like and has a very long snout. It takes rounded bits out of leaves, but most harm is done by the grubs. These are up to the same size with a grey/pink body and brown head, and destroy the roots of many plants. Adults are trapped in rolls of corrugated cardboard or bundles of sticks, or under saucers where they hide during the day. Vine weevils are difficult to control with chemicals, as the troublesome larval stage live in the soil, but you can water on a parasitic nematode to control them. For vines and plants in pots,

make an excluding lid that fits snugly around the stem or stand them in double saucers with a water moat between. Outdoors, trap them by clean cultivation – and by keeping chickens running around.

Eelworms or nematodes are microscopic, small 'worms' or the larger, saprophytic varieties that are mostly harmless. Good ones are sold commercially as controls for many other pests. Pest nematodes are too small to see, although they may cause visible damage. On potatoes, they form visible cysts on the roots. Many fungi attack eelworms, so organic soils rich with compost suffer much less. *Tagetes* marigolds give off secretions that kill nematodes and can be planted to clean the ground. *Crotalaria*, castor oil plants, and pot marigolds, *Calendula officinalis*, may discourage them.

Rabbits Only netting the area will keep rabbits out. If they get in, place a plank against the fence so that they don't eat even more by being trapped inside. If the perimeter cannot be secured, surround or wrap each plant in wire netting. If this is impossible, feed

the rabbits when snow stops them finding their own food and before they attack your plants! Just the smell of a ferret or its droppings will drive them away.

Moles Many plants are said to repel moles – find one that always works and you will have fame and fortune. Try spurges and castor oil plants but only if you like irritant and poisonous plants. Poke sharp, twiggy, thorny things down their runs, flood them, gas them with car exhaust, and pour disgusting things down their runs. You will only discourage them for a while or drive them to the neighbours temporarily! Why not accept them and appreciate the pest control, ventilation and fine soil they leave?

Children and people These can be the worst pests of all, and their senseless damage is worse than their thefts. Fences, barriers and locks are sadly now required, especially for succulent fruit. Signs saying, 'Beware of the wasps' nests!' can be singularly more effective than 'Keep out'. Dogs are considered the best guards, but geese are as good and have other benefits.

The safest and easiest methods for breaking new ground and killing off established weeds

At some point, most of us want to create a new bed or border where none has been before. Before embarking on the task, check for pipes or wires buried under the ground. Traditionally, you have to hack off the top growth, dig it all over and pull out the weed roots as you go. There are easier ways! Easiest of all is cutting it out of a lawn, so if possible put the whole area down to closely cut grass for a year or two. Then just cut the bed.

Good weed control is easy even though as organic gardeners we spurn chemical herbicides. These do not just kill the unwanted plants, but microscopic ones and other forms of life as well. Instead, we rely on mechanical means combined with wit and cunning. As with pests, the aim is control, not elimination, as weeds also have their uses. Vigorous, self-sown weeds have an advantage over our inbred, cosseted plants, rapidly out-competing and choking them. Thus, to get optimum yields, weeds must be controlled. Weed control is more effective the earlier it is done because crops receive most damage the earlier they are checked. However, intervening too early reduces the fertility created by weeds, so precise timing is needed. The timing and best method of control varies with the weed, situation and crop, so effort can be saved with a little planning and knowledge of weeds.

ABOVE *Weed control does not have to mean total permanent elimination, as they have their uses.*

Friendly and unfriendly weeds Weeds are just plants in the wrong place; many are valuable garden plants or even potential crops like poppies. Weeds may be the last remnants of the original flora and so help preserve insect and wildlife populations. A stand of weeds not only fixes and stabilises the soil, but also acts as a miniature hedge and windbreak, sheltering emerging seedlings. However, it needs eradication before it competes too much. Most of all, weeds are a useful free source of fertility. They produce a wealth of green manure at times when our crops cannot use the soil and act as valuable ground cover. Weeds are also superb mineral accumulators (see page 89), making these available to crops after incorporation. Some, like clovers and vetches, fix nitrogen; comfrey, nettles and thistles accumulate potassium; and fat hen, sorrel,

yarrow and thorn apple collect phosphorus. However, they also choke our crops, spoil the garden's appearance, lock up fertility in seeds and roots, and harbour pests and diseases. To be controlled effectively, it helps to recognise the two types of weed – annual weeds and perennial weeds – because once the latter have been eliminated, then the former are easy to control.

Annual and perennial weeds Annual weeds spring from seed as soon as soil is exposed to light, warmth and wet. Suppress them by mulching or deep burial. Allowed to germinate, they are relatively easy to kill by any method, but get tougher rapidly. Some can even set seed lying on the ground if they have reached flowering. It doesn't matter if the seedling weed is actually a biennial or perennial because it is easily killed when small and not long established. Established perennial weeds are more difficult. The worst ones creep, spread and regrow from pieces of root. Clearing every bit of these methodically reduces later weed control effort to seedlings, which are easily hoed or mulched. Planting up beds or borders without first removing or killing all perennial weeds allows them to interpenetrate the crop roots and then weeding is far more difficult. Once all the perennial weeds have been cleared from an area, there are certainly going to be thick flushes of weed seedlings for a year or two. Once the soil has had some seasons of regular weeding, though, there will be fewer seedlings and not sufficient to give good winter cover. Digging or deep raking will bring up more seeds, or selected weeds or other favoured plants can be allowed to seed to maintain populations on vegetable beds and other areas needing their cover and manuring. Where the weeds are being mulched, dug or hoed in, their goodness is retained in situ, but it can be transferred to the compost heap and concentrated for more important crops. All weeds can be composted, but those with pernicious roots should be withered on a path for some days first. Weeds, their roots and most seeds are also very efficiently killed by immersion under water for a week or two and can then be composted safely. Diseased weeds are best burnt.

Weeding methods Not all methods of weed control are suitable for every occasion or location. Some, like traditional grubbing up, are ideal initially for gaining control of small areas. Others, such as hoeing or flame-gunning, are better for maintaining control. Mulching is probably the most important, preventing weed seeds from germinating

and improving fertility and water conservation. Hygiene is also valuable for preventing undesirable new weeds. Dirty manures, uncomposted mulches, and bought-in plants in pots can smuggle in seeds and even live specimens. Protect sensitive areas, such as flowerbeds, gravel paths and drives, by never letting anything set seed nearby or upwind. Rotation is as useful for controlling weeds as for controlling pests and diseases. By moving the crop and changing the conditions, no weed species is favoured and allowed to establish, the conditions under peas or beans being different to those beneath brassicas or sweet corn, for example.

Digging is easy when starting a new bed or border whereby the ground has been under grass for a while. Regular cutting will have reduced weed populations, favouring grasses and rosette weeds. From late autumn until mid-spring, the turf can be skimmed off and stacked for loam, use elsewhere or dug in. Remove tap-rooted weeds and wilt them for compost. If there are many creeping weeds,

ABOVE AND BELOW *A borage green manure excludes weeds and can be harvested. I'm hoeing and collecting weeds, the geo-textile eliminates weeds but produces no material.*

digging up becomes laborious. Excluding light with mulches is easier. Digging in is suitable for green manures and overwintering ground-cover weeds in early spring (they will have time to decay before the crop is planted). Dig and chop small spits methodically rather than labour with larger pieces. Alternatively, the surface can be lifted and inverted in shallow slices, and the weeds prevented from re-rooting by later hoeing.

Rotary cultivating involves chopping up the weeds. Unfortunately, this kills earthworms and damages some soil textures. Also, most rotary cultivators have insufficient power to break up perennial-weed-infested ground and will chop each weed into bits that then re-grow. They are better for incorporating lush green manures and overwintered annual weeds, which are less likely to re-grow. Use them for regular weed control, provided your plot is laid out in long, straight,

wide-spaced rows. They are more suitable for larger gardens. To break up a large plot, rotary cultivate two or three times, a fortnight or so apart in spring, to incorporate the cover and any re-growth as it occurs.

Hand weeding is practised most amongst other plants, often when an earlier hoeing would have done. Gloves make hand weeding pleasanter. Kneeling pads protect the knees and a sharp knife helps cut stubborn roots. Use an old washing-up bowl or bucket to collect the weeds and transfer them to the barrow or heap when it's full. Remove the weeds amongst and near the plants first, and then the ones between. Small weed seedlings may be killed with the edge of a knife, a hand rake, onion hoe or scuffler, rather than by pulling up. Pulling destroys too many crop roots at the same time! Hand weeding, although laborious, converts perennial weeds into fertility if every new leaf is cut or pulled off each week as it appears until the root system expires. Some much-feared weeds, such as ground elder or bindweed, can be eliminated in a season if

every leaf and shoot is removed weekly. Any lapse, though, and they may recover from just one little piece.

Hoeing is the most widespread method of maintenance weed control. Using the hoe to sever the top growth just below ground level is most effective. This is difficult with a blunted hoe, so hoes must be sharp. In heavy, sticky or stony ground put a hoeing mulch of sharp sand or sieved compost on top of the soil to make the going easier. There are two basic types of hoe: the swan-necked or draw hoe and the Dutch hoe. The former is used with a chopping action and is good for incorporating seedling weeds and young green manures. The draw hoe is also good for pulling earth up to potatoes and can be used for making drills. The Dutch hoe's blade is pushed to and fro through the soil just below the surface. Although it doesn't incorporate seedlings as well after chopping them off, the Dutch hoe deals with bigger weeds more effectively than the draw hoe. Weeds are further damaged by its rolling action and this also makes a good

dust mulch. It is hard to draw soil up or make a drill with the Dutch hoe.

Hoeing is excellent for maintaining clean soil in beds and borders. If these only produce annual weeds, then hoe them fortnightly from early spring until mid-summer, but little thereafter. If the hoeing is left for longer than a fortnight, the weeds get more established and take more effort and time to weed. Hoeing to remove perennial weeds should be done at least weekly, so the top growth that sustains the weed is removed. However, this is hard work over a large area unless only a few perennial weeds are present.

Flame-gunning is not as horrendous as it sounds. A gas- or paraffin-powered blowtorch gives an intense blue flame that splays out over a foot square or so. This is passed over the weed leaves at a walking pace and then cooks but doesn't char the leaves, leaving them to further weaken the root system as they wither. It only warms the soil, but is effective against young seedlings as they are meagre. However, if the weeds are well established, some may recover from the roots and need a second treatment a week or so later. You can kill perennial weeds with repeated weekly applications, but this wastes potential composting material.

Timing a flame-gunning just before a crop emerges can be very useful as it removes the weed competition without disturbing the crop or soil and bringing up more weed seeds. For example, carrots take twelve to eighteen days to germinate, so if these are sown into a weeded seed bed, then all new weeds emerging in the next ten days can be removed in perfect safety on day eleven. The carrots then emerge and establish, deterring further weeds germinating.

Flame-gunning is most useful for weeding large areas such as seed beds and gravel drives, but should be kept away from cars, buildings and inflammable materials. It is possible to use flame guns under and up to trees and even tough-stemmed plants, but conifers, evergreens, dead leaves and hedges catch fire easily! Herbaceous plants can also be flame-gunned while dormant to kill winter weeds if the crowns are covered with sand. Small, hobby blow-torches are superb for weeding rockeries and can also be used on weeds growing in the cracks and crannies of paths and patios. Simply pouring the surplus hot water over weeds in a path or patio every time you make a cuppa will give you control for free.

Mulching is probably the most important, yet under-used, method of weed control. Although mulching materials are expensive, they save much time and effort by suppressing weeds. They all help water conservation and moderate and improve soil temperature, thus encouraging growth. Organic mulches also add fertility and improve the soil texture.

However, mulches may encourage pests such as voles and moles underneath, while loose ones are scattered onto lawns by birds. There is more danger of rotting crowns or bark in excessively damp conditions and grafts may disadvantageously root if the union is covered with mulch. Mulches also seal in the soil's warmth, so the growth above becomes more prone to frost than it would in bare soil. This is important to note for strawberries and bush peaches in flower, and also mulched potatoes. Mulches are an alternative to green manuring, whether with weeds or otherwise, but do not increase biomass because they don't utilise sunlight.

Mulches are the easiest way of breaking new ground, initially, as well as a good way of keeping weeds down later. As long as the top growth is not woody and has at least been cut with a rotary mower, then an area can be turned into weed-free clean soil in six months.

All weeds are killed by the exclusion of light – hence the effectiveness of impenetrable mulches. The tougher perennial weeds are only stopped by thick, opaque plastic or fabric, such as woven geo-textiles, but the majority of weeds will be killed off by a thick mulch of straw, hay or grass clippings on top of cardboard and newspaper. In any case, some hand weeding is needed if weeds appear through any holes. It helps if an isolation trench, a foot deep and wide, is dug round the perimeter first and the mulch continued over the edge.

Mulching new ground works best if the impenetrable mulch is put down just as the weeds have started into growth, flattening them underneath. This is most effective in

ABOVE *Simply excluding light rapidly kills any plant.*

about early spring when the soil is also full of water. The weeds turn yellow through lack of light and rapidly rot, followed by the root systems, thus feeding soil life and increasing fertility. After a month or so, expose any creatures for birds by rolling back the sheet of mulch in the morning. (Worms and beneficial insects move quickly and escape; most pests do not.) If an area is mulched in this way in early spring, it can be cropped from early summer, though the weeds may recover if the mulch is simply removed. Late spring into early summer is planting out time for many less hardy vegetables. Once hardened off, these can be planted through holes in the mulch where they will grow in the moist, enriched soil underneath. Tomatoes, courgettes, marrows, ridge cucumbers, melons under cloches and sweet corn all do well. The brassicas also thrive but most occupy the land through the winter, so do not fit in if the area is needed for the autumn.

In the autumn, after any catch crop has been removed, remove the mulch and dig over the area if necessary. Almost all the

ABOVE *Geo-textile under my vines and pumpkins saves a great deal of work.*

weeds and roots will have rotted and disappeared, leaving a rich texture and natural stratification that may be better left undisturbed. It is possible to plant through the mulch and leave it in place, providing it will not interfere with cultivation. In exactly the same way, green manures and overwintered weeds can be mulched in early spring with sheets of plastic or fabric, even grass clippings in quantity. You can then plant through these into the enriched soil. Compost can also be added before mulching for the best results with hungry feeders.

Impenetrable or loose mulches can be applied to bare soil or areas covered with annual weeds during autumn. This hibernates the bed, protects the soil from erosion and encourages soil life, especially earthworms. When removed or planted through in spring, the soil will be ready with excellent texture and fertility. Autumn mulching can benefit herbaceous and less hardy plants by

protecting them from frost, though plants subject to rot in damp conditions should only be mulched with light, airy materials such as loose straw or bracken.

All mulches can be applied at any time, but early spring before the winter rain has evaporated has the most benefits. Similarly, if there is a long dry period, rake or roll aside mulches when it rains and replace afterwards to prevent them soaking up all the water.

Different mulches, impenetrable and loose

Plastic sheets are a great aid to weed control, but costly in cash and environmentally undesirable. They vary in manufacture and use. The clear plastic, similar to that used for polytunnels, can be pinned to the ground to warm up the soil in spring and encourage flushes of weeds. Black or opaque plastic sheet, which is thick enough to exclude all light, warms the soil and kills weeds, even perennials. It can be laid permanently and covered with a loose mulch to improve the appearance, so becoming suitable for shrub borders, soft fruit, gravel paths and drives.

If all perennial weeds are dead, puncture the plastic sheets in many places to prevent water problems. Unperforated, they may cause flooding or a lack of aeration to the soil. Pre-perforated sheets can be bought ready-made but then cannot prevent weeds passing through. Black and white plastic can be reversed after the black has warmed the soil and killed the weeds; the white side reflects light onto the plants and confuses pests.

Large squares of plastic tucked into slits round the edge make a superb start for young trees, keeping them weed-free and preventing evaporation for a year or two. Long strips, a stride or so wide, are excellent for starting hedges. Cuttings of easy rooters, like quickthorn, can even be pushed through them. Strips of plastic can also be used for strawberries, vegetables and, particularly, lettuce and saladings, although slugs may become more of a problem.

Woven materials are similar to perforated plastic but heavier. Their porosity allows much better aeration of the soil and less water run-off than impermeable plastic. More expensive to buy, they are too costly to use where plain plastic will do. They are better, though, for growing valuable crops through, like strawberries, where their wear resistance will also be useful. Bed-sized pieces on the vegetable plot will kill and incorporate green manures for many years, and they are tough enough to have flaps cut for planting through.

Carpet is the best woven material, heavy, weed-resistant and not unattractive laid upside down. This is *the* material for breaking new ground – even a bramble can't push through a nice bit of Axminster or Wilton. Purely artificial carpets last forever and make good paths, especially in the fruit cage and polytunnel. Organic wool or cotton carpets rot after a year or two, so are perfect for establishing trees and shrubs. I must warn you otherwise sensible bodies that detest the use of old carpet and object to it as a mulch for somewhat spurious reasons; however, used for paths it is beyond compare!

Paper and cardboard are no good used alone as a mulch except in the greenhouse or polytunnel where they are safe from wind and keep lettuce and saladings clean. Outside, they blow away unless used with another mulch on top. Under a loose mulch, they kill weeds nearly as well as plastic or fabric materials, but rapidly rot. They also stop birds mixing weed-seed-infested soil into a loose mulch material if used underneath and improve the effectiveness of a thin plastic sheet that lets in some light. Wet them first and they lie flatter.

Peat, bark and coir are more attractive than any other mulches. Peat is considered as undesirable as kicking dogs in the UK, but, on a world scale, is in abundance and an excellent material. Bark by-products are better for the UK, as we produce these. Coir and other wastes are also replacing peat, but all are very similar. They do not add much to soil fertility, are expensive compared to the others and incur a carbon footprint as we rob the developing world of this material. However, they are generally weed-seed-free, of good texture and beneficial to most plants. Because of their cost, they are best used for ornamental areas. Use them on top of newspaper or cardboard to make them go further and to improve the appearance of plastic mulches. Used alone, a depth of at least two to three inches is needed which will need topping up every year. Also, lay down fine-grade material with a coarse top layer to prevent wind blow. Do not put these down unaided on top of weeds, as they will just grow through.

Compost, well-rotted muck and manures are all more applied for their fertility rather than as mulches. You can sieve them before-hand to make them look more attractive, but this is laborious and they are full of weed seeds. They are most useful on the vegetable bed and around trees and shrubs. In layers thicker than a few inches, they suppress many existing weeds, but not creeping or vigorous ones. These mulches disappear quickly and need continual topping up.

Straw and hay make good mulches under trees, in the fruit cage, and for strawberries. There tend to be quite a lot of annual grass seeds after these mulches, so be prepared to keep mulching once you start. Best placed on top of a newspaper layer, a three-inch-thick slab of straw will then last for two years or more. Put on loose, they cover less hardy plants in severe weather, although bracken fronds are better. Take care with mouldy straw or hay, and with bracken, as inhaling dust from these can be a health hazard.

Grass clippings are readily available at home. Put down in one place they make a wet smelly mess, but put in inch layers and topped up regularly they make one of the very best mulches. They feed the soil and encourage worms as 'greens', so benefit almost every area of the garden. Thicker layers are good for earthing up potatoes and soft fruit bushes and trees. Grass clippings 'glue' down the edge of plastic sheets and can help disguise them as a skim on top. They can be made more effective and longer lasting if put down over newspaper.

Sand and gravel are not usually regarded as mulches. They have many advantages, being attractive, cheap and sterile, although they add no fertility. They also keep moisture in the soil, but do not get wet themselves which makes them good for the winter protection of less hardy plants. They are

ABOVE *Sterile mulches suppress weeds and save moisture.* **BELOW** *Straw is the second choice mulch for strawberries, pine needles are better.*

TOP LEFT *These are not weeds at all but fertility waiting to be hoed in.* TOP RIGHT *Such perennials like celandines can be difficult to eliminate.* BOTTOM LEFT *Thick, lush growth is really a lot of useful compost material.* BOTTOM RIGHT *A hoe and a rake and it will be soon be clean soil.*

among the best mulches for fruit where they reflect up ripening heat and light. Sand is excellent for asparagus, but should be darkened with soot or it will not warm up quickly enough. Be warned, anything seeding into gravel germinates, so practise preventative hygiene nearby. It is a good idea to put gravel over perforated plastic, confining the worms and soil underneath.

Weed control in non-soil areas Paths, drives and patios are often a problem, as windblown seeds lodge in every niche. Prevention is better than cure, so either point up holes and cracks with cement or mastic after cleaning them out by hand with a knife and a pressure hose, or grow plants you want there. A mixture of potting compost and thyme and chamomile seeds will soon establish and prevent other plants getting in. A carpet or plastic sheet laid on top for a few weeks will also kill off many weeds. It can be permanent and covered with fresh gravel. I repeat my tip about using surplus boiling water from the kettle – it kills weeds in cracks most efficiently at no cost and little effort.

Ground cover Under shrubs and over large areas, mulching becomes expensive in materials and time, as some weeds will arrive on the wind. It then becomes more effective to grow ground-cover plants, which also add fertility from captured sunlight (especially grass which is simply maintained). In shady areas, ivy is better and easily weeded by shearing or nylon line trimming anything that grows out of it. Planting bulbs, primroses, violets and other naturalising plants can further improve the appearance and the wildlife habitat. Weed control can still be carried out by using a nylon line trimmer to cut up to and around the chosen plants and reducing the weeds to grass or ivy. The most vigorous and beneficial ground cover, wherever height allows, are the mints, which suppress most weeds and are loved by insects when in flower. They can be kept within bounds by a mown grass path.

Worst weeds and garden 'weeds' There are weeds and there are wildflowers. The least desirable weeds are annuals, which should not be allowed to increase, and perennial weeds that are very difficult to deal with. They include: annual meadow grass (*Poa* species); Canadian fleabane (*Conyza canadensis*); hairy bitter-cress (*Cardamine hirsute*); shepherd's purse or cress (*Capsella bursa-pastoris*); bindweed (*Polygonum convolvulus*); couch grass (*Agropyron repens*); ground elder (*Aegopodium podagraria*); horseradish (*Cochlearia armoracia*); horsetails (*Equisetum* species); Japanese knotweed (*Polygonum* species); lesser celandine (*Ranunculus ficaria*) and winter heliotrope (*Petasites fragrans*).

These garden plants are amongst the worst seeders and spreaders: *Allium, Ajuga*, bluebells, feverfew, forget-me-not, foxglove, goldenrod, Himalayan balsam, honesty, *Hypericum*, *Lamium*, loosestrife, mints, periwinkles, poppies, Russian vine, *Rhododendron ponticum*, Shasta daisies, *Sisyrinchium*.

An interesting experiment you could try is to put your garden soil in a pot, water it and put it on a windowsill. Then watch what comes up. You can remove many of the duplicates and anything as soon as you recognise it; these are your common annual weeds. Once you know them, you can spot the rare finds, such as tree and shrub seedlings.

What weeds are telling you are the conditions they are growing in. Any piece of ground gets covered with weeds very rapidly if left untended. These compete with each other and different species dominate temporarily. As weeds slowly build up the fertility of the soil, it becomes suitable for nettles, brambles and tree seedlings. Thus, a profusion of these, especially nettles, can indicate a potentially rich site. Deep-rooted weeds, such as dock and thistle, are good as they bring up nutrients from deep down, making them available for future crops.

BELOW *Here's a compost main ingredient – weeds are needed to add variety.*

The types of weed will always be those most suited to the conditions, so if the population consists of acid-lovers such as daisies, small nettles and sorrels, then the topsoil is probably acid. Lime-rich soils are indicated by cat's ears, cowslips, knapweed and silverweed, while damp conditions encourage nettles, buttercups, bugle and rushes. Lots of docks mean horses or their manure have been on the land, as the seeds pass through unchecked. Similarly, lots of tomato seedlings could mean sewage sludge has been used. Beware of any land that grows few weeds!

On prospective land you want to see masses of stinging nettles! Other favourable weeds are chickweed, docks, forget-me-not, goosegrass, groundsel, thistles and yarrow. What you most definitely do not want – and it may be best to move home – are white-flowered bindweed, *Equisetum*, horseradish, Japanese knotweed, lesser celandine, Leylandii hedges or poplars on or close to the sunny side of the garden, *Oxalis* or winter heliotrope. However, some generally feared weeds are common, very tough and require several attacks a week apart to die, but do succumb if you are persistent. They are: brambles, coltsfoot, couch grass, creeping buttercup, docks, ground elder, knotweed, any nettles, thistles and tree saplings.

Don't forget, the more growth the weeds make, the more material you have for the compost heap. A bed of nettles will get you up and running in fertility for the couple of years that it takes to kill them off by regular raids for their succulent growths.

The best of luck and keep on composting!

BELOW *A healthy soil should have plenty of weeds.* OPPOSITE *Red dead nettles are valuable flowering plants in late winter.*

THE MOST COMMON 'WEEDS'

'Weeds' or native plants that occur most frequently on acid soil:
Betony, birch, black bindweed, broom, cinquefoil, corn chamomile, cornflower, corn marigold, corn spurrey, daisy, foxglove, fumitory, gorse, harebell, heather, horse or marestail, lesser periwinkle, mercuries, pansy, rhododendrons, rowan, scabious, shepherd's cress or purse, small nettle, Scots pine, sorrels, spurrey and tormentil.

'Weeds' or native plants that occur most frequently on lime-rich soil:
Agrimony, bellflowers, black medick, candytuft, cat's ear, Clematis, cornelian cherry, cowslip, dogwood, goat's beard, greater hawkbit, hawthorn, hazel, horseshoe vetch, knapweed, lamb's lettuce, mignonette, ox-eye daisy, penny-

cress, privet, rose briar, salad Burnet, spindle, stonecrop, tansy, valerian, wallflower, white mustard, wild carrot and yarrow.

'Weeds' or native plants that occur most frequently on heavy clay:
Annual meadow grass, creeping buttercup, cowslip, goosegrass, hoary and ribwort plantain, meadow cranesbill, nipplewort, selfheal and silverweed.

'Weeds' or native plants that occur most frequently on light dry soil:
Annual nettle, bramble, broad dock, bulbous buttercup, charlock, dandelion, groundsel, knotgrass, mouse-eared chickweed, stinging nettle, petty spurge, poppies, red dead-nettle, rosebay willow-herb, shepherd's purse and speedwell.

'Weeds' or native plants that occur most frequently in wetter places:
Alder, bugle, bulrush, buttercups, comfrey, cuckoo flower, docks, great willowherb, hemp agrimony, Himalayan balsam, loosestrife, marsh marigold, meadowsweet, mints, plantains, primrose, ragged robin, sedge, stinging nettle, thistles, water avens and willows.

The yearly calendar

LATE WINTER

Empty insect traps and old bird boxes and hang up new bird boxes so that they are ready when the birds need them. Put out bird food, hang up fat and provide sources of water.

Make sure that no weeds get a hold – they pull up easily at this time. Hoe whenever it's dry enough.

Spray peaches and almonds with Bordeaux mixture when the buds are swelling, against peach leaf curl.

Cut the grass if no frosts are likely; set the blades high and return the clippings.

Put down impenetrable sheet mulches on top of new ground or green manures. Spread loose mulches under and around everything, preferably immediately after a period of heavy rain.

Plant out hardy trees and shrubs if the ground is workable. Firm in the roots of autumn plantings after hard frosts.

Check ties and stakes after gales.

Finish any major pruning work that needs to be done, but leave alone stone fruits or evergreens unless they are damaged by winter storms.

Chit early seed potatoes on trays in a light, frost-free place.

Tidy sheds and greenhouses and repair and clean tools and equipment.

If necessary, order seeds and plants and plan where you will put them.

Check your food stores and remove anything that is starting to rot before it infects others.

EARLY SPRING

Put out food, hang up fat and provide water for birds.

To stop any weeds getting away, hoe at least every other week and top up thin, weedy mulches.

Spray peaches and almonds for a second time with Bordeaux mixture. Examine every plant in the garden and under cover for pests, diseases and dieback before they start to leaf up.

Cut the grass at least fortnightly, preferably weekly, and return the clippings or put them as mulch around trees and bushes. Move, lay, sow and repair turf in non-frosty weather.

Once the soil becomes workable, plant out evergreens, soft fruit, artichokes, asparagus and rhubarb.

Spray the entire garden with diluted seaweed solution.

Hand-pollinate early-flowering plants under cover.

Cover blossoms and young fruitlets with net curtains or sheets to protect them from frost damage on still, cold nights.

Prune tender plants, evergreens, herbs and hollow-stemmed shrubs such as buddleias.

Outdoors, plant garlic, onion sets, shallots, potatoes.

Sow plants to be grown under cover: tomatoes, cucumbers, aubergines, peppers, hardy and half-hardy annuals.

Outdoors, sow in warm soil under cloches: peas, broad beans, onions, leeks, beetroot, kohlrabi, cabbages, cauliflowers, lettuce, spinach, turnips, carrots, chards, salsify, scorzonera, parsnips, herbs, radishes, spring onions, sweet peas and hardy annuals. Check your food stores and remove anything that is starting to rot before it infects others.

MID-SPRING

Plant out potatoes, onion seedlings and perennial herbs.

Spray everything with diluted seaweed solution; spray anything showing deficiency symptoms more heavily.

Firm in roots of earlier plantings after any hard frosts.

De-flower new fruit plants to give them time to establish.

Protect blossoms and young fruitlets from frost with net curtains, plastic sheeting or newspaper.

Feed and top-dress all plants in pots.

Tie in new growths of vines and climbing plants.

Once their flowers die, prune and cut back most early-flowering shrubs.

Cut the grass weekly and return the clippings or put them as mulches around trees and bushes.

Hoe weekly to ensure that no weeds get a hold.

Examine each plant for early signs of pests and diseases. Put out slug pubs and pheromone traps. Make night-time searches of your garden for pests – especially in sowing and propagation areas.

Sow plants under cover to plant out later: tomatoes, ridge cucumbers, gherkins, courgettes, marrows, pumpkins, sweetcorn and half-hardy flowers.

Outdoors, sow: peas, broad beans, most brassicas, lettuces and saladings, herbs, spinach, turnips, carrots, swedes, salsify, scorzonera, radishes, kohlrabi, fennel, leeks, parsnips, sweet peas and hardy annuals.

Use up stored fruits and vegetables and clean out stores once empty.

LATE SPRING
Hoe frequently to ensure that no weeds get away. Top up weedy mulches.

Examine every plant for pests and diseases, especially for aphids, caterpillars and, indoors, red spider mite or whitefly. Make night-time searches of your garden for pests – especially in sowing and propagation areas.

Cut the grass at least fortnightly, preferably weekly, and return the clippings or put them as mulch around potatoes.

Pot up any plant needing repotting.

Establish a daily watering round for all pot-grown plants. Feed indoor pot plants with comfrey liquid or seaweed solution weekly.

Spray everything with diluted seaweed solution; spray anything with deficiency symptoms more heavily.

Protect blossoms and young fruitlets from frost damage on still, cold nights.

Tie in and support climbers and the tallest herbaceous plants.

Cut back most flowering shrubs once their flowers die.

Harden off and plant out under cover; tomatoes, peppers, aubergines, melons, sweetcorn, ridge cucumbers, courgettes and marrows or plant them outside under cloches only if you are sure that the last frost is over.

Outdoors, sow in situ under cloches once you are sure that frosts have passed: tomatoes, ridge cucumbers, gherkins, courgettes, marrows, pumpkins, French beans, runner beans, sweetcorn and half-hardy flowers.

Sow outdoors without cloches: peas, most brassicas, lettuces and saladings, herbs, spinach, turnips, carrots, swedes, salsify, scorzonera, kohlrabi, fennel, leeks, parsnips and hardy annuals and biennials.

Harvest and use or store and preserve any crops.

EARLY SUMMER
Maintain good weed control so that no weeds get a hold; hoe fortnightly or weekly.

Examine every plant for pests and diseases, especially aphids, caterpillars and, indoors, red spider mite or whitefly.

Cut the grass at least fortnightly and preferably weekly, but raise the height of cut of the mower.

Pot up anything needing repotting.

Increase frequency of watering for all pot-grown plants to at least thrice daily!

Indoors, feed pot plants with comfrey liquid or seaweed solution weekly.

Plant or move out tender plants in pots for the summer.

Spray everything growing with diluted seaweed solution; spray anything with deficiency symptoms more heavily.

Deadhead roses and cut back most flowering plants after their flowers die.

Thin raspberry canes.

Prune grapevines, cutting back stems to three or five leaves after a flower truss.

Tie in new growths of climbing plants to their supports.

Fruit thinning, first stage: remove every diseased, decayed, damaged, misshapen, distorted and congested fruitlet.

Compost or burn rejected fruitlets immediately and protect the remainder from birds.

Outdoors, sow: lettuces and saladings, beetroot, kohlrabi, swedes, turnips, spinach, chicory, endive and herbaceous biennials and perennials.

Harvest and use or store and preserve everything that is ready, before it goes over.

MID-SUMMER

Hoe fortnightly to ensure that no weeds get away.

Make night-time inspections of your garden to catch pests on the prowl.

Cut the grass at least fortnightly and preferably weekly, but raise the height of cut of the mower even more.

Water all pot-grown plants at least thrice daily. Indoors, feed pot plants with comfrey liquid or seaweed solution weekly.

Spray everything growing with diluted seaweed solution, and anything with deficiency symptoms more heavily.

Deadhead roses and cut back most flowering plants after their flowers die.

If it is warm and humid, spray main crop potatoes with Bordeaux mixture.

Perform summer pruning: remove approximately one half to three quarters of each new shoot, except for leaders, of all red and white currants, gooseberries and all trained fruits. Prune grapevines, cutting back stems to three or five leaves after a flower truss; if there is no flower truss by the sixth leaf, cut it back anyway and mark it for removal during winter pruning. Take out old, fruited wood on blackcurrants and raspberries. Stone fruits are traditionally pruned now to avoid silver leaf disease.

Tie in new growths of climbing plants to their supports.

Cut back evergreens and conifer hedges.

Fruit thinning, second stage: remove damaged fruits. Harvest and eat or preserve ripe fruits and protect remaining fruit from birds and wasps.

Sow: lettuces and saladings, carrots, swedes,

turnips, Chinese cabbage, winter spinach, kohlrabi, Florence fennel, chards.

Harvest and use or store everything that is ready for picking.

LATE SUMMER

Hoe fortnightly to ensure that no weeds get away.

Make night-time inspections of your garden to catch pests on the prowl.

Protect every ripening fruit from birds and wasps.

Cut the grass at least fortnightly and preferably weekly, but reduce the height of cut of the mower a little.

Decrease watering for pot-grown plants to at least twice daily. Feed pot plants with comfrey liquid or seaweed solution weekly.

Spray everything growing with diluted seaweed solution, and anything with deficiency symptoms more heavily.

Deadhead roses and cut back most flowering plants after their flowers die.

Finish pruning all stone fruits to avoid silver leaf disease.

Tie in new growths of climbing plants to their supports.

Plant new strawberry plants, if you can get them.

Order hardy trees and shrubs for autumn planting.

Sow under cover: winter lettuces and saladings, early carrots.

Outdoors, sow: winter lettuces and saladings, Japanese and spring onions, winter spinach, turnips, Chinese greens and hardy and biennial flowering plants.

Sow green manures and winter ground cover on bare soil that is not mulched.

Harvest and eat, store or preserve everything that is ready.

EARLY AUTUMN

Hoe fortnightly or top up mulches to maintain good weed control.

Cut the grass at least fortnightly and preferably weekly; collect the clippings with any fallen leaves and put them around trees and bushes. Raise the height of cut again.

Decrease watering for all pot-grown plants, but still check them daily.

Transplant biennial flowering plants that are pot-grown, with a decent rootball.

Cut back herbaceous plants as their stems wither.

Remove old canes of all the berrying fruits and tie in new stems.

On still, cold nights, protect tender bedding plants from frost damage with sheeting.

Bring indoors tender plants in pots.

Collect and dry seeds.

Plant: garlic, daffodils and most other bulbs.

Sow hardy annuals to overwinter.

Sow green manures and grass.

Harvest and use or store everything before it goes over.

MID-AUTUMN

Control weeds by hoeing fortnightly or topping up mulches.

Cut the grass at least fortnightly and preferably weekly; collect clippings and fallen leaves together or rake them into rings around trees and bushes. Aerate and spike the grass if needed, brushing in sharp sand and grass seed if you are a workaholic.

Decrease watering again as growth slows more.

If necessary, make new beds and borders and move turf.

Spread mulches under and around everything possible.

Outdoors, plant: garlic and bulbs, deciduous shrubs, trees and soft fruit (preferably bare-rooted).

Check ties and stakes if gales are forecast.

Cut back herbaceous plants as their stems wither.

Winter-prune: apples, pears, grapes and non-stone fruits and other plants, once they drop their leaves.

Order seed catalogues and anything to plant soon. Collect and dry seeds and berries for sowing next year and to feed the birds.

Check food stores and remove anything that is starting to rot before it infects others.

Harvest and store late fruits and tender root vegetables.

LATE AUTUMN

Continue to hoe fortnightly or top up mulches to maintain weed control.

Cut the grass at least fortnightly; collect fallen leaves with the clippings or rake them onto now empty or dormant beds and borders.

Water all pot-grown plants only as needed.

Lime the vegetable beds.

Make and turn compost heaps and sieve and store finished compost.

Plant out bare-rooted deciduous shrubs, trees and soft fruit – if the soil is in good condition and the plants are dormant.

Winter-prune any plant that still needs it.

Check ties and stakes after any gales.

Take cuttings of hardy plants as they drop their leaves.

Harvest and store root vegetables under cover in cold areas. Check food stores and remove anything that is starting to rot before it infects others.

Take all hosepipes, plastic cans and so on under cover before hard frosts make them brittle.

EARLY WINTER

Cut the grass if the weather is still mild; collect the fallen leaves with the few clippings and bag them up to make leaf mould. Lime most tough grass swards every fourth year, but not among ericaceous or lime-hating plants.

Decrease watering to a minimum as plant growth almost ceases.

Plant out hardy trees and bushes, provided that the soil is still in good condition and not frozen.

Check ties and stakes after each gale.

Clean out gutters and drains once the last leaves have fallen. Clean the greenhouse, cold frames and glass and plastic cloches.

Prune hardy trees and bushes, including any major work necessary on trees and bushes (but not on stone fruits or evergreens.) Make a bonfire of diseased and thorny material.

Get in your seed orders early so that you get the best choice and they arrive in time for the new season. Order potatoes, evergreen and herbaceous plants for spring.

Check food stores and remove anything that is starting to rot before it infects others.

MID-WINTER

Make bird boxes, slug pubs, insect traps, hibernation quarters and plastic bottle cloches.

On clear bright days, make a health and hygiene check: examine every plant for damage and dieback, scale insects and mummified fruits.

Collect up and destroy hibernating snails.

Clean and repair the mower so it's ready to roll in the spring!

Check ties and stakes after any gales.

Make sure that your seed orders are in.

Check food stores and remove anything that is starting to rot.

Relax, take it easy for a while: note your successes and mishaps of the year, enjoy the fruits of your labours and plan the pleasure of next year and doing even less work.

Index

as a weed 251, 252
horses 76
    manure 90
horseshoe vetch 252
horsetails *see Equisetum*
hosepipies 94
Hosta 45, 53
hot water, weed control 247, 250
hotbeds 201
hounds's tongue 229
house martins 21
house plants 111
houseleeks 111
hoverflies 17
    encouraging 19–20, 236
    growing plants under cover 203
    pollination by 18
human liquid waste (urine) 90–1, 93
humus 13
Hungarian rye grass 88
Hyacinthus 39
hybrid berries 133–4
    cuttings 123
    pruning 126
hybrids, F1 98
Hydrangea petiolaris 23
hygiene
    pest and disease control 234
    weed control 245
Hypericum 229, 251
hyssop 168
    companion planting 160
    encouraging beneficial insects 19, 229
    household products 225

I

Iberis 20
    I. sempervirens 40
iceplant 171
Ilex 23, 47, 58, 70, 229
Impatiens 64
insecticides, disposing of 15
insulation 200, 202
intercropping 160
Iris 41
    I. foetidissima 41
    I. unguicularis 41
irrigation systems 94, 110–11, 202
isolation trenches
    pest control 238
    weed control 247

ivy 51
    to attract birds 23
    encouraging beneficial insects 59
    as ground-cover 68, 250

J

jams 220–1
Japanese cucumbers 191
Japanese knotweed 251, 252
Japanese wineberries 134
Jasminum (jasmine) 19
    J. nudiflorum 51–3
    J. officinale 53
    J. stephanense 58
jellies 220–1
Jerusalem artichokes 180
John Innes composts 101, 110
juicing fruit 220
Juniperus (juniper) 47

K

kale 156, 190
kingcups 53
kiwi fruit 137
knapweeds 19, 252
kneeling pads 246
Kniphofia 42
knives 234
knotgrass 252
knotweed, Japanese 251, 252
kohlrabi 156, 174
kumquats 211

L

lacewings
    encouraging 20, 236
    growing plants under cover 203
    as predators 17
ladybirds 19
    encouraging 20, 236, 237
    growing plants under cover 203
    as predators 17, 19, 239
lady's mantle 40
lamb's lettuce 171, 252
Lamium 251
land cress 169
large gardens 71, 72
Lathyrus odoratus 36
laurel 23
Laurus 229

L. nobilis 162
Lavandula 229
Lavatera maritima 49
lavender 164
    companion planting 124, 160
    cooking with 224
    cuttings 105
    encouraging beneficial insects 19
    household products 225
lawns 67–8
    liming 81
    mowing 68, 81
    pest control 237
    wildflower lawns 75
layering 105
lazy cuttings 105
leaf cutter bees 19
leaf mustards 172
leather jackets 237, 239
leaves *see* foliage
leeks 183
    companion crops 161
    comparative value 156
    sowing 101
legumes 181–2
    crop rotation 158
    green manures 87
    mineral accumulators 89
    see also individual types of legume
lemon balm 45, 168, 229
lemon grass 213
lemon verbena 164, 225
lemons, growing under cover 211
Lent roses 41
lettuces 171–2
    companion crops 161
    comparative value 155, 156
    growing under cover 204
    plastic mulches 248
    resistant varieties 235
Levisticum officinale 164
Leycesteria formosa 47
Leyland cypress 70, 157, 252
light
    growing plants under cover 202
    mulching and 247
    pest and disease control 234
    planning gardens 62
    seedlings and 102
Ligustrum ovalifolium 70
lilac 19, 48

Lilium (lilies) 39
    L. martagon 39
lily beetles 39
lily-of-the-valley 45
lime 91
    for acid soil 85
    Bordeaux mixture 13, 239
    encouraging worms 22
    improving soil 108
    lime-rich soils 108
    liming lawns 81
    weeds and 252
Limnanthes douglasii (poached egg plant) 229
    to attract predators 236
    as bedding plants 66
    companion planting 124
    encouraging beneficial insects 19
    as green manure 87, 88
Limonium 36, 229
Lincolnshire asparagus 167
lingonberries 134
Lippia citriodora 164
Liquidambar 229
liquid feeds 92–3, 111
Liriodendron 229
livestock 75, 226–8
lizards, encouraging 236
Lobelia 229
    L. cardinalis 53
loganberries 134
loggias 66
Lonicera 19, 23, 53
    L. caprifolium 53
    L. fragrantissima 48
    L. nitida 70
    L. periclymenum 53
    L. syringantha 48
loosestrife 42, 251, 252
lovage 164
lupins 42
    encouraging wildlife 17, 20
    green manures 88
Lupinus polyphyllus 42
lures, pest control 238
Lychnis 19, 229
    L. chalcedonica 41
    L. viscaria 'Splendens Plena' 41
Lycium 137
Lysimachia 229
    L. punctata 42
Lythrum 229